*Agents of Autonomy*

# Agents of Autonomy

MAORI COMMITTEES IN THE NINETEENTH CENTURY

*Vincent O'Malley*

HUIA

Issued by the Crown Forestry Rental Trust in 1997.
First published in 1998 by Huia Publishers,
39 Pipitea Street, PO Box 17-335,
Wellington, Aotearoa, New Zealand.

ISBN 1-877241-02-4

Text © Vincent O'Malley 1998
This edition © Huia Publishers 1998

All rights reserved. No part of this publication may be reproduced,
stored in a retrieval system, or transmitted in any form or by any means,
electronic, mechanical, including photocopying, recording or
otherwise, without prior permission of the copyright owner.

Published with the assistance of the Crown Forestry Rental Trust.
Designed, typeset and printed in Aotearoa New Zealand.

# Contents

Foreword, by Alan Ward

| | | |
|---|---|---|
| Page 11............ | 1. | Introduction |
| Page 15............ | 2. | The Native Land Court Assumes Control |
| Page 39............ | 3. | Early Proposals for Reform |
| Page 63............ | 4. | Unofficial Committees in the 1870s: Some Brief Regional Case Studies |
| | | 4.1  Wairarapa |
| | | 4.2  Hawke's Bay and the Influence of the Repudiation Movement |
| | | 4.3  Whanganui |
| Page 85............ | 5. | 'Unity is Strength': Te Arawa Committees of the 1870s: A More Detailed Case Study |
| Page 129......... | 6. | Autonomy Achieved? The Background to the Native Committees Act 1883 |
| Page 163......... | 7. | 'A Semblance of Authority': The Demise of the Official Native Committees |
| Page 193......... | 8. | Autonomy Denied : Continuing Maori Efforts |
| Page 217......... | 9. | 'To Keep Off the White Man and His Works': Te Urewera Committees and the Experiment of 1896 |
| Page 241......... | 10. | Tentative and Temporary Steps: The 1900 Legislation |
| Page 255......... | 11. | Conclusion |

| | |
|---|---|
| Page 267......... | Endnotes |
| Page 295......... | Select Bibliography |
| Page 301......... | Index |

# Foreword

This is a timely and important publication. It concerns the British undertaking in the Treaty of Waitangi to respect the 'tino rangatiratanga' of Maori chiefs, hapu and 'tangata katoa' over their land, kainga and other taonga. A great many of the 700 and more claims by Maori to the Waitangi Tribunal under the Treaty of Waitangi Act 1975 and its amendments refer to the failure of the Crown to respect and uphold tino rangatiratanga, asserting indeed that the Crown deliberately undermined it in its drive to secure land for Pakeha settlement.

Vincent O'Malley's study of 'Native Committees' is important because it gives a range of insights into many of the ways by which Maori themselves tried to express tino rangatiratanga, and to secure the Crown's recognition of those endeavours. The title 'Native Committees' is of course a kind of shorthand for a range of ideas and institutions which emerged after 1840, as Maori sought to adapt traditional social structures and institutions into forms which would meet new needs and which the British authorities and the settler government would recognise. Various proposals regarding the composition and powers of 'Native Committees' were debated from the 1850s. O'Malley discusses many of these in detail. The discussion is useful, not only for considering how well or badly the Crown honoured its Treaty obligations but also for informing current discussion about just how power could be devolved to Maori if there were to be a serious move to do so.

At the heart of Maori social order was a subtle relationship between rangatira (chiefs) and their kin. Chiefs were expected to lead, to take initiatives, but eventually they had to talk about what they had done and carry their people with them, or risk repudiation. The advent of the money economy and commodity markets imposed enormous pressures on the relationship, and still does. Colonisation added particularly intense pressures through the demand for land. Maori leaders were well aware of the threat to their society before 1840; that is why Tamati Waka Nene and others asked the Governor to stay and help Maori protect their chieftainship, their lands and their customs. After 1840 they became aware that the Crown itself, and the settler Parliaments created from 1846, were adding to the pressure, acquiring the land and threatening the whole Maori social order. Hence, from the mid-1850s, there developed movements amongst Maori communities in various parts of the country to strengthen their traditional runanga, to create runanganui and even to establish a Maori king, in order to control the increasingly chaotic situation surrounding the land and to mediate the relationship with the colonists in beneficial ways. Maori requests for official recognition of their runanga, komiti or committees therefore went to the heart of the relationship between Maori and settler and, most immediately, to the struggle for the land.

A form of official recognition of Maori runanga was indeed offered in settler legislation of 1858 and in Governor Grey's 'new institutions' of 1861–64. As O'Malley shows, however, the proposed devolution was confused with settler efforts to acquire land through the runanga, about which Maori were understandably suspicious. Then, with the passing of the Native Lands Act 1865 in the wake of British military advances, governments ceased to be seriously interested in devolving authority upon Maori committees.

The issue remained very alive for Maori, however, and O'Malley shows how succeeding decades saw proposal after proposal raised whereby Maori would recover some authority, firstly over the determination of title to land, then over the management of it. But governments were not willing to concede powers which might have closed the land to settlement. Indeed although official Native Committees were created under an Act of 1883, and although the kotahitanga and the kingitanga carried their effort through to the more substantial Maori Councils Act 1900, that Act was emasculated within a few years.

All the same, the capacities and achievements of the Maori leadership and people in the struggle, and in respect of matters where they were allowed some limited scope for officially recognised action, show what might have been possible under a less greedy and domineering colonisation, and what might yet be possible if fresh efforts were to be made at serious devolution. It is all to the good that much of the detail – including the problems and the negative experiences – is now being made available through O'Malley's work. Maori readers especially will doubtless find much of value in this study of the actions of their tupuna.

Alan Ward
*Emeritus Professor of History*
*University of Newcastle, NSW*

# 1. Introduction

In its 1996 *Taranaki Report*, the Waitangi Tribunal concluded that it was disempowerment, 'the denigration and destruction of Maori autonomy or self-government', that lay at the heart of the Taranaki claims. The Tribunal added that Maori autonomy, or rangatiratanga, is pivotal to the Treaty of Waitangi and the partnership concept it entails, and that:

> it is the right of peoples to determine themselves such domestic matters as their own membership, leadership, and land entitlements. Remarkably, it was presumed that the Government could determine matters of Maori custom and polity better than Maori and that it should have the exclusive right to rule on what Maori custom meant.
>
> The result was not only the distortion of Maori custom by those who did not understand it but the introduction of a profoundly wrong process. The process, which still applies today, is one where decisions particular to Maori are made not by Maori but on their behalf, even in the administration of their land or in the application of their traditions.[1]

Yet, as the Tribunal says, the fact that Maori attempts to engage with the new colonial order on terms mutually beneficial to both Maori and Pakeha were ultimately thwarted by settler self-interest does not mean that Maori were somehow passive victims of this process of disempowerment. Indeed, attempts by Maori to assert the autonomy they believed the Treaty had guaranteed them generally intensified as the process of marginalisation and disempowerment gathered force.

Maori committees, often adaptations of traditional runanga, were one obvious and important means by which Maori could attempt to retain some form of collective cohesion in the face of settler and Crown efforts to undermine the tribal basis of Maori society. The so-called 'beastly communism' of the Maori was, as both Maori and Pakeha quickly appreciated, the cornerstone of Maori autonomy. Without it, as the Tribunal says, 'the Government could divide and rule and Maori could not be strong'.[2] Formal structures derived both from the Pakeha and traditional Maori worlds were used to assert and defend this autonomy, although as Maori at the time realised, without legal authority the long-term prognosis for these committees was at best doubtful.

Committees set up by Maori in the nineteenth century were established at a number of levels: by kainga, hapu, iwi, district, or according to the goals and functions they were intended to fulfil. Some assumed social control functions, passing laws of local concern on matters such as adultery, the consumption of alcohol, the fencing of cultivations, and so on, and meting out appropriate punishment to offenders. Others, generally those established at a broader level, took on more political goals, such as gaining support for petitions to the Queen on Maori grievances or repudiating land transactions considered to be invalid.

Another primary function of some committees was to act as an alternative to the Native Land Court, adjudicating on land titles and settling boundary disputes. Some committees assumed all of these functions, and it is difficult to disentangle them. One of the primary political objectives of many committees in the nineteenth century, for example, was the abolition of the Native Land Court and its replacement by legally recognised committees elected by Maori, whilst one of the key social control functions of some committees was to maintain a tribal veto over land dealings and to punish individuals who dared to transgress this.

To the extent that it is possible to disentangle these various components, however, the primary focus of this paper concerns Maori efforts to investigate and adjudicate on land titles themselves, without the intervention of the Native Land Court, and the extent to which the Crown provided for or conversely undermined this widely held aspiration of nineteenth-century Maori. It will be seen that Maori consistently sought the right to

*Introduction*

determine ownership of their own lands themselves, often in conjunction with Crown officials, but were just as consistently denied this right and instead subjected to an institution which distorted their customs, denied them the tribal ownership guaranteed by the Treaty, and quietly and efficiently denuded them of their lands as a result.

# 2. The Native Land Court Assumes Control

Apart from a brief period in the mid-1840s, the pre-emptive right of the Crown to purchase Maori lands provided for by the Treaty of Waitangi remained a firm plank in government policy until the 1860s. Land purchases until the mid-1850s were generally conducted by agents of the Crown on the basis of tribal ownership, through tribal leaders acting with the sanction and in the presence of their people. Where problems arose, these often involved disputed claims to the same land, and in the absence of any established forum for settling such disputes, Crown purchase agents or other officials frequently found themselves forced to mediate between contending claimants before finalising transactions. This was a far from satisfactory method for determining the owners of land it was proposed to purchase, especially when Crown agents failed to fully inform all groups with possible claims on the block in question of their intention to purchase before entering negotiations.

Most of the South Island had been purchased from its owners by this time, but the North Island remained largely in the hands of Maori, who were increasingly not disposed to sell land. Although section 71 of the New Zealand Constitution Act 1852 had provided for predominantly Maori-owned areas to be proclaimed as districts in which Maori customs and laws might prevail, little interest in implementing this provision was shown at the colonial frontier.[1] Instead, the practical effect of the 1852 constitution was to grant self-government to the settlers, whose General Assembly became a vocal lobby for settler interests in matters pertaining to Maori, for whom the Governor retained official responsibility. This nominal division of responsibilities was hardly tenable in a colonial situation in which native affairs were inextricably linked with the general affairs of the colony, however, and in practice the Assembly showed little reluctance to legislate on Maori matters. As Alan Ward says, in the mid-1850s most Maori were concerned by their 'exclusion from any real share in a Government which appeared increasingly bent on the acquisition of their land, and increasingly under the control of the settler assemblies'.[2] This concern was compounded by fears about the continuing alienation of land and the effects of this on Maori society, which had produced resistance to further sales and prompted Crown land purchase agents, led by Donald McLean, to begin negotiating surreptitious purchases with compliant individuals, often against the wishes or without the knowledge of the rightful owners of the lands concerned. Civil warfare between rival owners to the same block had resulted at Hawke's Bay in 1857–58; at Waitara this policy led to armed conflict between the Crown and local Maori, whose objections to the purchase of land offered by a single chief had been deliberately ignored, in 1860.

The more fundamental response to these perceived threats, however, was to develop more formal tribal and supra-tribal structures aimed at retaining some measure of collective cohesion. At a meeting convened by the paramount Tuwharetoa chief, Iwikau Te Heuheu, at Pukawa late in 1856, which was attended by representatives of many North Island tribes, the idea of a Maori parliament was floated. G.S. Cooper, the Hawke's Bay land purchase officer, reported to McLean that the principal subject intended to be canvassed by such a parliament was:

> the devising [of] some plan by which a united action on the part of the Maories as a nation...[could take place and through which] some check may be applied to the growing influence of the colonists, whilst the power of the Native Chiefs which they perceive to be waning in proportion as that of the colonists increases shall be restored in as far as possible to its former status. As a principal means towards this end, it is to be proposed to put an immediate stop to all sales of land to the Government, and to use every possible means to induce squatters to settle with flocks and herds upon the extensive plains in the interior; such squatters to occupy the position

of vassals to the Chiefs under whose protection they may live, whose orders they are to obey in all matters, and to whom they are to afford a revenue, by way of rent for their runs, to assist in maintaining the power and the influence of their landlords.[3]

The notion of a Maori parliament was one which was to be revived in the late 1870s. Meanwhile, the concept of a Maori king, first promoted by Matene Te Whiwhi in 1853, was more popular, and after further meetings in 1858 Potatau Te Wherowhero was installed as the first Maori monarch.

As a number of writers have pointed out, the King movement envisaged being in a complementary, rather than antagonistic, relationship with the government. It was not opposed to controlled settlement of Maori districts, as Cooper's 1856 report makes clear. Yet although traditional tribal rivalries and chiefly jealousies prevented the Kingitanga from becoming the truly pan-tribal movement it aspired to be, the concerns which it reflected were widely shared. Thus although many tribes were not yet ready to embrace the King, a related movement aimed at reviving and adapting traditional runanga, which was underlain by similar motives, did receive wider support. East Coast Maori, for example, were divided on the question of support for the King, but at a meeting attended by Wiremu Tamihana Tarapipipi and other Kingitanga representatives in April 1859, resolved to establish runanga and that 'no more land should be sold to the Government; but that all sales already made should be respected, and that all bargains on which money had been paid in advance should be completed'.[4] The following year Cooper reported that ever since the visit of the Waikato deputation:

> the Runangas have been in constant and active operation, and I am bound to say, not without a good deal of beneficial result. As Petty Courts they are really useful; for although the fines and punishments they inflict are generally excessive, and, according to our ideas, quite disproportioned to the offences committed, they are always rigidly enforced; and the result has been that drunkenness, which had lately been increasing to a fearful extent among the Natives, has now almost disappeared; and acts of violence, such as

17

seizing horses, &c., amongst themselves, rarely now occur.

> The action of the Runangas will, however, I am sorry to say, effectually put a stop to sales of land to the Government in those parts of the district to which their influence extends. On this point they will listen to no argument, hear no reason. But the evil is not altogether unmixed; for they have, also, removed the chance of further bloodshed, by preventing lands from being sold by claimants with doubtful titles; or, what was still more dangerous, by rightful and acknowledged claimants, against the wishes of a majority of those interested.[5]

Ward points to the use of the traditional term 'runanga', rather than the 'komiti' of the missionaries, as suggesting 'a trend indicative of the Maori leaders' reassertion of their own culture and their independence of the Pakeha'.[6] For although there was certainly a social control element to these, as he adds:

> the Maori were concerned with much more than the control of petty crime. Their real concern was that they were losing control of their own destinies, and being subordinated to the political and economic power of the settlers. The official rhetoric of Waitangi, that Maori and settlers were one people, was increasingly considered false.[7]

Yet without any legal authority with which to enforce their decisions against recalcitrant kin, these runanga were in a precarious position, and some leaders looked to the government for support. As early as 1847 the Wesleyan missionary John Whiteley had urged that runanga be encouraged to revive, provided this was 'under the superintendence of the Government'.[8] In a situation where runanga were being spontaneously revived in modified form, the government now appears to have seen this as an opportunity to bring them under the aegis of the Crown whilst using them to counter the perceived threat of the proto-nationalist Kingitanga. Indirect rule rather than genuine self-government was the aim, and behind this lay the ulterior motive of individualising and investigating land titles, thereby facilitating alienation to the settlers.[9] After visiting

Kingite leaders in the Waikato in 1857 Governor Gore Browne decided to send F.D. Fenton to the district as Resident Magistrate, principally with a view to utilising the runanga as a state-sponsored rival authority to the King. Fenton's mission met with an encouraging response from some sections of Tainui, but once he began meddling with land claims he alienated the Waikato people and was withdrawn from the district early in 1858 before further damage could be done.[10]

Enough promise had been shown to suggest that, if applied more judiciously, this scheme of indirect rule might stand some chance of success, and in 1858 the Assembly passed a range of measures designed to provide the legislative framework for its more general application. The Native Districts Regulation Act provided for the Governor-in-Council to proclaim native districts within which runanga could issue by-laws on matters of local concern, under the chairmanship of a Pakeha. The Native Circuit Courts Act provided for the appointment of Resident Magistrates, who, along with local Maori assessors and juries, would enforce these by-laws as well as the common law. But one of the primary underlying motives behind this adoption of the runanga system was revealed by the third measure, the Native Territorial Rights Bill, which envisaged these magistrates, assisted by a jury, investigating customary land rights and awarding title either individually or tribally, with up to 50,000 acres a year in individual title permitted to be sold directly to settlers, subject to a 10s per acre tax.[11] Gore Browne insisted that the bill be reserved for the royal assent. Concurring in his objections to the proposed measure, the Colonial Office disallowed it.

Despite this, it was apparent even prior to the Waitara dispute that some more settled form for determining the rightful owners to Maori land prior to any purchase was required. Gore Browne's proposal that a Native Council composed of public figures such as Bishop Selwyn and the former Chief Justice, Sir William Martin, undertake responsibility for Maori affairs (including the investigation and extinction of native titles) did not gain support among settlers or their elected Assembly.[12] At the Kohimarama

Conference of 1860, which had been convened by the Governor largely with the aim of shoring up support for the Crown's actions with respect to Waitara, and thereby marginalising the Taranaki and Waikato tribes, this question was again raised. McLean read a message to the assembled chiefs in which Gore Browne stated that:

> It is very desirable that some general principles regulating the boundaries of land belonging to different Tribes should be generally received and adopted: for, until the rights of property are clearly defined, progress in civilization must be both slow and uncertain. When disputes arise between different Tribes in reference to land, they might be referred to a committee of disinterested and influential Chiefs, selected at a Conference similar to the one now held at Kohimarama.
>
> There is also a simpler plan universally adopted in Hindostan, which appears well suited to the circumstances of New Zealand, viz., when men cannot agree as to their respective rights, each party chooses two persons, and these four choose a chief of another tribe having no interest in the matter disputed. Then the five sit in judgement and decide who is right and who is wrong; but before they pronounce judgement, both the contending parties solemnly engage to abide by it.[13]

Paora Tuhaere of Ngati Whatua, however, pointed out that the government refused to issue Crown grants for customary Maori land like those that settlers were entitled to receive for land which they owned.[14] Clearly at least some participants at the conference considered that the government's primary concern was with acquiring Maori land, rather than protecting them in tribal ownership. Despite McLean's urging that the Governor was 'most anxious that some means should be devised by the chiefs of this Conference to define tribal boundaries', nothing substantial appears to have come from the Kohimarama meeting. And Gore Browne's proposal to call an annual conference of Maori leaders at which such issues might be discussed was dismissed by his successor, Sir George Grey, who believed that it would not be 'wise to call a number of semi-barbarous Natives together to frame a Constitution for themselves'.[15]

Meanwhile, Gore Browne wrote to the Judges of the Supreme Court to seek their advice on 'a subject which has long engaged his attention, but which is surrounded with difficulties'.[16] The Governor asked whether the constitution and mode of procedure of the Supreme Court could be successfully adapted to the investigation and determination of native title, and if not, whether an efficient court could be established for such a purpose, and with what constitution and procedure. In response to the first question Chief Justice Arney and his two colleagues responded that, 'Even with the element of a Maori jury introduced, and the treatment of Maori Customs as matters of fact and not of law...the Supreme Court could not be practically applied in such cases to the satisfaction and with the concurrence of particular litigants or the mass of the Native community'.[17] Essentially, then, the Judges believed that a formal court of law was not an appropriate mechanism for determining native title.

On the second part of the question, the Judges, though reluctant to comment on a matter 'so necessarily involved with political considerations', stated that:

> we feel justified in suggesting that a competent tribunal might probably be established by the formation of a Land Jury, selected by lot or otherwise, from members of the various tribes in previously defined districts, nominated by such tribes as competent to act in that capacity, to be presided over by a European Officer or Commissioner (not being an Agent of the Crown for the purchase of Land) conversant with the Maori language, and assisted if necessary by a Native Assessor, and whose duty it should be merely to propound the questions for the decision of the jury, to record their verdict, and to administer Oaths to witnesses.

Basically, then, the Judges of the Supreme Court advocated that Maori should determine land titles themselves, with a Pakeha official present to rubber-stamp their decisions and ensure that correct procedure was followed. This was remarkably close to what many Maori consistently advocated in following decades, although Gore Browne's belief that Maori would be incapable of deciding land rights in an impartial manner was unfortunately to become an equally common (if less than valid) counter-argument to this:

> it occurs to me that a judicial officer (query a Judge) residing in Auckland should have power to issue a Commission enabling the holder to associate two Native Assessors with himself, and then to empanel a Jury, as advised by the Judges. I am myself inclined to think that the decision of a Commissioner, with disinterested Native Assessors, would be safer and more likely to decide impartially than a Maori Jury; but I hesitate to advise anything not exactly in accordance with the opinion of the Judges, such a Court, however constituted, would be powerless unless both parties consent to abide by its decrees, but time and experience might give it additional influence.[18]

This was the crux of the matter. In the tense racial atmosphere that prevailed in the early 1860s any land titles court controlled by Pakeha would most likely have been interpreted by many Maori as just another ruse to obtain their lands. Convincing Maori that they would have effective control of any such tribunal was therefore the key to its success. Grey, who succeeded Gore Browne as Governor in October 1861, was informed by the Secretary of State for the Colonies that the British government would not object to 'any prudent plan for the individualization of Native title, and for direct purchase under proper safeguards' which the colonial administration might wish to adopt.[19] More astutely perhaps than Gore Browne, though, Grey realised that the best means of adopting such a policy was to work through Maori runanga. Thus in outlining a comprehensive scheme of 'new institutions' based on village and district runanga, to be overseen by Resident Magistrates and Civil Commissioners, Grey suggested that the district runanga should be empowered to decide 'the adjustment of disputed land boundaries, of tribes, of hapus, or of individuals, and for deciding who may be the true owners of any Native lands', as well as recommending the terms and conditions on which Crown grants might be issued, and controlling the alienation of lands once title had been ascertained.[20] Grey proposed that:

> So soon as the boundaries and ownership of any lands in any District have been ascertained and defined, in accordance with the regulations of the Runanga, and have been registered in the Civil Commissioner's office and approved by the Government, the Native owners will be permitted to dispose of any such lands, or part of such lands, not exceeding the extent of one farm, by direct sale to any purchaser who may be approved of by the Government on the recommendation of the Runanga, on such conditions as may be agreed on between the seller and purchaser.[21]

Importantly, too, given that the Native Land Purchase Ordinance of 1846 prohibited Maori from leasing their lands to the settlers (as many tribes were anxious to do), Grey also advocated that those found to be the rightful owners should be permitted to lease their lands on such terms as might be decided upon by the government after consultation with the district runanga. Although the Fox ministry took exception to some parts of Grey's scheme, the essential feature of allowing runanga to determine land titles and control alienations was not disputed. William Fox made it clear that to a large extent this was a matter of necessity. Any attempt to impose alien institutions on Maori would be fraught with danger, and as the Colonial Secretary noted:

> much jealousy exists at the present moment in the minds of the Natives on the subject. There seems to be only one method of removing that feeling, without at the same time absolutely abstaining from all further purchase: and that is to leave the matter substantially in the hands of the Runangas. A title sifted through the investigation of these bodies (whose knowledge on the subject will in all except a comparatively small number of disputed cases be found complete), and made the subject of publicity, may be considered as pretty well ascertained.[22]

Fox maintained that, once title had been ascertained, 'the Natives should then be left to hold, sell, lease, or otherwise dispose of their lands in such manner as they themselves might choose'.

Governor Grey was prepared to compromise on this point, stating that all he desired was that 'no one should be allowed to grasp more land than he can use'. Only bona fide settlers should be permitted to purchase land from Maori and even then only with the concurrence of the runanga. He would, Grey added, 'fear at present to go further. The great object is to devise a system which, at this critical time, both Natives and Europeans will gratefully accept'.[23] This was as close as the colony had come to having a single, coherent policy on native affairs since responsible government had been granted to the settlers, and Fox even suggested a very sensible amendment to Grey's scheme in the case of disputed titles:

> Ministers conceive that, when once confidence in our rule shall have been established, no great difficulty will be found in inducing the Natives to refer these to some tribunal, to be hereafter constituted, of a certain number of the great Chiefs of the country, whose decisions, on receiving the ultimate sanction of the Government, may become final.[24]

As Ward says, this proposal:

> envisaged the preservation of corporate tribal authority over land, during both the determination of title and alienation. It therefore contrasted with the alternative view, widely favoured among the settlers, that Maori title should be individualised as quickly as possible and direct dealing between individual Maori and settlers permitted.[25]

Even if both Grey's and Fox's correspondence on this question suggests that tribal authority was being recognised only reluctantly and until such time as the Crown might be in a position to enforce a European system of land tenure on Maori, there is no doubt that such a policy if persevered with and used to bring about a reconciliation with moderate leaders of the Kingitanga such as Wiremu Tamihana, might have prevented nearly a decade of bloody fighting and racial conflict. Controlled settlement of Maori districts on terms not inconsistent with the Treaty of Waitangi might have been possible. Unfortunately settler self-interest remained a major obstacle to this. As soon as it became clear that few runanga were willing to throw open their lands to full-scale colonisation, the runanga scheme became discredited, and a showdown with the King movement began to be spoken of as inevitable. And whether or not Grey genuinely believed that the plan of 'new institutions' might avert a looming showdown with the Kingites, or had merely intended these to buy time while he made preparations for an attack on Waikato (as some historians have suggested), the fact that the official runanga scheme was used in an effort to undermine the King movement contributed substantially to its ultimate failure to prevent such a conflict.

Early in July 1862 Fox introduced a Native Lands Bill which essentially confirmed the power of the runanga to determine titles and control alienations to bona fide settlers (who would receive freehold title only after ten years occupancy).[26] Attempting to justify this policy to an increasingly belligerent Assembly, Fox informed its members that:

> we look to the runanga, or Native council, as the *point d'appui* to which to attach the machinery of self-government, and by which to connect them with our own institutions...We have no choice but to use it, it exists as a fact, it is part of the very existence of the Maori – we can nor more put it down than we can stay the advancing waves of the rising tide; and, if we do not use it for good purposes, it will assuredly be used against us for bad.[27]

With its native policies roundly under attack both inside and outside the Assembly, the Fox ministry resigned a few weeks later, and was replaced by a new hard-line administration (led by Alfred Domett, with Francis Dillon Bell as Native Minister) which was entirely unsympathetic to the runanga system. The Native Lands Act passed by this administration during the same session contained few of the safeguards which Fox's bill had sought to put in place before waiving the Crown's right of pre-emption. No limit was placed on the amount of land any settler could buy, and there was no requirement to prove occupation before freehold title was granted, opening the door for speculators such as

Thomas Russell and Frederick Whitaker – both members of the Domett ministry – to trade in Maori lands. The attraction of such speculation was heightened further by the fact that the Act did not put in place any mechanism for ensuring Maori received a fair value for their lands, such as a requirement to sell by public auction.[28]

The clearest indication that this Act was intended to undermine rather than acknowledge tribal authority with respect to land was the fact that any individual awarded title was free to dispose of this without reference to the runanga. Moreover, the Act was also vague as to the constitution of the 'Courts' to be established to determine titles, merely specifying that every such court was to be presided over by a European magistrate and that the Governor was empowered to make rules for their conduct, including the empanelling of juries. This was a long way from the explicit acknowledgement of the right of runanga to determine titles and control alienations which Fox's bill had provided for, and gave the government considerable discretion to decide the make-up of any courts that were established. Despite this, Bell claimed in Parliament that:

> we desire, subject to proper safeguards, that the Natives themselves should be empowered to ascertain and define their own titles; and we therefore propose to constitute Courts which, after a proper survey, a careful inquiry, and confirmation of their proceedings by the Governor, shall have the power of certifying who, according to Native custom, are the owners of any land.[29]

Curiously, though, Bell cited Royal Instructions from 1841 that Commissioners be vested with 'an effectual and summary jurisdiction' to determine land titles, and Earl Grey's 1846 Instructions (never implemented) for the compulsory registration of all Maori land once investigated by a land court, in support of the Crown's right to 'take a part in the ascertainment and determination of Native title'. It would appear that the Act was framed and justified in such a way that although Maori involvement in the investigation of titles might be conceded where necessary, this could always be reduced where circumstances allowed.

Initially, however, those tribes informed of the Act's provisions were told that they themselves would be responsible for determining titles. At Whanganui, for example, the local Resident Magistrate, John White, informed Maori that:

> the Government had sent a Bill home to get the Queen's consent to let the Maori lease or sell his land to anyone. After the claim by Maoris, to Maori land, had been investigated by, and proved before, the Native Assessors, guided by Maori custom respecting land under the supervision of the European Resident Magistrate...the Governor would issue Crown grants to those who the court gave the land.[30]

Whanganui Maori were reportedly well satisfied with the process of determining title which White had outlined. As Ward says, although the Act failed to provide for tribal control over the alienation of lands, the concept of a Native Land Court consisting of panels of chiefs in each district meeting under the chairmanship of the local Resident Magistrate 'envisaged working through existing Maori leadership, determining, as far as possible, the various customary rights in the land, and agreeing, after exchange and arbitration of claims, who would share in the grant of a legal title'.[31] It seems likely, too, that, notwithstanding the provisions allowing individuals to apply for investigations before selling their interests, courts sitting on the marae might have dissuaded all but the most recalcitrant from ignoring the wishes of their kin. Selling the family jewels in defiance of the rest of one's hapu was made much easier when courts were later convened in alien environments, far from the lands under investigation.

By the time that the royal assent to the Native Lands Act 1862 was received the Waikato War was all but imminent, rendering its provisions largely redundant, other than for a handful of claims heard in the more settled north. Yet these few hearings brought about encouraging results. At Kaipara, for example, the local Resident Magistrate, John Rogan, convened a panel of Assessors from the district in June 1864 to determine titles to two blocks earmarked for sale. According to one correspondent's report, 'The

Court was conducted with all the decorum and order that could be found in any European assembly', and:

> the native Judges appeared well suited for the important task they have to perform. They well know that all the responsibility will fall upon themselves should they award certificates to any but the rightful owners – hence the examinations are extremely minute and well and ably conducted.[32]

At the end of proceedings lists of owners were announced and the blocks were made out in the name of just one chief, to simplify the transfer to the purchasing settlers. Rogan reported that the Court's decisions afforded 'general satisfaction', with the owners unanimously acknowledging the sales.[33]

The 1862 Act was not entirely satisfactory from a Maori point of view, particularly when compared to earlier proposals to allow runanga to determine titles and control alienations, but it was undoubtedly far superior to the 1865 Act which repealed and replaced it. Early in January 1865 F.D. Fenton was appointed as the first Chief Judge of a newly constituted Native Land Court. At the same time all existing districts proclaimed under the 1862 Act were annulled and the entire country was placed under the jurisdiction of one court, to which Rogan and a number of others were appointed Judges.[34] This did not bode well for the future of a flexible, localised 'court' with Maori essentially determining ownership themselves, and indeed the bill which Fenton proceeded to draft (passed into law after surprisingly little debate as the Native Lands Act in October 1865) was far more precise in the constitution of the court to be established, which was to be one with minimal Maori involvement in the determination of titles.

In 1861 Chief Justice Arney and his colleagues had informed the Governor that a formal court of law was not an appropriate mechanism for determining native title, and Fenton, apparently concurring with this view on the basis of his experiences in Waikato, had helped to draft the 1862 Act, which envisaged local Resident Magistrates meeting with the chiefs of a district and mediating in the settlement of tribal boundaries.[35] Yet having been given a virtual free hand in drafting fresh legislation and reorganising the system of land title adjudication, Fenton, once appointed Chief Judge, set about creating a formal institution based on the Supreme Court, 'whereby a roving Judge could sit in any centre, summon witnesses, hear evidence and hand down a judgment with due pomp and formality'.[36] The contrast with the 1862 legislation, which had been successfully implemented by Rogan at Kaipara, was considerable. As Ward says:

> The 1862 Act envisaged what was essentially a commission of the leading chiefs of the area under consideration, meeting under the chairmanship of the R.M. or Civil Commissioner of the district, and arguing out a consensus. This would have been an open flexible institution, not too removed from traditional mechanisms for resolving land disputes, and little relevant information would have escaped it. But the 1865 Act established a very different court, one in which the Judge called hearings in the nearest comfortable town, sat in dignified station, heard evidence marshalled by lawyers according to complex legal formalities, and handed down *ex cathedra* decisions which, on occasion, were so far short of the realities of customary rights that they ignored the claims of villagers within sight of the court because they had not been properly presented in evidence. This highly formal tribunal had been created partly because it was believed necessary to overawe the contending Maori claimants into acceptance of its decisions, but also because its creator, F.D. Fenton, Chief Judge of the court from 1865 to 1882, was very much concerned with power and status seeking and wanted to make his own position analogous to that of a Supreme Court Judge. A Maori Assessor, sometimes two, sat with the court but the extent of his influence depended very much on the attitude of the presiding judge. For example, Judge Maning...boasted that he took no account of his Assessors' opinions and bemoaned his misfortune at having to sit 'cheek by jowl' with them for days on end in the court. Wiremu Te Wheoro, a high-ranking Waikato chief of progressive opinions, who had supported the establishment of the 'new institutions' in 1861, had taken up arms on the government side during the wars, and had become an Assessor both of the R.M.'s

court and the Native Land Court in the belief that the government genuinely meant to give Maoris a full share in the administration and the economy, began to experience his disillusionment on the Land Court bench. 'It would appear', he said, 'when a block was going through the Native Land Court, as if the block was owned by the Court itself, and not by the litigants.' He shortly resigned his office, saying it was a sham.[37]

Although the 1865 Act provided for juries to be appointed either at the discretion of the presiding Judge or upon application by interested parties, the former were unwilling to relinquish their powers of adjudication, whilst few Maori were familiar with the provisions of the legislation. In the one instance in which a jury was requested, in the Wairarapa district, none was convened, because the necessary regulations had not been promulgated.[38]

The method of investigating land titles introduced by the 1865 Act was one which ignored the complex and fluid customary land usages of Maori, whereby more than one party might be recognised as having overlapping interests in an area, or might have rights to specific resources, rather than absolute ownership of all resources in a particular locality.[39] In a runanga environment the emphasis was on pragmatic compromise, with the potential for these varying interests to be acknowledged and a peaceful resolution made between contending parties. Instead, the adversarial, winner-takes-all nature of the Native Land Court system imposed a rigid set of rules for awarding title based on simplistic notions of the traditional bases of native title in Maori society, with conquest elevated over whakapapa and no allowance made for tribal variations in custom.[40] As Ward says, this system was one which:

> invited not co-operation but contention between parties who – although the Court frequently divided the land – could win all, or lose all, on the Judge's nod. It ushered in an era of bitter contesting, of lying and false evidence. The legalistic nature of the Court also instituted a costly and tedious paraphernalia of lawyers, agents, legal rules and precedents – a morass in which the Maori floundered for

decades, frittering away their estates in ruinous expenses and still all too often not getting equitable awards.[41]

There was certainly some justification for Pakeha officials such as Resident Magistrates to assist in settling land titles, and ratifying agreements reached between contending parties in a modified runanga situation, provided this was done with the consent of all interested parties. This was in line with what many Maori themselves later requested and, as a number of nineteenth-century observers asserted, would have produced a fairer, less adversarial resolution of disputed land titles. Instead, as the Native Land Laws Commission commented in 1891:

> The Natives, being compelled to enter the arena of the Court and contest the title to land, which they could with ease have settled in their own runangas, learned to look upon our method of getting land as merely another form of their old wars. Formerly they fought with guns, and spears, and clubs; now, to accomplish the same end, the defeat of opponents and the conquering of territory, they learned to fight with the brain and the tongue. As in the olden time all means were fair in war, so, pitted by our laws against each other in the Courts, they held all stratagems to be honest, all testimony justifiable, which conduced to success. ...
>
> So utterly unreliable have many of the Maoris become during late years that it is now the fashion amongst some of them not only to spoil the living, but to plunder the dead. The fabrication of spurious wills has, in the words of several witnesses, like the false swearing in the Native Land Court, 'become a fine art.' Natives who, speaking in their own runangas, will testify with strict and impartial truth, often against their own interests, when speaking in the Native Land Court will not hesitate to swear deliberately to a narrative false and groundless from beginning to end.[42]

It is little wonder that many Maori felt obliged to advance false evidence in support of their claims before the Native Land Court, given that even those with valid claims according to customary Maori law risked losing all because of a Pakeha Judge's ignorance of, unwillingness to comply with, or – most importantly –

inability to implement according to the laws under which the Land Court operated, traditional land rights in respect of usually arbitrarily defined land 'blocks'. Tailoring evidence to comply with the distorted application of customary land tenure laws used in the Land Court became an essential survival tactic for many Maori in the nineteenth century.

The crux of the matter lay in the fact that the Native Land Court was intended not merely to determine native title to Maori lands but to extinguish this and replace it with a transferable title which would expedite the alienation of land to the settlers. And while the 1862 Act had sought to do this by cautious means, by 1865 settler attitudes had hardened, as had the government's confidence, in the wake of a generally successful Waikato campaign against the Kingitanga, that it could impose this tenurial reform on Maori without endangering the peace of the colony unnecessarily. This 'reform' and the encouragement of alienation would inevitably involve distortions of customary land tenure. As T.W. Lewis, Native Under-Secretary for more than a decade, informed the Rees–Carroll Commission in 1891:

> the whole object of appointing a Court for the ascertainment of Native title was to enable alienation for settlement. Unless this object is attained the Court serves no good purpose, and the Natives would be better without it, as, in my opinion, fairer Native occupation would be had under the Maoris' own customs and usages without any intervention whatever from outside.[43]

With most North Island iwi still solidly opposed to the alienation of their lands, the process by which this was to be achieved was one which deliberately aimed at the abolition of traditional Maori social structures and tribal ownership of lands. As Henry Sewell, the Attorney-General at the time that both the 1862 and 1865 Acts were passed, later commented:

> The object of the Native Lands Act was two-fold: to bring the great bulk of the lands of the Northern Island which belonged to the Natives, and which, before the passing of that Act, were *extra commercium* – except through the means of the old land purchase

system, which had entirely broken down – within the reach of colonization. The other great object was, the detribalization of the Natives – to destroy, if it were possible, the principle of communism which ran through the whole of their institutions, upon which their social system was based, and which stood as a barrier in the way of all attempts to amalgamate the Native race into our own social and political system. It was hoped that by the individualization of titles to land, giving them the same individual ownership which we ourselves possessed, they would lose their communistic character, and that their social status would become assimilated to our own.[44]

Not only did the Act seek to create an individual title in law where none existed in Maori custom, but it required just one claimant to apply for investigation of title to set in train the whole costly and disruptive process of a Land Court hearing. Thus there was little voluntary about the implementation of the Act, which grievously undermined tribal authority in land dealings.[45] 'Rightful Maori owners', as Ward says, 'could not avoid litigation and expensive surveys if false claims were put forward, since Fenton, seeking to inflate the status of the Court, insisted that judgments be based only upon evidence presented before it'.[46] And although provision was made in the Act for blocks of more than 5000 acres to be awarded to tribes, rather than individuals, this provision was rarely adopted by the Court's Judges, who saw their primary function as extinguishing, not perpetuating, tribal ownership of lands. H.A.H. Monro, one of the first appointees to the Land Court bench, believed, for example, that the communal ownership of Maori lands 'recognised by the Crown in the Treaty of Waitangi' was 'too much at variance with the habits of a civilized community' to be taken cognisance of in the Court's operations.[47]

Instead of granting land to specified tribes in accordance with the principles of collective ownership which underlay customary Maori land tenure, the Court's Judges instead awarded blocks to ten or fewer chiefs, regardless of the number of owners or the extent of the blocks. As the Rees–Carroll Commission reported:

> It was believed that these ten were trustees for the whole body. It was so stated in many cases to the Maoris by the Judges of the Native Land Court...The certificate, however, erroneously alleged that they were the absolute owners of the land according to Native custom, and the Crown grants, which were issued to them by name, vested an absolute estate of freehold in possession, unencumbered by any trusts or conditions whatever. Thus, in Hawke's Bay 569,220 acres of the finest land in New Zealand... which belonged to nearly four thousand Natives, who were living upon and cultivating small homesteads, were vested in about two hundred and fifty grantees, without any trust being declared in favour of the vast majority of the persons ascertained by the Native Land Court to be its owners according to Native custom.[48]

Although an 1867 amendment to the Native Lands Act provided for the names of all owners to be endorsed on the back of the certificate of title, this was ignored by Chief Judge Fenton, who believed that 'To recognise the kind of agency contended for would be to build up communal ownership, and would tend to perpetuate the evil instead of removing it'.[49] And while the Native Land Act of 1873 marked the end of the 'ten-owner system' by specifying that every owner was to be named on the memorial of ownership, since it was to be on this basis that each individual's proportionate share was to be defined, this new legislation took the whole process of individualisation a step further. Europeans could negotiate piecemeal purchases of the interests of each individual, and although theoretically requiring the consent of all owners before an alienation could be completed, in practice frequently found it more convenient to seek a partition of the block if any interests could not be acquired. Thus the 1873 Act was probably an even greater departure from the basis of customary Maori ownership, since it supposed that the proportionate interests of each individual could be defined and marked on the ground when all the weight of evidence pointed to the absurdity of such a suggestion.[50] As W.L. Rees commented in 1884:

> A very gross act of cruelty and bad faith as well as folly was perpetrated by us when we compelled the Natives to hold their lands as individuals. The Treaty of Waitangi assured them of 'all their rights in their lands'. The chief right of all was the right of tribal ownership – but a tribe of five hundred persons is totally different from five hundred distinct and opposing claimants. It is the tribe which owns the land, and it is the tribe which, in justice, ought to have sole power to use it or to deal with it.[51]

Indeed the 1873 Act further breached the rangatiratanga principle in that those chiefs who had managed to resist the pressures of alienation and remained good trustees for their people were unable to prevent piecemeal and surreptitious sales of individual shares.[52] As Ward says:

> The Crown Grants awarded after an order of the Native Land Court extinguished customary tenure and substituted rights of a totally different order – including the right of an individual title-holder to sell his interest to any settler who wished to buy it. This led to a judicial raupatu as devastating as any confiscations...but directed without distinction against allies and opponents of the government...The reciprocal relationship implied in the tino rangatiratanga guaranteed by the Treaty was destroyed. Neither chiefs nor people were able any longer to check each other. Maori society was fundamentally disrupted and exposed to half a century and more of land-sharking.[53]

On the basis of the certificates of title issued by the Court, Maori land could for the first time be used as security for debts. As M.P.K. Sorrenson says: 'This was a fundamental factor that sooner or later coerced even strong opponents of sale into disposing of land'.[54] Speculators or land agents could always find one or two individuals from a tribe willing to sell land, or to accept credit on supplies from the local hotelier or storekeeper. Once they did, any form of collective opposition to land sales or the Court system proved almost impossible. Compelled to enter the Native Land Court arena by applications for investigation of title by others, non-sellers frequently found that, even if successful in defending their claims, the costs involved in attending Court sittings in faraway towns, often for months on end, swallowed up the land. In fact, Wi Pere informed the Rees–Carroll Commission in 1891 that in many instances the rightful owners were dissuaded from attending the Court's hearing simply by the high costs involved in doing so.[55] Either way, as many Maori soon realised, the net outcome was likely to be much the same regardless of whether they attended or not.

Not only did Native Land Court sittings facilitate the alienation of land to the settlers, they also endangered Maori health. Sorrenson, Ian Pool and others have shown that the drastic decline in the total Maori population during the second half of the nineteenth century was underlain by regional variations reflecting different levels of Land Court and purchase activity.[56] In districts where both were high, the rate of decrease was correspondingly accelerated. Conversely, those districts which remained closed to the Land Court and would-be purchasers (such as the King Country and Te Urewera) retained relatively stable populations until their eventual 'opening up' to these harbingers of colonisation in the late 1880s. The deleterious consequences of Land Court sittings on Maori society were regularly brought to the notice of politicians and Native Department officials. The member of Parliament Robert Bruce informed the House in 1885, for example, that:

> we could not devise a more ingenious method of destroying the whole of the Maori race than by these Courts. The Natives come from their villages in the interior, and have to hang about sometimes for months in our centres of population, where they are exposed to many demoralizing influences. They are brought into contact with the lowest class of society, and are exposed to temptation, and the result is that a great number contract diseases and die...Some little time ago I was taking a ride through the interior, and I was perfectly astonished at hearing that a subject of conversation at each hapu I visited was the number of Natives who had died in consequence of attendance at the Native Land Court at Wanganui. That has always appeared to me to be a disgrace to the colony.[57]

## The Native Land Court Assumes Control

Despite frequent reports of this nature, little was done to alleviate Land Court conditions.

Just as damaging in the longer term was the stipulation that hereditary succession was to be determined 'according to [English] law as nearly as it can be reconciled with Native Custom'. In the precedent-setting Papakura succession case Fenton announced that

> Instead of subordinating English tenures to Maori customs, it will be the duty of the Court, in administering this Act, to cause as rapid an introduction amongst the Maoris, not only of English tenures, but of the English rules of descent, as can be secured without violently shocking Maori prejudices.[58]

This involved creating the new and entirely arbitrary precedent that all children of the deceased were to succeed to titles in approximately equal shares, completely ignoring complex Maori rules of succession based on factors such as occupancy, sex and rank. The result of this deliberate suppression of Maori custom was that:

> titles soon became divided into an infinite number of shares, smaller and less economic with each succeeding generation, until they were soon so over-crowded and fragmented as to put the actual land almost beyond efficient use. Moreover, the whole Maori population was encouraged to indulge in the pursuit of inheritances from both sides of their ancestry and in districts remote from where they lived.[59]

And as the Waitangi Tribunal has pointed out in its *Taranaki Report*, if this conversion of customary Maori land tenure was justified on the basis that titles should be held on the same basis as European freehold land, the enforced tenurial reform brought about by the Native Land Court has been a signal failure, since even today:

> there is no general land in such a similar state of multiple ownership and fragmentation. These results would not have happened had the Government acknowledged the right of Maori autonomy and had it allowed Maori to make their own decisions on how to manage their lands.[60]

This is the key point about the Native Land Court system imposed on Maori from 1865. Maori were not represented in Parliament at the time that the Court was introduced and were not consulted on the question. Thus Maori were effectively denied a voice in the framing of laws concerning customary Maori lands, despite the Treaty of Waitangi's clear guarantee that they should be allowed to hold for so long as they wished such customary lands and other resources as they might 'collectively or individually possess'. This stands in marked contrast to the preamble to the 1865 Act which stated as one of the principal aims of the measure, 'to encourage the extinction of such proprietary customs and to provide for the conversion of such modes of ownership into titles derived from the Crown'.

Maori lands were 'collectively' or tribally owned. And despite the Crown's arguments that the Native Land Court was not compulsory and that Maori 'were and are at liberty to avail themselves of the powers conferred, or to abstain from doing so, at their pleasure',[61] the tribal veto over individual land dealings which Wiremu Kingi had sought to uphold at Waitara was deliberately and grievously undermined by the Native Land Court system. From a tribal perspective there was little voluntary about this process and, given its quickly perceived consequences for Maori society, it is hardly surprising that many tribes soon became stern critics of the Court and sought to promote their own institutions for determining titles to, and controlling the alienation of, tribally owned lands.

# 3. Early Proposals for Reform

With warfare still ravaging many parts of the North Island in the 1860s, the Native Land Court's operations were initially confined to more settled districts such as Northland and Hawke's Bay. But in the early 1870s, with the resumption of peace, the Court's sphere of activity widened considerably. Many former 'rebel' tribes, still smarting at the confiscation of large tracts of territory, remained actively hostile to the Crown, and initially at least it was the government's former allies who came under immense pressure to pass their lands through the Court as a sign of their continuing loyalty to the Queen. By the early 1880s, however, after nearly a decade of concerted pressure from government and private land purchase agents, even the tribes of the King Country Rohe Potae were writing that 'the practices carried on at the Land Courts have become a source of anxiety to us and a burden upon us', adding rhetorically:

> What possible benefit would we derive from roads, railways and Land Courts if they became the means of depriving us of our lands? We can live as we are situated at present, without roads, railways, or Courts, but we could not live without our lands.[1]

Many Hawke's Bay Maori, finding their lands effectively confiscated and granted to a handful of chiefs by the Court's ten-owner rule, had asked similar questions in the 1860s, especially given overwhelming evidence that these individuals were unable to resist the cynical ploys of land speculators. In 1867 G.S. Cooper reported that:

> The chiefs are allowed, indeed sometimes tempted to take credit without stint from merchants, tradesmen, and often from their own tenants, and this they do with the utmost readiness, and to an extent

almost incredible. Some of the principal landowners are at this moment in debt to the amount of many thousands of pounds.

Then pressure is put upon them, and, seeing no other means of raising the money, they have begun to sell their land in every direction.[2]

The Hawke's Bay Resident Magistrate warned the government that a 'future of pauperism' awaited Maori in the district unless something was done to halt this process. Fenton, though, was less sympathetic, writing that:

The intemperance and waste so noticeable amongst the Maori landlords of Hawke's Bay are matters much to be regretted; but, in my judgement, it is not part of our duty to stop eminently good processes because certain bad and unpreventable results may collaterally flow from them, nor can it be averred that it is the duty of the Legislature to make people careful of their property by Act of Parliament, so long as their profligacy injures no one but themselves. It is well that all the money squandered by the Maori landlords is spent in the place whence it is drawn. Education will cure the evil, for drunkenness is the vice of the uncultivated and brutish man.[3]

The 1867 amendment to the Native Lands Act requiring all owners to be listed on the certificate of title proved largely ineffectual thanks to Fenton's reluctance to 'stop eminently good processes'. Many Maori did not even know of this provision, and the Chief Judge, claiming a 'discretion' as to whether to apply it, made no effort to inform them.[4] By 1870, though, land dealings at Hawke's Bay had become a colonial scandal. Donald McLean, the Native Minister and a considerable landowner in the district himself, moved to allay this concern by passing the Native Lands Frauds Prevention Act, but opposed an amendment to allow the Trust Commissioners to investigate prior transactions. This, along with the part-time appointments made and evidence of political bias in the decisions of the Commissioners, largely negated the worth of the legislation.[5]

In a further move prompted by evidence of increasing Maori opposition to the work of the Native Land Court, McLean also appointed T.M. Haultain, a former soldier and Minister for Colonial Defence, to investigate the working of the Native Lands Act. Haultain reported back in 1871, maintaining rather unconvincingly that Maori were generally happy with the Native Land Court per se and at most sought a few minor reforms to the system introduced in 1865.[6] This is not borne out by the evidence of most of the Maori witnesses Haultain had consulted, whose views were published as appendices to his report. Te Wheoro of Waikato and Paora Tuhaere of Ngati Whatua, for example, in joint evidence advocated that:

> Instead of the present system of investigating titles to Native land, the Judges and Assessors should be done away with, and six Maori arbitrators should be appointed by opposing claimants, three by each side, who should hear and decide the cases; and if they agreed, their decision should be ratified by an officer of the Government. This officer might be the Resident Magistrate of the district, and should certainly be a local officer. Three of the present Judges might be appointed to districts for this purpose, but they should not move from place to place.[7]

Te Wheoro had been an Assessor of the Native Land Court since 1865, and Tuhaere was appointed as a special member of the Auckland provincial government in 1867.[8] Yet incredibly the pair informed Haultain that they did not know that juries might be appointed under the 1865 Act, and had not even seen a Maori translation of it.[9] How Te Wheoro, as an Assessor of the Court, was to implement a law the contents of which he had no means of knowing defies imagination. In view of this obvious indifference on the part of the government and Land Court Judges to the Assessors, it is hardly surprising that Te Wheoro also announced his intention to resign from the position in his evidence with Tuhaere, adding by way of valedictory remarks that he had been opposed to the Native Land Court from the outset and that it was 'a pity that the Maoris were not consulted before the Act was brought into the General Assembly'. In fact, Te

Wheoro and Tuhaere remarked with respect to the Assessors that they would do away with them altogether. 'They are of no use', the pair stated, 'and have little or nothing to say to the cases that are being tried; they sit like dummies, and only think of the pay they are going to get'. Many more complaints were levied against the Court by the pair, including insufficient notice of its sittings, its failure to 'sit as near as possible to the place where the claims are situated, so that the boundaries may be viewed or pointed out', the ten-owner system, the cost of surveys, the refusal of some Judges to impose alienation restrictions, even when requested by the owners, and the involvement of lawyers and interpreters in the process of determining title. Lawyers, the two chiefs remarked, 'know nothing of Maori custom, and go into all sorts of irrelevant questions, and cause a great deal of unnecessary expense. If one side has a lawyer, the other must employ one also'. Interpreters were even worse, in their view, 'for they prompt the witnesses as to what they are to say, and often advise them to state falsehoods; they also are an unnecessary expense'.[10]

Te Wheoro also forwarded to Haultain separate and more detailed proposals for an alternative runanga-based system of land title adjudication. This differed slightly from what he had advocated with Tuhaere, but he still argued that 'it would be by far the best plan to let the Maoris prove their titles themselves'.[11] Under this plan six members would be selected for each runanga, with a seventh acting as a chairman. These runanga, comprising persons with no interests in the area, would meet on or near the lands under consideration. Te Wheoro added:

> Let it be for the Magistrates of the different districts to carry out or give effect to the decision of that Maori runanga. Let three of the Judges of the Court be retained to act within different districts, namely, Mr. Rogan for Kaipara; Mr. Fenton for Auckland; and Mr. Smith for the South; and let each Judge (Magistrate) act within his own district. The runanga should go into the cases, and submit them to the Judge. Should he have any statement to make it should be made before the runanga, who should then give consideration to it; and if they all approve, let the matter be finally settled.[12]

Had such a system been adopted from the outset, Te Wheoro remarked, 'all that the law would have had to do would have been to give legal effect to the decisions' of the runanga. As it was under the Native Land Court system, though:

> no matter where the land is, it is not inspected, and the land becomes the property of him who has made the most plausible statement; it goes, together with the houses and cultivations which are upon it, to a stranger. In some cases, perhaps, the Judge of the Court has seen the cultivations and the houses, but he only pays attention to the statements made by the parties before him, and says that it would not be right for him to speak of what he has seen, but only to take what is stated in the Court.[13]

Te Wheoro was not exaggerating. Native Land Court Judges were bound by the Chief Judge's ruling that only evidence presented in court could be considered. The impact of this was only compounded by inadequate notice of hearings, or courts convened at distant townships, meaning that many owners were excluded from titles through non-attendance. Judges were indeed, in theory at least, obliged to ignore what they had seen (or knew to be the case from personal experience).[14]

Even northern Maori, who, according to official reports, were well satisfied with the work of the Court and anxious to obtain Crown grants in order to farm their lands,[15] informed Haultain that they wished to see lawyers and private interpreters excluded from the Court, and sought to have individuals prevented from applying for investigations of title without tribal support. Many also stated that they wanted to see the provision allowing for juries to decide cases to be implemented. Hemi Tautari, an Assessor from the Bay of Islands, for example, stated that it was 'not advisable that a claim should be investigated at the instance of a decided minority' and that 'Native jurors could be depended upon when not directly interested in a case'.[16] Hone Mohi Tawhai of Waima considered that the Judges and Assessors of the Court had no faults except that 'the laws lead them to sin', perhaps cryptically suggesting a lack of flexibility in the Court's procedures, whilst Wiremu Pomare, of Ngapuhi, also objected to any one person being able to demand an investigation into any block of land. No man should be able to make a claim for investigation without the consent of the majority of those interested, he maintained, adding that he would like to see the jury system implemented and that:

> The Maoris would like all the laws connected with Natives and their lands translated and circulated, as newspapers are amongst the Europeans. In the same way, what the Maori Members say in the Assembly should be told to us. We know nothing of the laws, they are never sent to us; they are stowed away in the pigeon-holes of the Government, and we never see them.[17]

Clearly if the 1865 Act and its amendments had been translated into Maori, this information had not been circulated widely. Most Maori were reliant on word of mouth or conscientious Judges to fully explain the provisions of the legislation (such as the right to request a jury) to them – neither particularly efficient or effective ways to convey the laws of the land. This helped to further marginalise Maori from the process of adjudicating titles to their lands, and was quite clearly contrary to the principles of Article Three of the Treaty of Waitangi, which had promised Maori 'all the rights and privileges' of British citizens.

That this failure to distribute Maori translations of the legislation had helped to deprive rightful claimants of land was evident from the evidence of Henare Tomoana, a prominent Ngati Kahungunu chief, who informed Haultain that it was not until late in 1870 that he had become aware of the fact that legislation had been passed three years previously providing for the names of all owners to be included on certificates of title. Tomoana also stated that his request to have the Heretaunga block made inalienable had been ignored by the presiding Judge, and outlined the highly dubious tactics used by prominent Hawke's Bay settlers in their notorious 'purchase' of the land.[18] Other Maori witnesses from the district were, not surprisingly, also scathing in their condemnation of the way in which the Court had operated at Hawke's Bay. Karaitiana Takamoana, for example, wrote:

> Let me here speak of one thing – a disapproval by me of this institution, the Native Land Court. Its fault is this: listening to the false statements of men who have no just claim to the land. Friends, this is a very bad practice. Our Maori custom is much preferable to this.
>
> This is another thing, the regulation of Crown grants. The fault in that is this: do you listen! Where there are one hundred or more men (as claimants), the Court only admits of ten being inserted in the Crown grant, while the one hundred are thrown carelessly out of their land. This is the fault of that regulation.
>
> Another fault of the Crown grant is, the European invites the man to whom the Crown grant belongs to drink spirits, and that Maori then says, 'I have no money'. Then the European says, 'Your money is your Crown grant – your land is your money'. I look upon this as being a cruelty to the Maoris (so that they may cease to have any land).[19]

He had, Takamoana added, only taken his lands before the Court that their ownership might be permanently settled and the lands prevented from being sold. Yet despite this, it appeared the land could be sold regardless of whether this was desired.

The thrust of almost all of the Maori submissions made before Haultain was that some measure of tribal control ought to be retained in the investigation of titles to and subsequent alienation of lands. Even those supportive of the Court desired this. Wiremu Patene of Waikato, for example, stated that although the Native Land Court was generally approved of, he did 'not think that any Native should be allowed to make a claim to the Court without the knowledge of all those who are interested; he should acquaint the tribe, who will consider whether his claim is right or wrong'. No land should be permitted to be sold without the full knowledge of the tribe.[20]

It was, though, Wiremu Hikairo, a Te Arawa (Ngati Rangiwewehi) Assessor of the Court and clerk in the Chief Judge's office, who presented the most detailed critique of the Native Land Court and suggestions for its reform. Hikairo stated that although he had worked in Fenton's office for three years, he had never seen a translation of the 1865 Native Lands Act or its amendments. Many of the defects complained of might have been remedied, he believed, had the Acts been translated and circulated amongst Maori. Hikairo believed that Judges ought to be confined to particular districts, so that they could become familiar with them, and suggested that the North Island be divided into five Court districts. On the question of juries, Hikairo stated that he was aware of only one case in which a jury had been applied for (hardly surprising, given that few Maori were aware of the provision in the Act for these), and that on that occasion only five jurors had been empanelled from amongst the bystanders, with a further twelve objected to. The jurors had proved of no use on this occasion, he added, because European lawyers had been employed in the case and much of their conversation had not been interpreted. Jurors should, he believed, be brought from a distance, especially for important cases (such as the recent and highly contentious Te Aroha block hearing), although if the merits of that particular case 'could have been discussed by an ordinary Maori runanga they would perhaps have arrived at a right conclusion...and they could have brought it to the Judge for ratification'.[21] This was in fact the sort of system Hikairo envisaged in outlining a plan which would:

> be a means of hindering single individuals, who may have claims in blocks of land, from bringing on an investigation in the Court without the previous knowledge of the majority of those concerned, and would also encourage the others to agree to a settlement of disputed boundaries amongst themselves, lest their lands should not be investigated at all.[22]

In support of this, Hikairo cited a case at Maketu, the Pukaingateru Block, in respect of which one individual had applied for an investigation of his claim 'when the whole of the Arawa were unwilling that the case should be brought before the Court' but had instead 'proposed to partition the land by Maori runanga'. 'The chiefs were very angry,' according to Hikairo, 'but they could not prevent it, because the Court always listened to what the applicants said. 'In a similar way,' he added, 'most of the Arawa lands [at Maketu] were brought into Court against the wishes of the majority, who wanted to settle amongst themselves how the land was to be divided, and then to bring it into the Court for ratification'.[23] Under Hikairo's proposal, the Judge appointed to each of the five proposed Land Court districts would subdivide it and appoint an individual to be referred to as a 'Kaiwhaka Komiti' for each subdivision. The duties of Kaiwhaka Komiti would be to identify those anxious to bring claims before the Court, to call meetings of all interested parties:

> to attend himself to hear these discussions, to ascertain the names of those whose claims in any particular block are admitted or rejected, and to report fully what takes place to the European Judge of the district. He would also ascertain and inform the Judge what were the opinions of the meeting with regard to the boundaries of such blocks; and no claims for investigation should be received by the Judge without the indorsement of the Kaiwhaka Komiti.[24]

Hikairo did not specify whether the Court's Judges would be bound by the decisions reached by these runanga under the supervision of the Kaiwhaka Komiti, but stated that 'the Natives will always be able themselves to settle disputed questions of land if sufficient time is allowed them'.[25] It would appear that he wished to retain the Native Land Court as a mechanism for ratifying decisions reached in a tribal forum, whereas others such as Tuhaere and Te Wheoro wanted to abolish the Court altogether, but still sought some sort of Crown ratification of land titles decided by runanga. This latter position was increasingly to dominate Maori thinking, whilst various governments, in the face of concerted pressure for the abolition of the Land Court, flirted with the former notion of allowing Maori to at least undertake some kind of preliminary investigation of titles prior to the Court's adjudication.

There was, in fact, support from influential thinkers such as Sir William Martin, the retired Chief Justice of the Supreme Court, and Edward Shortland, a former Native Secretary, for a midway position which would involve remodelling the Court along the lines of a Commission, with Maori juries convened under the supervision of a European official deciding questions of title on the lands concerned. Lawyers and agents were to be excluded from these hearings, under the proposals of Martin and Shortland, succession decided strictly according to Maori custom, and sales made only by public auction.[26] These sensible reforms might have gone some way to meeting Maori wishes, at least with respect to the investigation of titles, though of course they did nothing to alter the fact that individualised titles issued subsequent to any inquiry, however conducted, were grossly at variance with Maori custom.

C.W. Richmond, chairman of the Hawke's Bay Native Lands Alienation Commission of 1873 (the unsatisfactory nature of whose inquiries, from the petitioners' perspective, fuelled the fires of the emerging Repudiation movement, discussed below), while expressing some sympathy with the suggestions of Martin and Shortland, particularly in the view that 'Commissioners of Inquiry, prosecuting their investigations on or near the spot, would be better suited for the ascertainment of native ownership than a tribunal on the model of an English Court of Judicature', at the same time considered that the abolition of the Native Land Court would be 'inexpedient'.[27] Richmond, who had been responsible for the unsuccessful Native Territorial Rights Bill of 1858, considered it, 'a great point gained to have secured any sort of submission to such a jurisdiction'. Thus rather than the remodelling of the Native Land Court, Richmond suggested that District Officers be appointed to undertake preliminary inquiries into the bona fides of claims for investigation of title prior to these being referred to the Court.

Richmond and Haultain's proposals for minor reform were preferred by the General Assembly over those of Martin and Shortland for a radical reshaping of the Native Land Court, and incorporated in the Native Land Act of 1873. Yet as the Rees–Carroll Commission commented in 1891:

> All this was in vain. The tendency in the Act to individualise Native tenure was too strong to admit of any prudential check. Neither

> Parliament, nor Government, nor even the Court itself, paid attention to the...principles of the Act. No District Officers were appointed; no reports were made; no Domesday Book, founded upon evidence fast dying out, was prepared; no reserves were set aside; no division of tribes into hapus before dealing was attended to: the desire to purchase Native estates overruled all other considerations.[28]

District Officers were in fact appointed for some regions, but this hardly detracts from the general thrust of Rees and Carroll's arguments. As already mentioned, the 1873 Act took the whole process of individualisation a step further, and scarcely assuaged Maori desires to retain tribal control in the process of investigating titles to and alienating tribally-owned lands. Haultain's 1871 commission of inquiry was novel in the sense that it was the first time that Maori had officially been consulted concerning Maori land legislation. Yet increasingly tribal leaders were taking every opportunity they could to express their dissatisfaction with the Native Land Court system. In January 1871, for example, McLean meet with Te Arawa leaders at Maketu, where he was informed by one tribal representative, Te Pokiha Taranui, that 'instead of the Native Land Court being a boon to us, it is a source of trouble and expense'. A serious internal quarrel had developed between rival sections of Arawa concerning the Court's decision with respect to a disputed piece of land, and many speakers pinned the blame for this on the government, Petera Te Pukuatua adding that:

> the coming of the Native Land Court is premature. It would be far better if we met amongst ourselves, and, with the assistance of the Resident Magistrate, determined our subdividing boundary lines; these all settled, then the Native Land Court could, as a matter of form, do the rest.[29]

McLean's advice that Te Arawa could always leave the Native Land Court alone if they found it unsatisfactory was, as David Armstrong points out, especially disingenuous given that 'if even one of their number could be induced to make application to it by a designing Pakeha or a Crown land purchase officer the whole costly and disruptive process would be set in motion, with the inevitable land sales soon following'.[30]

By 1872 the desire expressed by Tuhaere and Te Wheoro to have Maori runanga or committees determine titles with the assistance of the Resident Magistrate (in some cases retaining the Native Land Court to hear appeals or ratify the runanga's decisions) was gaining widespread support amongst Maori communities throughout the country. This apparently spontaneous movement was perhaps strongest in the Bay of Plenty, where the Native Land Court was only just beginning to gain a foothold with the conclusion of hostilities in the district. In February 1872 nearly 1000 Maori from several Bay of Plenty tribes gathered at Ohinemutu to attend the opening of the Tamatekapua meeting house. Henry Tacy Clarke, the Bay of Plenty Civil Commissioner, also attended the gathering and reported that the occasion had been used to discuss issues of mutual concern. 'Land disputes and the mode in which it was suggested that they should be settled provoked much discussion', according to Clarke, who added that:

> The Honorable the Native Minister is aware of the dissatisfaction expressed by the Natives generally in this district as to the working of the Native Lands Act. They not only complain of the expenses of the Court, but the heavy expense of the Surveys, and also of the disputes that arise amongst themselves. They gave prominence to the fact that a clever schemer who had money could set up a claim against any poor man who had not the means of paying a Lawyer and the Court and survey expenses. They suggested that a permanent *Runanga* should be elected by themselves, who should take cognizance of all land disputes and who should finally settle them. ...
>
> With regard to a *Runanga* to settle the Land disputes, I informed them that my own idea was that it would be a very good arrangement provided that the disputants would bind themselves to abide by the decision of the Arbitrators or *Runanga*, and I also suggested that rather than have a permanent body of men, that the Civil Commissioner or the Resident Magistrate should nominate

chiefs of well known standing and influence to assist them in settling these troublesome disputes. I then appealed to them whether they would adhere to the decisions of such a *Runanga* This caused further discussion and it was decided that Ngatiwhakaue as the proposers of the scheme should first give their consent. This they did unanimously.[31]

F.E. Hamlin, the Maketu Resident Magistrate, also urged 'the advisability of adopting some plan by which the tribal claims, if not the individual ones, might be amicably settled and their titles and boundaries decided on and defined'.[32] And from Opotiki, Herbert Brabant reported that:

> The principal subjects I have heard discussed at the Native 'kainga' lately, are Representation, Land disputes, Road Boards, and Confiscated Lands. Great attention is given to Native Parliamentary representation. Some are of opinion that they are not fairly represented in Parliament in proportion to their numbers, and that there should be more Maori members in the House, whilst others are of opinion that the Parliament should not deal with matters affecting the Native race only, but that these should be arranged by a Native Council. Akin to the subject of the Native Council is the question, 'How are Native land disputes to be settled?' of which there are more than one of long standing in this district...Many Natives think that the 'Council', if established, could deal with these cases. The Native Land Court is unpopular, on account of the expense attending it, which in Native idea is unnecessary; they also think its machinery cumbersome.[33]

Support for these ideas was not confined to the Bay of Plenty district. Samuel Locke reported with reference to Taupo, for example, 'a desire springing up among the Natives to have local government, or District Runangas, composed of their leading chiefs, elected by themselves, with an officer of the Government as their chairman, to discuss their requirements and represent them to the Government',[34] whilst Marsden Clarke wrote from Waimate of a wish to have 'a Native and European Runanga, which should be empowered by the Government to settle disputes, and to assist the Magistrates in enforcing the law'.[35] Clearly the notion of self-government for Maori, with the assistance and patronage of the Crown, was one which was gaining widespread support. Some tribes had gone further than simply discussing the issue. Tuhoe and neighbouring iwi of the Urewera district, for example, had convened a meeting in June 1872 at which a council of 70 (Te Whitu Tekau) had been chosen. Informing McLean of this development, several tribal leaders wrote that they had decided on 'the uniting of the tribe – that their words should be one and that they should have one canoe, Matatua'. They had, it was added, decided on the 'apportionment of chiefs among Tuhoe'. There would be seventy who would be responsible for carrying out 'the work of this bird of peace and quietness' within their rohe, from which were banned 'roads, leasing and selling land'.[36]

In view of the fact that Maori were already beginning to elect their own committees and runanga, and in the light of favourable comments from figures such as Clarke and other district officers, the notion of granting limited powers to Maori to administer their lands and other affairs began to receive serious consideration. In October 1872 Parliament's Native Affairs Committee, reporting on a petition from nearly 200 Maori of Wairarapa and Hawke's Bay for the Native Land Court to be abolished and replaced by elected committees, while declining to proffer any recommendation on the former request, stated that 'the petitioners' prayer for the privilege to elect a committee from among themselves should be granted'.[37] And in the same month George Waterhouse, upon being appointed Premier, informed the Assembly in his first speech that:

> A matter that has excited great interest in the Native mind is what is by themselves called 'Local Committees'. There is among the Natives a general desire that matters simply affecting...the ownership of land, and various kindred matters, shall be settled by means of Committees, to be elected by the Natives in the various districts. I am told by those who are thoroughly competent to give an opinion upon this matter, that so firm a hold on the Native mind

has this question obtained, that it has now risen to the prominence the king movement did some years ago. It may be now availed of beneficially, or, if it be allowed to be disregarded, this agitation may be attended with injurious consequences.[38]

Waterhouse added that McLean, who remained Native Minister, had had his attention directed to the subject, and 'in accordance with public opinion amongst the Natives themselves' would by 'directing this movement' endeavour to make it a 'source of strength' to the colony.

Just over a week later McLean introduced a Native Councils Bill, which provided for local councils to be elected in any district where Maori were the main residents. The preamble to this bill referred to the fact that 'reiterated applications' had been made for 'some simple machinery of local self-government', and stated that 'it would conduce to the civilization and contentment of the Natives themselves if they were authorized and encouraged in such laudable desires'. For these purposes, upon application the Governor could declare any district where the majority of the population were Maori to be subject to its provisions, upon which a Native Council consisting of between six and twelve members plus a president and the Resident Magistrate would be elected to pass by-laws on matters of local concern, such as sanitation, drunkenness, dog and cattle trespass, and other common nuisances in Maori villages. Within such districts, all applications to the Native Land Court would first be required to be submitted to the Native Council, whose decisions would be binding on the Court in the event that agreement was reached between the contending parties. Moreover, the Councils were also to recommend to the Governor regulations relating to the 'use occupation and receipt of the profits of lands and hereditaments'.[39]

In introducing the bill in the House, McLean again referred to the large number of petitions and letters the government had received from Maori requesting that they be allowed to form committees to manage their own local affairs, subject to the advice and direction of the Resident Magistrates. It was intended that the bill would apply only to Native districts, the Minister added, and the government would not attempt to 'force' the measure, but would apply it in a 'tentative' manner in districts where Maori desired it. These committees, McLean believed, 'would materially assist the Native Lands Court' and would obviate the difficulties which Maori experienced in preparing their cases to bring before the Court. 'In the Wairarapa district', he added:

> there were a great number of cases which the Natives desired to bring before the Native Lands Court, and, prior to their doing so, they asked that a Committee of Inquiry should first settle some of the difficulties of a private character among themselves. They were the best judges of questions of dispute existing among them. No English lawyer or Judge could so fully understand those questions as the Natives themselves, and they believed that they could arrive at an adjustment of the differences connected with the land in their own Council or Committee, very much better than it would be possible for Europeans to do.[40]

William Kelly, the member for East Coast, supported the proposed measure, referring to a meeting held at Taupo earlier in the year at which a petition had been drawn up in favour of legally-constituted committees to investigate land titles. John Williamson also spoke in favour of the bill, warning that the Native Land Court had 'given great dissatisfaction' to many Maori, which was 'a dangerous matter', since 'If dissatisfaction existed, it would lead to disaffection, and it was hard to say where it would end'.[41]

The Maori members, more often than not strong opponents of government-sponsored legislation, were on this occasion warmly receptive of McLean's bill. Wi Parata, the member for Western Maori, believed that if the committees were appointed 'the Natives should have the management of their lands given back to them'.[42] Hori Taiaroa urged that the bill should be tried as an experiment, while Wiremu Katene asked those who opposed the measure 'if it was for the Europeans alone to conduct Native affairs'.[43]

McLean's proposed bill, although giving Maori a greater involvement in the investigation of titles and other matters of local concern, made no provision for tribal control over the disposal or otherwise of their lands, beyond allowing the Councils to recommend a 'general plan' for this to the Governor. Yet despite this, even the very limited powers which the bill proposed giving Maori were enough to spark fears among many settler politicians that it would destroy the authority of the Native Land Court and lead to the Councils assuming a much wider sway than they were to be given. Thomas Gillies undoubtedly spoke for many members in stating that, were the bill passed, 'The effect would be to destroy the Native Lands Court',[44] while Arthur Collins' strong objections to Pakeha living in predominantly Maori districts being subject to the by-laws of Native Councils were also widely shared.[45]

In the face of considerable opposition, McLean was forced to withdraw the bill until the following year. Meanwhile, officers in Maori districts throughout the North Island reported considerable support for the proposed measure. Richard Woon reported from Wanganui that local Maori had 'for the most part...expressed themselves as much pleased with the intent and meaning' of the bill.[46] Brabant reported similarly from Opotiki and J.H. Campbell from Waiapu,[47] while Clarke informed his superiors in Wellington that the proposed bill had met with the cordial approval of Tauranga Maori.[48] Clarke added that:

> The principal matter which has occupied the attention of the Arawa is the Native Councils Bill. I need not say that they are warm advocates for it, inasmuch as it embodies most of their well-known views. There are several important land disputes being held over till the proposed measure has become law. Some few disputes have already been partially inquired into on the principles of the Bill, with favourable results. The serious consequences at one time imminent have been averted, and the causes for irritation in most cases have been removed. ...
>
> Some of the tribes, and especially the Ngatiwhakaue, have been rather premature in the steps they have taken in regard to the

proposed measure. They have, I am led to understand, laid down the boundaries of a district, and selected individuals for nomination. The Tuhourangi have not gone quite so far as this, but they have repeatedly called meetings and discussed boundary lines. They will watch with some interest the proceedings of Parliament in regard to this measure, and I devoutly hope they will not be disappointed.[49]

With this evidence of significant Maori support for the bill, McLean sought to appease critics of the proposed legislation by toning down some of the provisions they objected to. Whereas in the original bill any six Maori could apply to the Governor for a Council to be elected, under the revised proposals a majority of the Maori residents would have to sign a petition requesting this before it could be brought into operation, and as soon as native title was extinguished in any district, the Council would cease to have any jurisdiction with respect to the region. Europeans could opt to come under the Council's provisions in mixed districts, and it would no longer be a requirement that all lands be referred to it before being passed through the Native Land Court.[50] Seeking to justify the revised bill, McLean noted that many matters of Maori custom could not be dealt with adequately by English laws, adding:

> I hold that it is a matter of sound policy to lead the Natives gradually from a state of social anarchy by gentle means, and through the agency of the more intelligent men of the Native population, rather than force upon them our enactments which nine tenths of ourselves do not fully understand and which to them are utterly incomprehensible.
>
> In one direction will the Bill now introduced be of immense service – that is in settling the numerous intertribal disputes to land which are continually arising, and thus facilitating the harmonious working of the Native Lands Act.[51]

McLean's assertion that the bill would help to facilitate the work of the Native Land Court was not enough to reassure its critics (who included Chief Judge Fenton) that it would not in fact do the opposite.⁵² Edward Jerningham Wakefield, for example, condemned what he saw as a proposal to:

> throw off the responsibility of deciding upon Native titles from the Native Lands Court to a set of outside Republics, presided over by Government officials...and the Native Lands Court was to be bound by the decision of these Republics.⁵³

Rather than attempting to persevere with the proposal, McLean opted instead to withdraw the bill, partly on the dubious grounds that the new Native Land Act had rendered many of its provisions redundant.⁵⁴ In fact, Hawke's Bay and East Coast Maori, J.D. Ormond informed McLean shortly after this, considered 'the Native Councils Bill was never intended by you to be passed and was only put forward to get your land taking measures secured'.⁵⁵ Whether this was true or not, Katene's query as to whether Europeans alone were to administer Maori affairs had implicitly been answered in the affirmative by the settler-dominated Assembly. For Maori already exposed to the depradations of the Native Land Court, a certain cynicism as to the government's motives must have come too easily.

*Paora Tuhaere*
PHOTOGRAPH MUSEUM OF NEW ZEALAND TE PAPA TONGAREWA, C.010093

*Karaitiana Takamoana*
ALEXANDER TURNBULL LIBRARY, F- 944 )3-1/2 -

*Petera Te Pukuatua*
ALEXANDER TURNBULL LIBRARY, F- 73830-1/2 -

*Mita Taupopoki, Te Arawa*
RAILWAY COLLECTION, ALEXANDER TURNBULL LIBRARY, G- 23794-1/2 -

# 4. Unofficial Committees in the 1870s: Some Brief Regional Case Studies

Parliament's hostile response to the Native Councils Bill of 1872–73 indicated that it was unwilling to grant even limited powers to Maori to determine land titles and administer local affairs themselves. Concern that legally recognised Maori institutions might hinder the Native Land Court's great task of individualising the titles to and expediting the European settlement of Maori lands prevailed over all other considerations, it seems, notwithstanding the more than plausible counter-argument that providing legal standing for such bodies might have led eventually to the controlled settlement of districts where the Court had yet to penetrate and tribal cohesion remained relatively strong. In withdrawing his bill, McLean had stated that he intended the following year to introduce a revised version of it which would apply only to regions such as the Urewera, Waiapu, and parts of Waikato.[1] There was, however, to be no further measure along these lines introduced in the Assembly in the 1870s.

Despite this, however, Maori efforts to gain the legal right to determine land titles themselves if anything intensified during the remainder of the 1870s and in the absence of such authority unofficial bodies were continually being established and re-formed in an effort to maintain some kind of tribal control in the face of overwhelming pressures towards individualisation. Interestingly, too, whereas the revival of runanga in the 1850s suggested a reassertion of traditional Maori structures, in the 1870s it was the komiti which came to the fore, possibly signifying a recognition of the need to adapt to the new challenges posed by the Native Land Court. Yet so long as the Court remained in existence the authority of the committees was tenuous. Groups dissatisfied with the outcome of a committee's decision could find solace in the fact that this carried no legal weight and that they were therefore free to try their luck in the Land Court. And although the Court's Judges sometimes took cognisance of resolutions of disputed claims reached out-of-court by the contending claimants, more formal Maori structures for deciding titles were generally looked on with a contempt that was underlain by a strong vein of jealousy of what were seen as rival bodies.

In fact, the districts where the committees survived best seem to have been those which the Native Land Court had yet to fully reach, such as Rotorua, Taupo, Urewera, the King Country and Upper Whanganui; and to a lesser extent (and more tentatively), those where a large amount of land had been alienated prior to 1865, leaving for the most part smaller blocks to be dealt with, such as Wairarapa, Hawke's Bay and the Bay of Islands. Once the Court reached the first group of districts the tribal cohesion underpinning the relative success of these committees was soon dealt a grievous blow, as were the hopes of local Maori that they could determine titles and control the subsequent fate of their own lands. Committees in these areas often met stern opposition from the government because they were perceived as obstacles to the introduction of the Native Land Court, whereas in districts where the Court was already firmly implanted, the committees could do little to change that reality.

## 4.1 Wairarapa

By 1865 between 70 and 80 per cent of the Wairarapa district had been alienated to the Crown.[2] Despite, or perhaps because of, this, Wairarapa was one of the areas in which unofficial Maori committees were most active and successful in the 1870s. The introduction of the Native Land Court, renewed Crown efforts to purchase land in the district, and strong support for the Hawke's Bay-based Repudiation movement all appear to have been contributing factors.

Yet Wairarapa also provides an early example of the problems confronted by unofficial committees attempting to retain some form of tribal control over the determination of land titles. In 1871 a committee met at Te Ore Ore to establish the rightful owners of a block of land due to be considered by the Native Land Court. Witnesses examined before the committee had their evidence transcribed so that it could be given again in court. But when one witness inadvertently referred to the existence of the committee, the presiding Judge immediately informed the claimants that the Court in no way recognised such bodies and would therefore disregard its findings.[3]

What little information is readily available concerning the Wairarapa committees suggests that notwithstanding the Court's dismissive attitude towards them, they were able to resolve difficult land disputes in a peaceful way and that these decisions were accepted by contending claimants in most instances. In 1877, for example, a complex dispute between contending hapu over land at Papawai was settled by a committee consisting of about 50 men to the apparent satisfaction of all parties.[4] *Te Wananga*, the newspaper of the Repudiation movement, was of the opinion that 'no European Court could have dealt so fully, or so satisfactorily with the difficult questions of title involved...We doubt also whether such a clear decision would have been given'.[5]

While the unofficial nature of these committees often makes it difficult to unearth reliable information concerning their internal dynamics (such as, for example, whether the apparently quite deliberate use of the term 'komiti' symbolised more than merely a semantic change from the old-style 'runanga'), a further account of a 'great meeting' of the Wairarapa committee, 'called to nominate and to vote for chiefs who are to act as Magistrates in matters which may rise in regard to dispute and other offences in the midst of the Maori people', suggests that there was a more or less formal structure adapted from that of the Pakeha. Boundaries were defined within which each magistrate would be empowered to issue summonses and hear disputes involving sums of less than £20. Three 'chief heads' were to hear cases for

65

between £20 and £50, while the magistrates and their superiors would sit on claims of greater than £50. No case was to be heard until the cost of the summons was paid, and at a future meeting 'the books of the laws' would be given to the 'chief heads' to distribute to the magistrates.[6]

One of the key functions of these committees was to try to retain some kind of tribal veto over applications to the Native Land Court, although it would seem that they had limited success in this regard. E.S. Maunsell, the Wairarapa district officer, wrote in 1880 that:

> A strong objection still pervades their minds against the Native Land Court as a means of acquiring land titles, the process being vexatious and incomprehensible to them. They have on many occasions of sittings of the Court withdrawn their applications for investigations through this objection, and in anticipation of a more simple tribunal being substituted. Even now, Natives withhold their land from the operation of the Native Land Acts, except in cases of claims to succeed deceased grantees, and of disputed titles forced into Court by one party having animosity towards the other, and of mercenary motives, when sullenness and indisposition to allow the hearing to proceed on the objecting side result.[7]

With disgruntled parties free to take their claims before the Native Land Court, it was difficult, if not impossible, to maintain any kind of tribal control over the determination of titles. Yet Maunsell's report also revealed the nature of the 'more simple tribunal' which Wairarapa Maori wished to replace the Court with:

> Their attention is principally occupied by land disputes and social questions, which they inquire into and decide at meetings held periodically. These meetings are styled 'committees' – constituted of no particular members, but of those who choose to meet on these occasions. Their decisions are invariably accepted, and fines imposed are paid to the aggrieved persons. Recently a committee decided against a man for eloping with another's wife, and fined him £50, which was paid by cheque upon a bank to the injured

husband, the wife forfeiting also her horses to him. After having disbursed the liability under this dictum, they departed, and now live together and are recognized as husband and wife, the discarded and former husband being satisfied with the exchange. Instances of similar acts of the committee and its influence are of frequent occurrence.

Purely Maori disputes over matters such as adultery might be successfully settled by committees in accordance with a communal consensus of opinion, but when it came to land their jurisdiction tended to be undermined by the intervention of outside interests, including a Court anxious to guard its powers against any unwanted challenges, and would-be Pakeha purchasers keen to ensure that legal title was obtained through the Court's mechanisms. Te Whatahoro, a Wairarapa chief, probably spoke for many in describing the Native Land Court as 'verily the monster who swallows the most land in this world, and by which the Maori people will be most certainly impoverished'. In a lengthy letter outlining the successes of the Wairarapa committee, Te Whatahoro added that:

> Not one law has been passed by which the land or the Maori people of these Islands could be saved. ...
>
> And the European is not related to you. (If he had been related to you) he might have had some misgivings or doubts (in his mind) when he passed laws by which you (the Maori) were made poor. ...
>
> Hence, I say to all the tribes of these islands, let us have our voice in respect to the European laws, and in respect to selling land, in accordance with the Government laws, we should then see some of the teeth of this monster broken. ...
>
> Let us cease to take our lands into the Native Lands Court, but let us act together, so that the European judges of the Court may be put away. The reason I say this is, that the European does not know how to adjudicate on Maori claims to land. And hence, I say, let the Maori people investigate the claims, and say who are the real owners of the land. ...

> I have been at many sittings of the Court, and have observed how the Court conducts its investigation of matters laid before it. And I have seen that it is wrong, and is not in accordance with the Maori knowledge of such matters, but it (the investigation) is conducted in accordance with the rules which guide the Courts where pure European disputes are discussed.[8]

Te Whatahoro then went on to outline many of the familiar complaints of Maori concerning the Native Land Court. Lands were lost by their real owners when they lacked the ability to conduct their claims before the Court, whilst those who presented plausible but false claims gained the lands of others. Native custom was distorted by the Court; and those who failed to appear before it also lost their lands. The Maori who claimed to understand Pakeha laws was, Te Whatahoro stated, speaking 'that which is very fiction', while the Pakeha who claimed to understand Maori laws was 'the second man who speaks fiction'. All that was required was a Pakeha clerk 'empowered by law to seal and give effect to the decision, come to by the Maori investigators'.

This was in effect what Wairarapa Maori sought in 1879 in writing to the Native Minister, John Bryce, to request that he:

> appoint and empower a Maori committee for our District of Wairarapa, to investigate and conduct matters which arise from the land (land disputes) between us, the Europeans and the Government.
>
> Let Mr. Maunsell be an associate for such committee and he will nominate those from us who are to constitute the committee.[9]

Bryce's reply that the Native Land Court was really the committee appointed by law can hardly have been the kind of response they had hoped for, and ironically when an official Wairarapa Committee with limited powers was eventually appointed in the 1880s its first meeting was rendered null and void by the absence of half its members, who were attending Land Court hearings around the country.[10] The Court remained the 'committee' appointed by law. Non-attendance, just as before, might have deprived them of their land interests, even if attendance more often than not produced a similar result.

## 4.2 Hawke's Bay and the Influence of the Repudiation Movement

Hawke's Bay Maori knew better than most exactly how the Native Land Court's operations worked to deprive them of their lands. According to M.P.K. Sorrenson, by 1873 nearly 4,000,000 acres of Maori land in Hawke's Bay had been purchased by fewer than 50 Europeans, among them the Native Minister since 1869, Donald McLean.[11] By the early 1870s simmering discontent was beginning to boil over into outright repudiation of the usually unscrupulous and sometimes fraudulent purchases that had been transacted by the wealthy and politically influential Hawke's Bay elite under the Court's blatantly unjust ten-owner rule. The repudiation of what were perceived as unjust purchases was for many just a starting point. Led by the energetic young chief Henare Matua, many advocated the abolition of the Native Land Court and the determination of land titles by Maori alone. As Matua put it to a huge intertribal gathering at Te Waiohiki, which was attended by about 1200 Maori from all over the North Island, in 1876:

> Why is it, and what is the reason that we, the Maori race cannot, or are not allowed to work with the Government, in regard to the adjudication of Maori claims to land. We, the Maori people, are fully enlightened, and know all our own old customs in regard to land claims, and by us alone can a full and clear, and true judgement be given in our own land disputes. And we, the Maori alone, are competent to sit as Judges in Maori disputes or claims to land as we are guided by our perfect knowledge of our own laws and customs to our own land. The European is ignorant of our ancient laws in regard to our Maori lands, and the European is wrong in his mode of investigation, also in his judgement and decision given by him in all Maori land claims, as the landless man obtains by the foolish acts

69

of the European, as Judge, the lands of the rightful Maori owner. The European laws are not a right guide by which claims to Maori lands are to be investigated. Let the claims to Maori lands be heard and decided ascending [*sic*] to the old custom of the Maori in respect to his land, and when such is done, then let the European law step in and carry on the right of ownership.[12]

Matua's forthright support for the abolition of the Native Land Court and for the repudiation of dubious purchases was initially not shared by more pragmatic Hawke's Bay Maori leaders such as Karaitiana Takamoana, who sought to settle grievances through Parliament.[13] Agitation from both factions induced the government to appoint a Hawke's Bay Native Lands Alienation Commission in December 1872; but the refusal of its two European members to condemn any of the purchases investigated, notwithstanding the abundant evidence presented to it of highly dubious and sometimes fraudulent dealings, strengthened the hand of Matua's party, with even Karaitiana, the member of Parliament for Eastern Maori, becoming a committed repudiationist.[14]

With the support of influential settlers such as Henry Robert Russell and John Sheehan, Hawke's Bay Maori continued to press for a fresh commission of inquiry to investigate their grievances, while Matua travelled throughout the North Island, seeking support for an end to land sales and to the jurisdiction of the Native Land Court and Pakeha Judges over Maori lands. In August 1873, for example, he appeared in Gisborne, where he led 300 local Maori into a sitting of the Poverty Bay Commission (which had been convened to determine the ownership of lands confiscated in 1868) to demand that these be returned forthwith without adjudication. The ensuing scuffle in the courtroom compelled the two commissioners to adjourn their hearings; they advised the Native Minister that although they might proceed at bayonet point, to do so would in their opinion 'probably be disastrous'. The refusal of Poverty Bay Maori to cooperate with the Commission eventually compelled the Crown to return the confiscated lands without adjudication in November 1873, a small but significant victory for the repudiationists.[15]

In the Repudiation movement may be seen the seeds of the more successful Kotahitanga movement of the 1890s. J.D. Ormond, the Hawke's Bay Superintendent, informed McLean in 1873 that Matua had 'shown considerable ability in working up what he calls the Committee', the aim of which, Ormond considered, was to 'get up a Maori national movement'.[16] From Taupo, Upper Whanganui, and the Bay of Plenty, district officers reported apprehensively on the growing influence of the Repudiation movement. It seems likely, too, that thanks to the extensive publicity given to Hawke's Bay land dealings and Maori opposition to these in the colony's press, the Repudiation movement's influence extended beyond those districts which Matua had visited. In 1873, for example, 'the Committee of all the Runangas of Ngaitahu' wrote a remarkable letter to Parliament, informing its members that the committee had 'enquired into and fully considered the causes which led to the loss' of their lands, and had decided that these had been acquired in an unjust manner:

> it is because the people are few in number and their eyes were closed, also the ready consent of a small portion of the tribe – those are the real causes which led to the loss of this Island, the payment being schools and Hospitals and the protection by Government of the Maori people.

But because of the smallness of their numbers, the letter added, Ngai Tahu had not received the promised payments for their lands:

> consequently the Runanga decided upon drawing a line through the centre of the Island and defining the two boundaries, one for the Poutini on [the] West Coast and the other according to Wakefield's purchase for the Otago people.

The committee was to have full power to arrange this division, and the government was asked to 'give notice to the various runholders in the centre of the Island to remove their sheep &c. to the Coast'.[17] Whether or not Ngai Tahu had been influenced by reports about the Repudiation movement in the North Island, it is at least clear from this and similar letters from this period that they too were looking to reassert some kind of autonomy through the mechanism of a tribal committee. There is little evidence of sullen demoralisation here, but rather a recognition of the need to find some more flexible and adaptable body through which to press their claims for redress.

By contrast, the political goals pursued by North Island committees were directed as much at preventing future land loss as towards gaining redress for that of the past. Allied with the goal of abolishing the Land Court and putting an end to land sales was (at the local level) that of providing an alternative method of determining titles and holding lands tribally. In fulfilling the latter goal the committees were implicitly also aiding the achievement of the former, since if tribal cohesion could be maintained, the Court could be boycotted, at least temporarily, while the existence of a popular, inexpensive and efficient alternative stood in marked contrast to the cumbersome, costly and widely despised Court.

The importance of the 'Committee of Kahungunu', which appears to have emerged from a meeting of more than 500 local Maori at Pakowhai in July 1872,[18] lay primarily in the galvanising effect which it had in rallying opposition to the Court and encouraging other tribes to follow the Hawke's Bay example and elect their own committees. Several large hui attended by tribes from all over the country were organised by the Ngati Kahungunu committee in the 1870s. The panui for one held at Pakowhai in 1876 provides a typical example of the topics that were regularly debated:

> 1. First subject! A Parliament for Maori people to organise their Land should take place.
>
> 2. Second. The tribes should unite in this Land, and its organisations.
>
> 3. Third. The time for Maori members of Parliament has ended. They are not for the future. What should we do?

4. Fourth. The decision of the Land has emerged that land sales should stop. They will not stop. How are we to stop them?

5. Fifth. Notices have come out to the Land that the Court should stop. It will not stop. How are we to stop it?

6. Sixth. Are we surviving or perishing through the operations of Parliament in these years that are passing?

7. Seventh. Will we not agree to petition the Queen to look into the troubles that oppress us?

8. Eighth. What ideas are there about Elections?[19]

Parliamentary representation was certainly a subject which attracted considerable attention, but by the mid-1870s the attitude of many to the paltry representation of Maori in the Assembly was decidedly cynical. Renata Kawepo informed the meeting at Te Waiohiki in 1876, for example, that the only reason four Maori MPs had been granted in 1867 was because:

> the time might come when the acts of the Government would be condemned by the public, when they (the Government) could point to the Maori members and say: "The Native tribes being represented in the Parliament, participated in all the acts of the Government, and therefore all wrong acts were sanctioned by the Native race, as such then the Maori people mislead themselves. Also if Her Majesty the Queen should say to the present Government that they have acted in a wrong way to the Maori race, then our present Government could say to Her Majesty: 'O but our acts were sanctioned by the tribes and chiefs of the Maori people'".[20]

Although some saw salvation in the dumping of McLean as Native Minister and the instalment of a government led by Sir George Grey, a Maori parliament, essentially involving regular intertribal meetings of the kind that had already begun to be held but with the addition of some recognised authority, was also a popular concept.[21] In fact, although almost all of these meetings passed universal resolutions condemning the Native Land Court and in favour of committees, a strong element of tribal rivalry also seems to have entered proceedings, with various chiefs jostling verbally for the right to stage the next meeting.

By 1878 the Repudiation movement, struggling financially and disillusioned by the Grey government's failure to settle its grievances, faded from the scene. In December its mouthpiece for the past four years, *Te Wananga*, folded, and the following year Henare Matua came only third in the election for the Eastern Maori seat.[22] Despite this, its efforts had not been in vain. Inspired by the repudiationists, several tribes around the country had elected their own committees, and many of these continued to function until the early 1880s. Grand ambitions of repudiation were, moreover, replaced by more moderate and potentially successful ones. Henare Tomoana, for example, who had been largely responsible for establishing *Te Wananga* and who had, like many other Ngati Kahungunu leaders, thrown his full weight behind the Repudiation movement after the disillusionment of the 1873 commission of inquiry, later went on to sponsor a bill providing legal recognition for the election of Maori committees throughout the country, a watered-down version of which the government was eventually compelled to accept. And the push for kotahitanga which the repudiationists had made was to be taken up again on a wider level in the 1880s and 1890s, as Maori sought to gain real and effective powers for these committees.[23]

## 4.3 Whanganui

Much land had been alienated in the Whanganui district prior to the 1860s, primarily along the lower reaches of the river, near the township of Wanganui. Extensive fighting had put a stop to this process during that decade, but with the cessation of conflict in the early 1870s numerous meetings were held in an attempt to achieve a united approach to the land question.[24] Deep divisions between Kingite and kupapa, and between lower Whanganui and upriver Maori, made this a difficult task. Upper Whanganui tribes were generally opposed to the Native Land Court and to any form of land dealings and were warmly receptive to the Hawke's Bay Repudiation movement, while those living further down the river were generally more anxious to obtain legal titles for their lands and were not opposed in principle to leasing or selling if the price was right.[25]

Notwithstanding these divisions, tentative intertribal boundaries were apparently agreed to at a meeting held at Parikino in May 1871.[26] The following year a hui attended by residents from all parts of the river reportedly agreed to set aside a tract of country between the Whanganui and Turakina rivers of some eighteen miles by twelve miles in extent as a reserve in perpetuity for its owners. Richard Woon, the Resident Magistrate, noted that:

> The reason assigned for adopting such a course is an apprehension which exists amongst the Natives here (one founded on reason), that unless some steps are taken to check the wholesale alienation of land by the Natives, a danger exists of the owners thereof eventually disposing of the whole of their lands, thereby rendering themselves homeless and poverty stricken.[27]

These concerns were indeed reasonable ones. In September 1871 James Booth, a government land purchase agent, had been instructed to ascertain whether Whanganui Maori were 'inclined to alienate any tract of land available for settlement'. The government had already signalled its intention to acquire as much land between Whanganui and Taupo as possible and by 1872 Booth was reportedly engaged in negotiations for the purchase of extensive tracts of land in the district.[28] Land Court sittings also became frequent from the mid-1870s, with even some former 'rebels' submitting claims for investigation. Woon, while encouraging this, also sought to mediate in land disputes and argued that these could be settled through runanga or committees. In 1873 he informed the Native Department that:

> The system of Native Councils in connection with the settlement of Maori titles to land might...be beneficially introduced, the Natives for the most part having expressed themselves as being much pleased with the intent and meaning of the Act [the Native Councils Bill] introduced at last sittings of Parliament, which would have

> provided the machinery requisite for affording the Natives a further and more effectual means of adjusting many of their differences and disputes (particularly land quarrels) in a manner satisfactory to themselves and without the risk of future complications.[29]

The failure of McLean's bill did not dissuade Whanganui Maori from continuing to attempt to settle disputed tribal boundaries, however, and in 1874 Woon reported that 'the all-absorbing topic of the proper administration of their landed estates' occupied much of their energies, with 'several local land disputes...amicably settled by...the Natives themselves'. The Resident Magistrate added that:

> They have, as a first step in the matter (and a very necessary one too), commenced to adopt measures whereby all tribal differences as to boundaries, &c., may be adjusted; and in April last a highly-important meeting was held at Putiki, whereat an arrangement was come to by Major Kemp and Renata Kawepo,...representing the Whanganui and Ngatikahungunu Tribes, whereby the disputed tribal boundary of the Murimotu country is likely to be settled; said chiefs having consented to take charge of the survey of said boundary line...and to use their united influence in settling individual claims of members of each tribe to land on either side of such boundary.[30]

But with both Booth and James Buller, another government land purchase agent, attempting to secure the Murimotu lands for the Crown, this was far from the end of the matter. By the late 1870s the 'ground bait' laid by these agents in the form of advance payments was being used to good effect as the Murimotu lands began to be passed through the Court against the wishes of many of the owners.[31]

In fact, despite their determined efforts to settle intertribal disputes themselves, Woon's 1874 report noted that the land question continued to 'agitate and perplex' Whanganui Maori 'in an inordinate manner'. And with the Land Court and Crown agents continuing to undermine tribal efforts to administer their lands, it is not surprising that the Repudiation movement gained significant support in the district. In May 1874 Henare Matua and 'a cavalcade of one hundred or more' had attended a week-long hui at Kaiwhaiki, about twelve miles up the Whanganui River, where some 800 Maori from surrounding districts had gathered. Woon believed that:

> Disaffection, bordering on rebellion, is at the root of this agitation, and the effect has already been to unsettle the Natives, and influence them with the belief that our rule over them is an unjust and oppressive one. Should this combination gain the support of any more of the tribes and its adherents increase in number (of which there is some likelihood), the result of this organization is likely to prove dangerous to the peace of the country, for it can be looked upon as nothing more nor less than a fresh development of the Land League and King movement, only under another phase or garb; and if their demands are not acceded to, there will be a danger of their openly casting off their allegiance to the Queen and setting up an authority of their own, utterly antagonistic to good government and the extension of peace and quietness throughout the country.[32]

Matua had told them to 'look to the law alone for redress' of their 'imaginary' (according to Woon) grievances, and had 'expressed his approval of both European and Maori Courts of justice – the one to have authority over the land of the Queen, and the other over that of the Maori'. He had 'succeeded in impressing them with the idea that they...have and are being victimized through their ignorance of our laws', Woon added. These grievances included the Native Land Court, which Matua said should be abolished, and unequal parliamentary representation, which could be remedied by allowing every large tribe to have its own representative in the Assembly. Woon, probably correctly, considered that:

> this movement is a final effort of the Maoris in these parts to stem the tide of advancement on the part of their European neighbours, as they are becoming alarmed at the inroads made upon them and their domains by the continued acquisition of large tracts of country by the Government in the interior, and they do not like the idea of losing the authority and power formerly held by them over the inland districts of this Island, one of the propositions of Henare

> Matua being that all land selling should cease, and also leasing, till they become wiser and better able to look after their own interests...[33]

More than 300 local Maori had identified themselves as active supporters of Matua, according to Woon, and the majority were 'favourably impressed with his views, upon his assurance that he looked to the law alone for redress'. A council of twelve was to be selected to attend the next sitting of the Assembly, where they would argue their grievances alongside Matua and his other supporters.

A year later, Woon reported that:

> Some dissatisfaction still exists among several of the river Natives and coast districts, consequent upon the action taken by Henry Matua, who has led them to believe that they have been victimized in their former sales of land to the Government, and has succeeded in setting them against our Courts (Land and Judicial); and the Maori Runanga is constantly at work, settling land disputes, and trying offences amongst the disaffected and disappointed members of the Maori community.

Woon considered that this movement would eventually die out, but was forced to admit that:

> In some instances, where local differences about title to land have arisen,...the Runanga has been the means of doing some good, by investigating and promptly settling, to the satisfaction of the Maori disputants, quarrels about land, which might otherwise, through the tardy operation of the Land Court, have resulted in a breach of the peace. The Runanga, however, is not satisfied with merely settling the disputes, but arrogates to itself the power of granting a certificate of title and taking fees, and professes to ignore entirely the operation of the Native Land Court, whose awards, in many instances, the Maoris decline to accept, by refusing to take up the Crown grants, which Henry Matua has set them strongly against.[34]

The runanga had, Woon added, taken it upon itself to settle all Maori debts and claims, and was trying and punishing offences, appropriating the fees and fines. Yet although the Whanganui runanga appears to have been quite explicit in its rejection of the Native Land Court, it seems to have been more tolerant of Woon's judicial work. On one occasion, the Resident Magistrate reported, he had found the runanga sitting in the assembly house at Parikino, at the same time that he was scheduled to hold his own court there. Woon speedily adjourned to a nearby schoolhouse, even though the runanga had offered to adjourn their proceedings until his court was held, 'feeling they had stolen a march upon me, and that it would be derogatory to my position as a Queen's Magistrate to in any way submit to, or countenance their unlawful proceedings'. Obviously the runanga saw itself as in peaceful co-existence rather than competition with Woon's court. Thus a dual system of law operated, Woon being forced to rely heavily on Maori custom to avoid outright rejection of his own court, and the runanga finding its own authority undermined by those who saw more advantage in pressing their claims under Pakeha tikanga. There was, therefore, a de facto rivalry between the two systems, although as Ward says:

> the *runanga* persisted. It enjoyed favour because it embodied Maori, not alien, authority, because its proceedings and decisions in some respects were more appropriate than English law (even as modified by Woon) to traditional Maori offences and Maori notions of justice, and because the fines and fees it levied remained in the district instead of going to Wellington. In fact Woon's court and the *runanga* tended to alternate in popularity owing to the influence of faction and according to whether a somewhat fickle local opinion believed one or the other to be giving the more satisfactory judgements.[35]

Despite Woon's occasional clashes with the runanga, he remained flexible and astute enough to realise that it did fulfil some useful functions, and generally tolerated its existence. In 1877, for example he reported that Whanganui Maori:

> arrange many quarrels and differences by a recourse to the Maori runanga, a body of men selected by the tribe to investigate any matter brought to them by the people for adjustment; said runangas

being an imitation of our Courts of justice, and which are not without a beneficial influence on the mind of the Natives, as, by their arbitrament, strife and contention of a serious nature are often assuaged and prevented.

Sometimes, however, the runanga or committee commits an excess of authority, by enforcing its decisions in an illegal and irregular way against members of the Maori community who do not recognize its authority; and it was only the other day that I fined one of its policemen £5 for distraining upon the goods of other Natives than those of the defendant in the case. I treated the affair as one of Maori *muru* (robbery), and had not the fine been paid by the chairman of the committee, who issued the process to the constable, I should have sent the offender to prison, in terms of the Act in such case made and provided. This is the only time the runanga has come into direct collision with my Court, and it came off second-best in the business, and had to acknowledge a maladministration of its affairs.[36]

Yet as members of the runanga undoubtedly appreciated in seeking entirely to supplant the Native Land Court, the two institutions could not coexist without some legal obligation on the Court to take cognisance of the runanga's decisions. And with government and private land purchase agents active in the region, it was almost impossible for the runanga to maintain any kind of tribal veto over land dealings for any length of time. In these circumstances, regular meetings over tribal boundaries were being held in anticipation of one or other party referring their claims to the Court, and schemes for setting aside inalienable reserves were regularly discussed. Woon reported a 'wide-spread apprehension...that injustice, sooner or later, will be done to them in the matter of forcing them to part with their lands'. At one hui the question of sending a delegation to England 'with the view of securing a just administration' of their lands had been discussed, whilst the establishment of a Maori Council was in Woon's opinion one way in which 'the reasonable claims of the Maori population' might be met, at the same time 'occupying their active and restless minds, and thereby preventing disaffection and perhaps overt rebellion'. With respect to the land question, however, Woon believed that:

> Fresh legislation is urgently required to meet the case – an all-important one, – and every help and facility should be afforded to the Natives to secure a settlement of their conflicting land claims, and a registry of their tribal, family, and individual titles – not with the immediate view of hastening a disposition by way of sale or lease of their lands (which will follow as a matter of course), but with the object of settling a matter, and removing an element, that causes constant excitement and disturbance to the Maori mind throughout the country.[37]

Woon advocated more frequent sittings of the Native Land Court and the establishment of a court of appeal 'to which dissatisfied Maori litigants could have recourse for a final and exhaustive inquiry into the nature of their conflicting land claims'. Whanganui Maori had their own ideas on the subject, however, and in 1878 the Resident Magistrate reported on the erection by Mete Kingi and other local Maori, of a 'quasi parliament house...wherein the Wanganui tribes might meet periodically for the discussion of all matters affecting the Natives'. The first meeting, held at Te Paku-o-te-Rangi, opposite the township of Wanganui, had lasted more than a week, with land issues as usual 'the principal topic of conversation and debate'. Woon reported that at this meeting:

> an effort was made to 'tapu' several large tracts of country, and to forbid their being surveyed for lease or sale. The majority of the meeting agreed to this policy, being a last effort in opposition to the selling proclivities of an influential number of Natives. A short time has proved that such a determination could not be carried out, as, owing to the persistent acts of the land-sellers and others, Mete Kingi, Kemp, and other leading chiefs, who were asked to hold the interdicted land for the tribes, publicly, at the last meeting, gave up their charge of same, and announced to the assembled Natives that for the future the Native landowners must use their own discretion, and hold or sell as they thought proper; that they were free to

exercise their own right in the matter. The result has been an openly-manifested desire on the part of the Natives here to deal with their land, and numerous fresh surveys of blocks are being undertaken in all directions.[38]

Woon, like most other Crown officials of the time, attributed this apparent willingness to sell lands to Maori 'improvidence', and suggested that 'it will yet become the duty of the Government to step in and prevent many of them from parting with every inch of soil, and thus becoming paupers and a burden to the country'.[39] The increased traffic in Maori lands in the region would, Woon predicted, give rise to many disputes between contending claimants, notwithstanding the efforts of the government-appointed Native Assessors to mediate in these. The informal efforts of Whanganui leaders such as Kemp and Mete Kingi to resolve these disputes and to check wholesale alienation of the tribal estate had proven unsuccessful, and by the time of the second big hui at Te Paku-o-te-Rangi the emphasis had shifted to discussing how the law might be altered to allow for continued tribal control over these lands. Woon's report referred to three main topics considered by the meeting:

> 1. A more complete representation, and a status in Parliament. 2. A share in the administration of their land, to include the investigation into title thereof by a Maori committee in connection with the Native Land Court, and by authority of law. 3. An amendment in the form of Crown grant for Native reserves, whereby same could be secured to their lineal descendants by entail general.[40]

Yet despite numerous petitions and appeals to Parliament, by 1880 there was still little indication that the government was willing to allow Maori any real say in the adjudication of titles to and subsequent administration of their lands. Prompted by an attempted government survey of lands which he laid claim to in the Murimotu area, in February of that year Major Kemp (Te Keepa Te Rangihiwinui) took an armed party of 70 onto the block and built a pa on it. Dismissed from government employment as a result, Kemp responded by endeavouring to set up a 'trust' covering an area of nearly one and a half million acres, which was to be administered by a council of chiefs for the benefit of all those with ancestral rights to it.[41] European solicitors were appointed to act on behalf of the trust, and a formal ceremony was held to mark the placing of the first of four huge boundary poles. As Ward says:

> This was, in effect, an attempt to form a Rohe along the lines of the Kingitanga, to control the actions of land-selling chiefs, and engage, on more favourable terms, with the processes of settlement. At the same time Kemp became one of the active leaders to try to have the land-laws changed, so that such efforts as his Trust could become more stable and effective. But the traditional divisions on the Whanganui remained strong. Without a major change in the land laws, and while the purchase of individual interests in land went on, it was impossible for organisations attempting to straddle tribal lines to retain control for long.[42]

Kemp's Trust soon faded from the scene under the weight of these pressures, and by 1883 Whanganui Maori were, along with their Kingitanga neighbours, once more petitioning for the right to determine land titles themselves, without the intervention of the Native Land Court.[43] Yet despite their reassurances that they did not desire to keep their lands permanently locked up from European settlement, or from roads and other public works, but merely wished to have some say in the rate with and manner in which these were introduced, even this was too much for Pakeha politicians to accept. The efforts of Kemp and others to administer their own lands themselves ultimately came to little, and instead the 1880s saw extensive Crown purchasing in the district.[44]

## 5. 'Unity is Strength': Te Arawa Committees of the 1870s: A More Detailed Case Study[1]

Perhaps the best documented and most active committees of the 1870s were those of the Rotorua district, which encompassed the tribal lands of the Te Arawa people. Prior to the 1870s the Rotorua region was highly unsettled and scarcely considered a prime site for would-be settlers, because of a combination of inter- and intra-tribal tensions, its relative inaccessibility, and the hostile attitudes of its inhabitants towards wholesale alienation of their lands. But with the gradual restoration of peace in the district, the need to acquire more land for a settler population which was burgeoning under the immigration and public works policies of the Colonial Treasurer, Julius Vogel, and the increasing realisation of Rotorua's potential as a tourist destination, Te Arawa soon found themselves under immense pressure to part with their lands. Indeed, although the tribe's perceived status as 'loyalists' was in many ways misleading, since Te Arawa had allied their fortunes with those of the Crown in the 1860s for a combination of tribal and pragmatic reasons, it brought its own pressures for the government's former allies, who were frequently targeted by land purchase officers in the following decade, and pressured to consent to the alienation of their lands as a symbol of their continuing loyalty and adherence to the Queen. In 1874 a delegation of Arawa chiefs travelled to Wellington to lay their grievances before Parliament. Members of the Native Affairs Committee were informed that:

> The Arawa people have from the foundation of the colony consistently refused to lease or sell their lands; and while all the other great tribes have divested themselves of the greater portion of their tribal lands, the Arawa country has remained almost untouched in the hands of the aboriginal owners. When the Native

85

Land Court was established, the tribe refused to take advantage of it for a long time, but ultimately, upon the repeated assurances of the Government that the survey and investigation of the titles to their lands would not facilitate leases or sales, they allowed one or two pieces to be surveyed and put through the Court. At once trouble and confusion arose. Men of no standing in the tribe began to lease or sell without the knowledge or consent of the acknowledged leaders of the people. The result was, that at subsequent sittings of the Court no lands were allowed to be put through. Then the tribe complained to the Government, and asked that their lands should be entirely tied up, so that in future no sales or leases could take place. The Government did this, but at the same time land-buyers and surveyors were sent into the district on Government account, and commenced leasing, selling, and surveying on all sides.[2]

In a clear reference to the Waitara dispute, the Arawa delegation added that:

> The Government is still persisting in this course, and their agents are adopting the old system which in days gone by led to trouble and bloodshed; for, in their eagerness to acquire lands, they are negotiating with and paying moneys to men of inferior rank, despite the protests and remonstrances of the principal chiefs.
>
> The chiefs are now willing to allow lands to be taken upon lease to the extent of the moneys already paid; they decline to confirm any sales of freehold; they complain that Government is dealing with land before investigation of title; and they ask that the land-buyers should be withdrawn, and that no further attempts should be made to purchase or lease their lands.[3]

Wiremu Maihi Te Rangikaheke, the prominent Ngati Rangiwewehi leader, in a remarkably forthright piece of evidence to the Committee, informed its members that:

> the word of the Arawa...was against disposing of their lands. The Ngapuhi, Ngatikahungunu and other tribes were disposing of their lands, but the Arawa were firm to keep one principle which was against disposing of their lands. In 1863 they laid down a boundary of their district within which their lands should not be disposed of,

and should prevent them from being confiscated. The Arawa chiefs heard that the Treaty of Waitangi had been broken. The Queen of England said she would preserve to the Maoris their rights, their forests, their fisheries, their rivers. When the Arawa chiefs heard that the Treaty had been broken they arranged that they would lay down a boundary within which the Government should not have any power to take their lands.[4]

Te Rangikaheke added that 'the Government are robbing the Arawa of their lands, and causing trouble among the tribe.' They would have had no objections to the restrictions 'if the Government had not deceived them, and commenced to buy the land'. Nor, in theory, would they have objected to the leasing of their lands:

> only we imagine these leases are simply made by the Government for the purpose of purchasing. The lease is the bait, the hook is the purchase.

The Arawa people had been loyal to the Crown; why then, Te Rangikaheke asked, was it committing an 'act of treachery' against them?

Te Arawa had, according to C.O. Davis and Henry Mitchell, land purchase agents appointed by the Crown for the Bay of Plenty district in 1873, 'long before the origin of the famous land league of the Waikatos' come to 'the unanimous decision that no lands should be alienated to either Government or private individuals'.[5] Yet the difficulty of maintaining such a united front when confronted with the reality of Land Court sittings and government and private land purchase agents in their midst, as they were from the early 1870s, was apparent from a counter-petition to that presented to the Native Affairs Committee in 1874, one which supported government efforts to exclude private speculators from the region. The Committee reported with respect to this petition that the people behind it were 'now leasing and selling to the Government against the wish of the other sections of the Arawa Tribe, and that the large majority of the tribe are entirely opposed to the granting of the prayer of this petition'.[6] In fact, although the Court had endeavoured to sit at

Rotorua as early as 1865, the unsettled state of the district and the fact that many of the tribe opposed having their lands adjudicated on had resulted in little being done. Davis and Mitchell later recalled that:

> Up to the year 1871 the various attempts made by the Judges of the Native Lands Court to investigate the titles of land at Maketu and Rotorua signally failed, and the proceedings of the Arawas were of so violent a character as to preclude the possibility of further action being taken in their country, a circumstance which induced the authorities to transfer from Maketu and Rotorua to Tauranga the sitting of the Lands Court, in the hope that the spirit of turbulence in regard to the Arawa land matters would be subdued; but even here, to prevent the outbreak of hostilities, Sir Donald McLean was compelled to order the closing of the Court, and the withdrawal from the district of all surveyors.[7]

It has already been seen that Te Arawa were prominent in the agitation of the early 1870s for the right to determine land titles themselves. Wiremu Hikairo of Ngati Rangiwewehi had advanced detailed proposals for a runanga or committee-based system in his evidence before Haultain's commission of inquiry into the operations of the Native Land Court, and other Arawa tribal leaders had informed McLean during his 1871 visit to Maketu that the Court's coming was premature and that they should instead meet and discuss tribal boundaries themselves, with the Court ratifying their decisions 'as a matter of form'. In 1872 H.T. Clarke reported that Arawa leaders had been formulating plans for runanga to settle land disputes well before the introduction of McLean's unsuccessful Native Councils Bill, of which they were reported to be 'warm advocates'. This bill coincided with the appointment of Davis and Mitchell to conduct negotiations for the acquisition of Taupo and Bay of Plenty lands by the Crown early in 1873. Clarke reported that some sections of Arawa had 'been rather premature' in appointing committees and laying down boundaries in anticipation of McLean's bill being successful. Te Keepa Te Rangipuawhe, the paramount chief of the Tuhourangi people of the Tarawera district, later informed the Native Minister that it was the arrival of Davis and Mitchell which had provided the spur for action:

> In 1873 the Government Land Purchase Policy commenced in the Arawa District, and because of that system the chiefs of Rotorua, Tarawera, Te Rotoiti and Kaingaroa began to consider the case of their ancestral grounds for fear lest [these lands] should go to Te Reinga (be entirely lost to them) through the cost of the surveys and the sale by other persons hapus or tribes, and it was in consequence of that that the Arawa established committees in each of the hapus which committees were to hold the lands and adjudicate upon them, and it was also in consequence of that that the committees so strenuously opposed the sitting of the Native Land Court in that District, and surveys and leases also.[8]

In one of their first reports to the government, dated 23 August 1873, Davis and Mitchell stated that they were making some progress, despite opposition from Ngati Whakaue and 'private agents with their surveyors &c. in various parts of the country'.[9] The same report omitted to mention, though, that the pair had apparently been forcibly expelled from Ohinemutu by resident Maori just days earlier.[10]

Although Davis and Mitchell's negotiations with Te Arawa appeared, on the face of it, to be public and open ones, they used tactics which included tying up lands by making advance payments to compliant individuals, and negotiating leases as a preliminary to purchase when opposition to the latter was strong, whilst generally ignoring the claims of objectors on the basis of a distorted and rigid view of customary Maori land rights. In 1874 the pair informed the Native Minister that:

> the method adopted by us at the commencement of the land negotiations in Arawa and Taupo countries, and sought to be carried out in its entirety was the securing of every available block of land on behalf of the Government by making preliminary Agreements with and paying deposits to sections of the recognised owners thereby binding the Tribes, and shutting out private speculators.
>
> On reaching this stage it was then our intention to enter upon the

elucidation of the title to each block by organising a series of public meetings, the time and place to be fixed by the various contending claimants and ourselves. At these public meetings we deemed it wise and advisable to call in the aid of certain native chief[s] and Assessors so that full justice might be secured both as regards absentees and all the claimants who should present themselves at these tribal gatherings.[11]

Exactly how Davis and Mitchell went about determining the 'recognised owners' to whom advance payments could be made prior to such meetings (or, indeed, how the rights of those who failed to attend their meetings were to be secured) is not at all clear. In practice it seems that the 'recognised owners' were all those who were willing to accept such payments, which locked up the land from private competition and bound the owners to sell to the Crown.[12]

Because of the 'general indisposition' on the part of Te Arawa to alienate their lands, the pair noted that they had 'deemed it advisable...to exercise some caution in introducing the question of purchase', and had mainly confined their proposals to leasing. This would, they believed, 'render purchase hereafter if desirable relatively easy'. However, it would appear that at least some sections of Te Arawa felt that they were being deceived by Davis and Mitchell as to their real goals with respect to the Bay of Plenty district. The pair noted in one early report that 'Ngatiwhakaue were dissatisfied on account of our purchasing lands at Maketu, saying that the avowed object of the Government they supposed to be leasing only of lands'.[13]

Ngati Whakaue (and Tuhourangi) opposition to the activities of Davis and Mitchell was to become a common theme over the next few years. Yet the two agents were dismissive of the claims of these tribes, which they believed were based on the outdated and unfair concept of mana:

> It has been our practice from the first to ignore the *mana*, because it professes to be perfectly distinct from the ownership of the soil, and moreover the assumed *mana* by these dominant tribes is repudiated by the genuine owners of the soil. It does seem strange

indeed that in these times, when Maori rule is almost annihilated by European usages, that any chiefs or tribes in the Arawa country should be found to assert their *mana* and to base their pretentions on it, and this seems doubly strange when we take into consideration the fact that all the leading chiefs of the Arawa are receiving Government salaries, by which act they have to all intents and purposes virtually abandoned the Maori notions of authority.[14]

The Crown's Bay of Plenty land purchase agents believed that the basis of mana was 'the more powerful domineering over the weak; the power arising from birth, intellect, and other fortuitous circumstances'. More astute observers might have drawn comparisons with the English class system, but Davis and Mitchell instead deemed it entirely inappropriate to recognise claims based on mana, which had 'induced the chiefs and tribes claiming *mana* to deluge the Government with letters and telegrams, in the hope that they would be able to extort money on the ground of this Maori *mana*, forfeited long ago and fully ignored by all parties'. The agents considered that Te Arawa's 'repeated endeavours' to base their claims for recognition on mana to be 'simply the reiterated cry, "Give, give;" and they assure themselves that nothing is lost by making the demand'.

The concept of mana in relation to land dealings essentially allowed some chiefly and tribal control over these important matters. Yet Davis and Mitchell's dismissive attitude towards customary Maori concepts of land tenure and leadership, and their practice of making advance payments to individuals, does not appear to have won them many friends amongst Te Arawa, prompting the government to suspend the operations of the Native Lands Act over their lands in August 1873, in an effort to protect the Crown's interests in respect of lands on which the pair had managed to make some advances.[15] This proclamation was not lifted until 1877, and during this period the Native Land Court was unable to sit in the district, so that private speculators could not obtain legal title to any lands they had negotiated purchases or leases for. The proclamation did not, however, prevent Davis and Mitchell from continuing their policy of 'binding' Te Arawa by making advances to individuals for as much of the district as possible.

In November 1873 the *Bay of Plenty Times* reported considerable dissatisfaction amongst the Tuhourangi section of Te Arawa about the activities of Davis and Mitchell in their district.[16] The following month Donald McLean travelled to Tarawera, where he heard several complaints concerning the work of the government's agents. McLean was informed that Tuhourangi had long ago defined their rohe and recently established a committee to protect their interests in these lands, despite which Davis and Mitchell had continued to deal with individuals. Aporo told McLean:

> The tribal boundaries...were laid out long ago: twelve people have been selected to take the charge of *(kaitiaki)* those boundaries, and protect our interests from the Pakehas, who were wishing to negotiate for the purchase or lease of land within the same, and from the encroachment and interference of outsiders.[17]

Hori Taiawhio confirmed what Aporo had said, and added that:

> That boundary was defined in Governor Grey's time,[18] and though a person was outside and had a title to land inside the boundary, his title was recognized, for Tuhourangi considered that their *mana* should be over the land. Individuals have been disposing of land, by leasing or otherwise, which Tuhourangi have not; what has been sold should not be charged against Tuhourangi. Tuhourangi are very well aware that other parties have been endeavouring to dispose of their land. This is wrong.[19]

Pauru, though, pointed the finger at the Crown's own agents, stating:

> Tuhourangi's *mana* is over those lands which are being treated for with individuals; formerly Government entered into negotiations with the whole tribe, now they treat with individuals, which is a very objectionable proceeding. Tuhourangi now wish each individual to return the money that he has received. These difficulties about the disposal of lands have arisen through the

action of Pakehas; if you wish to *tapahi* the *kaki* [chop the neck] of Tuhourangi, do so; Tuhourangi have nothing to do with money paid to individuals.

Hohepa Tamamatu agreed with the boundaries laid down by Tuhourangi but stated that the people who had suffered most were Ngati Whakaue, at the same time urging McLean to ensure that future negotiations were conducted publicly to avoid further trouble, which he considered had so far largely been the fault of Davis rather than Mitchell.

The mana of Tuhourangi over their lands was, as has been seen, rejected by Davis and Mitchell, who considered that with 'Maori rule...almost annihilated by European usages' they were free to ignore such 'absurd' notions of land rights. Yet the practice of both Crown and private agents of making advance payments to individuals who would accept these in defiance of those seeking to maintain some measure of tribal control over their lands was one which created serious rifts in Te Arawa society during the 1870s. This was further hinted at during the Tarawera meeting after Himiona stated that he wished to have Rotomahana adjudicated on by the Native Land Court, since some of the hapu of Tuhourangi were 'desirous of appointing certain chiefs to undertake the management of that place'. Petera disputed this, informing McLean that Tuhourangi did not wish to have the title to Rotomahana investigated.

The Native Minister told those present that 'no land questions will be entertained until thoroughly investigated', ignoring the fact that Davis and Mitchell were doing the exact opposite, advancing payments to all and sundry – or at least those who were prepared to accept them – prior to any investigation of title. And H.T. Clarke, who accompanied McLean to the meeting, made it clear to Tuhourangi that the authority of the twelve persons appointed to kaitiaki their lands would not be recognised:

> You know quite well that it is an easy matter for people to describe large boundaries, which invariably on investigation prove to be incorrect, other people being found to be better claimants;

therefore, it will be impossible for the Government, before investigation, to recognize the *Rohe Potae*.

This placed Tuhourangi in an impossible position. In order to have their efforts to maintain the rangatiratanga of the chiefs over their lands recognised, they would first have to have the title investigated by the Native Land Court. Yet once this had been done, and the title had been individualised, it would be virtually impossible to maintain any sort of tribal control over their lands.

Yet despite the government's reluctance to deal with, or to recognise in any manner, Tuhourangi's chosen leadership, efforts to maintain some tribal cohesion in the face of a system seeking to undermine this continued. In June 1874 F.E. Hamlin, the Resident Magistrate at Maketu, provided more information on the committee appointed by Tuhourangi to kaitiaki their lands, stating with respect to the 'reputed loyalty of the Arawa as a whole' that:

> the Tuhourangi, one of the strongest tribes, have of late endeavoured to establish a system of self-government, by forming a sect called Putaiki, the literal meaning of which is concentration or unity of strength, coinciding with the old proverb, 'Unity is strength', and taken from the backbone, which, being the concentration of the ribs and supporting the human frame, causes it to become a body. I am, however, of opinion that this will die a natural death.[20]

Hamlin's prognosis was, as it turned out, somewhat astray. The Putaiki did not die a natural death so much as succumb to overwhelming forces, most of which were of the government's making. For the remainder of the 1870s it proved a formidable obstacle to those seeking to acquire Tarawera lands against the wishes of the Tuhourangi tribe, and at the same time provided a spur for other sections of Arawa to also mobilise in opposition to land sales and the Court through tribal institutions of their own making.

In fact, the Putaiki's proselytising role extended beyond the tribal rohe of Te Arawa, and within a month of the publication of the first issue of *Te Wananga* in August 1874 members of the

Putaiki were writing to inform its readers that Tuhourangi had 'Elected a Committee to hold their land, which is called a (Putaiki) to prevent the laws which are hurtful to our districts', at the same time urging the 'tribes and chiefs of the Island' to 'see and elect a large Committee for this Island which is to be called the Great Heart of New Zealand'.[21] They did not, readers of the Repudiation movement's newspaper were informed, 'put the Laws of the Queen on one side', but had merely set up a committee 'as a guard' and to administer their own lands. In 1873, it was explained:

> The buying and leasing of the Government came to the boundary of the Arawa, but we could not push it a side, it was the rule that came from the administers of the Law, so some of the tribes of the Arawa agreed. But when the Land was consumed, when others saw that we are overcome by this rules of the Government, so this tribe thought it was best to hold the portions that was left, the Committee is called a (Putaiki) to keep the said boundary, it is not against the Law.[22]

The only wealth a Maori had, the members of the Putaiki wrote, was the land, and if this was consumed, 'he has no reason to be called a Maori tribe', but was like 'a dying person'. Thus Europeans wishing to purchase or lease lands within the rohe potae of Tuhourangi were not to go to the hapu or chiefs, who had no authority to let or sell land, but would instead have to go to the Putaiki, which had 'the word of the whole tribe' and would decide land matters as it saw fit. Moreover, in urging 'one rule for the tribes and chiefs of this Island', supporters of the Putaiki drew no distinction between those who had fought for or against the Crown in the 1860s, instead advocating that all tribes should appoint their own committee to hold their lands, and that a 'joint Committee' should be elected 'for us for the Maori people of this Island, whether Kingites, Hauhaus, or Government...like one family residing in the one house'.[23] This message of kotahitanga, coming as it did just a few years after the wars had ended, proved too premature for some to accept in the still tense intertribal atmosphere that prevailed in many areas. Yet there were those ready to support Tuhourangi's initiatives. Hone Mohi Tawhai of Ngapuhi, for example, wrote to a Tuhourangi chief that:

> The following are what the Ngapuhi have agreed to:– That the Native Lands Court be done away with. That the lands which we have not passed through the Native Lands Court, shall be held by us in the same way as they were held by our ancestors. And if the Native Lands Court is done away with, your council of Tuhourangi will be an accomplished fact. Then there will be no land sold or surveyed.[24]

Tawhai added that the effect of the Native Land Court was to 'make it appear that the law is the owner of the land, and the Maori people are to buy land from the law, so that the Maori may become the owner of the land'.

Other sections of Te Arawa certainly seem to have been receptive to Tuhourangi's message. In May 1874 Taekata Rawiri informed the Native Minister that 'A new system has sprung up among the Ngatiwhakaue and the Uenukukopako tribes..., namely that the control of the land is vested in that Committee and your administration thus done away with.'[25] Hamlin's report for the same year confirmed that a runanga had been established at Ohinemutu, to which the Native Assessors gave their allegiance, and that he had 'not been called upon by any hapu or tribe to arbitrate on any question of land dispute'.[26] In fact, Hamlin reported that at a recent 'great political meeting' held at Ohinemutu the subjects brought forward for discussion by Ngati Whakaue were 'indicative of a strong desire to support the King'. H.T. Clarke, by this time Native Under-Secretary, was also concerned by the state of affairs in the Rotorua district, informing McLean in the same month that:

> since the Government Agents have been negotiating for the purchase of lands in the Arawa Country a great change has come over many of the most influential and powerful hapus in their attachment to the Government.[27]

Te Arawa had always clung to their lands with 'extreme tenacity', Clarke told McLean, and 'As a people they have prided themselves in holding their land in tact as handed down to them by their ancestors'. Because of this, Clarke viewed with 'great anxiety' the operations of Davis and Mitchell in their country, noting that he was being 'continually appealed to by the chiefs and people...to interfere in their behalf as against the Government Agents'. The Native Under-Secretary pointed out that 'hostilities amongst the different tribes of Arawas arising out of the operations of Government Agents coupled with open disaffection to the Government would be most disastrous to the Country' and urged that steps be taken to avert this before it was too late. He recommended that Davis and Mitchell should be instructed to enter into no new negotiations, but to 'complete all those engagements that can be done with safety' before leaving the district. McLean approved of this suggestion, and the pair were told pointedly that it was 'a noticeable fact that we have not received a single deed in the office of a completed transaction from you'.[28] Advance payments had been made for a large portion of the Rotorua district, generally in the form of a few small sums paid to one or two chiefs early in 1873, but there had been little progress since then.[29]

When Donald McLean attended a lengthy meeting with more than a thousand Maori from all sections of Te Arawa at Maketu in March 1875, he heard more complaints against Davis and Mitchell. In May Hamlin reported that McLean's visit had 'resulted in instructions being issued to the Land Purchase Commissioners engaged in the Arawa territory to discontinue their negotiations for the present'.[30] There is no indication that these instructions, if indeed they were issued, were complied with. Davis and Mitchell's subsequent reports made no reference to them, but instead pointed to continuing opposition to the completion of their purchases. In July 1875 the pair reported that:

> we have had some difficulties to encounter in our land operations which at times threatened to bring about a collapse. Some of the Arawa chiefs acting under the advice of the Hawkes Bay natives and their pakeha friends whose opposition to the present Government is well known, have by petitions to the Assembly, by numerous letters,

and telegrams, and by various other means endeavoured to stay our land proceedings in the Arawa Country. The various petitions and other communications forwarded by the Arawas generally have been notable only for the gross misrepresentations they contained, and in these demonstrations they have borne out the ancient proverb accorded to them by the universal voice of the Maori tribes 'Te Arawa Mangai nui' – 'The big mouthed Arawa'. Added to the wanted troublesomeness of these Arawa tribes, their cupidity has been excited and their known character of dishonesty encouraged by private individuals who persistently endeavour to lease and buy Maori lands within our district, although they well know that it is impossible under the circumstances to obtain a legal title, and that by foolishly bargaining with unscrupulous Arawas they are but wasting time and money, and no doubt at some future period when driven to their wits end, they will fall back as their predecessors have done on the Government for compensation with what show of justice remains to be seen.[31]

The 'unscrupulous Arawas' opposing their efforts in the district were, as Davis and Mitchell saw it, insignificant landholders whose interests could safely be ignored. Referring to the meeting at Maketu in March, the pair stated that they were:

> present at daily meetings held by Sir Donald & the main hapus of the District for the purpose of inquiring into the nature and extent of the Arawa grievances which we are inclined to think were of the most delusive character, and brought forward with the pure desire of extorting Government money, which to the credit of Sir Donald be it recorded, they utterly failed in obtaining. In justice to the Arawas generally, it becomes necessary to draw the line of demarkation between the two prominent sections, namely the 'Anti-Leasing and Selling' party, and those who sell and lease…In fact the land holders generally throughout the Arawa Country favour both selling and leasing, and it is found that the opposing party as a rule have little or no land either to sell or lease. Consequently the genuine owners of the soil view the acts and interference of the clamorous anti sellers with extreme bitterness.

Davis and Mitchell reported that they had 'succeeded in arguing down the opposition of the body of Tuhourangi chiefs who call themselves the "Putaiki"', and that:

> notwithstanding the violence of the opposition and the various obstacles referred to with which we have had to contend, land matters at present throughout the whole of our district, as far as our operations are concerned are standing upon a most satisfactory basis.

Neither assertion proved to be correct. From the government's perspective land matters in the Rotorua district were in a far from satisfactory state, and Putaiki and other opposition to the activities of Davis and Mitchell was far from quashed. In September 1875 the pair 'met numerous deputations of Ngatiwhakaue, Ngatituara, Ngatiraukawa, Ngatitahu, Ngatiwhaoa, Ngatiwahiao, and others, who expressed their general approval of the system adopted by us in relation to the land transactions throughout the district, and pleaded the necessity of settling the land titles by ourselves and local committees'.[32] This 'general approval' was little in evidence beyond Davis and Mitchell's own reports to their employer. The same report referred to a meeting held at Te Wairoa in November 1875 to discuss advances made on land at Kairgaroa and Paeroa. 'No decision was arrived at regarding surveys and the inquiry into Maori titles of land, in consequence of the opposition pertinaciously adhered to by the Tuhourangis'. In February 1876 more trouble developed over the disputed Te Puke Block, and in March the Governor, the Marquis of Normanby, spent nearly a fortnight at Rotorua listening to lengthy complaints from local Maori over land matters.[33] During the same month a large intertribal hui was held at Paeroa to discuss land questions. According to the report of the government agent present, J.C. Young:

> The originators of the meeting, Ngatitaha and Ngatiwhaoa, opened the proceedings by reading a paper to the assembled tribes, numbering in all about 600 persons, consisting of Ngatiwhaoa, Ngatitahu, Ngatimanawa, Te Urewera, Ngatihineuru,

Ngatitutewha, Ngatituwharetoa, Ngatiwhakaue, Ngatirangitihi, Ngatihinewai, Ngatiraukawa, Ngatituara, and Tuhourangi, under the leadership of its Putaiki or Council of Twelve. The land policy of the Government was keenly argued before one of its representatives, and notwithstanding the audacity of Tuhourangi in proclaiming itself the sole dictator of the proceedings, its pretentious assumptions were at once repudiated by the confederate tribes in the following terms:– 'Who has constituted you an authority to dictate to us as to what we shall do respecting our land matters? We refuse to acknowledge your pretentions in any way, and let your interference in our land matters cease'.

Notwithstanding the fierce opposition to all general measures in the district by the Tuhourangis, the twelve confederate tribes declared for the Government, affirming their determination to keep inviolable all their bargains, and to facilitate in every possible way the settlement of the lands in the Arawa country; adding, with emphatic outspokeness, the land agents of the Government have acted throughout the negotiations in an open straightforward manner. After four days' continuous discussion the meeting was brought to a conclusion, the anti-selling Tuhourangi tribe retiring completely crestfallen to its home at the Wairoa, threatening to convene another monster meeting to defend itself, which meeting is still in abeyance.[34]

The Putaiki's zealous opposition to the work of Davis and Mitchell may have upset some neighbouring tribes resentful of Tuhourangi's perceived 'interference' in their land matters, but this ringing endorsement of government land purchase policies is hardly apparent from other sources. Indeed, by May matters had reached such a state as to prompt H.T. Clarke to write:

> I trust that the Hon. Native Minister will not consider that I am stepping beyond the bounds of my duty if I again urge upon the Government the expediency of removing the land purchase Agents from the Arawa Country. The tone of feeling as expressed by both parties (those who are obstructing the completion of the purchases and those who are anxious to fulfil their obligations) is anything but favourable to the Government.

> The fact is that the Agents employed by the Government are suspected by both parties, and [they] are accused by some of being actuated by party and political motives. ...
>
> The reason which weighs most with me and compels me to urge the withdrawal of the land purchase Agents from Arawa Country is that I apprehend, if causes of irritation are not removed, that a serious collision will be the result. I say that advisedly. A determined old chief has on more than one occasion suggested that the Government withdraw and let them settle in their own way the question of title.[35]

Davis and Mitchell were officially informed a few days later that 'owing to the Native difficulties' which continued to beset their operations it had been deemed expedient to suspend their negotiations for the present. The government's alleged 'taihoa' policy with respect to Arawa lands was condemned in the local press, and by November Mitchell had been re-employed to complete outstanding land negotiations in the Rotorua and Taupo districts. In February 1877 the proclamation over Arawa lands in place since 1873 was lifted and the Native Land Court's jurisdiction over the district was reinstated.[36] This did not herald any great shift in Arawa attitudes towards the Land Court. In April 1877, for example, the *Bay of Plenty Times*' correspondent reported that:

> The Ngatiwhakaue and Rotorua natives generally look upon the Court with suspicion; they having been informed by some unscrupulous European that the individualisation of their land will speedily be followed by taxation. It is very hard to combat with this idea, to which they seem to have given the blindest credence. They have given way so far that they agree to hold a general meeting of the tribe shortly, after which individuals, should they be so inclined, will not be opposed by the tribe in passing their small pieces of land through the Court. Of course no steps can be taken to force these people to do what is contrary to their inclinations, and in the mean time the progress of the district is retarded, and Europeans only remain here on sufferance. The 'Putaiki', or Council of Tuhourangi, are at present on the 'wallaby'; they are visiting all the principal settlements in the Bay of Plenty, endeavouring to unite the tribes in

strenuously opposing all surveys, Government sales and leases, and the introduction of the Lands Court.[37]

Mitchell, writing at the end of June 1877, confirmed that the government's land dealings in the Rotorua district were not in a 'forward condition', and added that 'the opposition of many of the Tuhourangi, including the anti-land leasing organization called "Te Putaiki", and some Ngatiwhakaue chiefs, to the completion of the Government leases remains in much the same state as at the beginning'.[38] Despite this, he detected a 'better feeling' towards the government's operations among Tuhourangi 'and other obstructionists', and remained hopeful of 'being able to report some definite evidence of this change in the way of a general application for adjudication of the disputed land titles by the established tribunals of the country'. Chief Judge Fenton visited Rotorua later in the same year, and reported that local Maori were willing to have the Land Court sit in their district, an event which would be delayed only if disputes regarding the completion of surveys arose between contending claimants.[39]

There appeared to be no inter-hapu dispute as to surveys, however, but rather a more general one with the government. Early in November a government surveyor arrived in the district unannounced and started work, but was soon stopped by a deputation of local Maori, who also levelled the trig stations he had begun erecting. One correspondent for the *New Zealand Times* reported that Rotorua Maori blamed Gilbert Mair, the district officer for the Bay of Plenty region under the Native Lands Act 1873, who they said had insisted that trig stations be erected before any other survey work was undertaken.[40] Mair wrote in his defence that:

> the opposition to surveys is a political, not a personal movement. The Rotorua natives will not allow any surveys to be proceeded with under any circumstances, tho' constant communication has been kept up with them on the subject for many months.[41]

Early in 1878 Mair informed the Native Minister, in response to letters from Maori complaining about him in the local press (written at the instigation of troublesome Europeans, according to Mair) that:

> the Arawa – and the Ngatiwhakaue Hapu in particular, are the most troublesome natives in New Zealand to deal with and no officer who tries to carry out his instructions can avoid, at times, clashing with them. The Ngatiwhakaue, I believe, have at different times, petitioned for the removal of every Govt. officer who has been sent amongst them. At the present time, and indeed for the past three years, they are the only people who have given any trouble to speak of. There are many reasons for this, one being that from the first Govt. Land Purchase Officers in their District have refused (and I think wrongly) ever to recognise the 'mana' of the Ngatiwhakaue, and their general claims over Land under negotiation to Govt. I have heard them say repeatedly that this is the real reason of their obstruction.[42]

Since their involvement in the survey disturbance, Mair added:

> The Ngatiwhakaue have formed a committee, and are now busy erecting a great flag staff to be called 'Te Puru o Houtaiki'. (after a sort of estoppel or 'Aukati', which they placed upon their war paths &c. in the old days, and which if broken, was punished with death). This flagstaff will be finished in February, after which the Committee state they will decide whether surveys &c. are to be proceeded with or not. They fully admit that the applicants for surveys are the real owners of the land they wish surveyed, but they consider that the minority have no right to exercise private rights against the wishes of the majority. In addition to the reasons already given why the Committee object to surveys &c, they also quote the Treaty of Waitangi, Governor Browne's speech at Kohimarama in 1860, Sir Donald McLean's speech at Maketu in 1875, Dr Pollen's visit to Tauranga last year and Mr. Fenton's advice to them when in Ohinemutu in October last.

These reasons were, in Mair's opinion, nothing but 'pretexts to gain time'. Maori committees were, he warned, as a rule 'productive of far more harm than good'. Clearly, though, Ngati Whakaue, had determined to set the agenda for surveys, land title investigations and alienations themselves, rather than being pushed one way or another by the government and private parties.

It is apparent, however, that just like the Putaiki, this Ngati Whakaue committee was not looking to set itself up in opposition to the colonial government, or the European settlement of the region, but merely claimed the right to be recognised as the body through which the government and settlers would have to deal in matters pertaining to their district. Mair and other Pakeha residents of Ohinemutu were in fact invited to the initial meeting of this new body, at which, according to one correspondent's report:

> The Rotorua 'Committee of Management' declared that the surveys were not to go on until after the meeting of January, when the Rotorua Native Council would declare their policy...The Council reserves to itself power to deal with the Land and Law Courts, and all matters wherein the natives are interested. They declare allegiance to Queen Victoria, but claim the right to manage their own affairs without interference, and that this conduct has been forced on them by the late Government.[43]

Within a week of this first meeting the Ngati Whakaue committee had received at least five applications for investigations of title, and had publicly declared that it would commence hearing these at Ohinemutu on 1 January 1878, as well as apparently passing several 'laws' to take effect on the same date.[44] Some settlers complained of the 'powerful combination...formed to obstruct all Government work in the Rotorua District', and wrote scathingly that 'even the Treaty of Waitangi has been referred to' in justification of Te Arawa's opposition to the continuation of surveys.[45] Others, though, whilst appearing to have some reservations about the wide powers assumed by the committee, argued that its investigations of title would be quicker, less expensive, and less fraught with difficulties than any attempted sitting of the Native Land Court in the district. And one settler referred to the remarks of committee members at the initial meeting, when it had been pointed out that the land in question was, after all, private property, the owners of which had authorised the committee to act on their behalf as they saw fit.⁴⁶

Conflicting reports as to the success of Ngati Whakaue's committee appear to have reflected differing ideas as to the appropriateness of its investigations of title. One correspondent to the *Bay of Plenty Times* reported that during its first week of hearings the committee had achieved 'very satisfactory results', in passing through its 'Titles Court' 160,000 acres which were to be 'thrown open for leases with Crown Title'.⁴⁷ The paper's editor, however, failed to see anything 'satisfactory' in the decisions of this 'self-constituted Court', and a later correspondent described this report as 'utterly false', adding:

> It is quite true that the self-constituted Committee of the Ngatiwhakaue have arrogated to themselves the right to hold Land Courts, Civil Courts, &c., and that they held a meeting during the first part of this month, lasting for a week; but the piece of land under investigation was a small bit...and even that case was adjourned till February next, when this farce will be continued. The Committee have passed a number of obnoxious bye-laws, prohibiting surveys, Land Courts, leases, Civil courts, &c., and the only activity they have displayed has been in levying 'black mail' upon the unfortunate European residents of Ohinemutu...⁴⁸

By March 1878 further trouble had occurred, with a private survey party from Cambridge, reportedly working on behalf of a great Auckland 'Land Ring', caught attempting clandestinely to survey lands near Niho-o-te-Kiore. Its members were captured and imprisoned by an armed Tuhourangi contingent before being released unharmed.⁴⁹ Just over a week later a large meeting was held at the Tuhourangi settlement of Parekarangi to discuss this and other incidents. One correspondent reported that:

> The Parekarangi meeting proved a failure. Tuhourangi, Tupaika, and Ngatiwhakaue Committees combine to prevent the Land Courts, sittings &c., and repudiate all Government land negotiations.

The *Bay of Plenty Times* was perhaps more astute, however, in describing this outcome as 'from a Maori point of view...anything but a "failure"'.⁵⁰

The united opposition of the Rotorua tribes to the surveying of their lands meant that there was now little prospect of a Native Land Court sitting in the district in the near future, and meanwhile Ngati Whakaue's committee continued with its own investigations of title. In May it was reported that the Rotorua 'Committee of Management' had forwarded its quarterly report to the Chief Judge of the Native Land Court (whose response is unknown), and the same correspondent noted that 'They have plenty of work in hand, and so far seem to have gained the confidence of the Europeans and Natives who have submitted land disputes for their settlement'.[51]

Concurrent with the committee's investigations of title at Rotorua, in April 1878 the first Native Land Court sitting within Arawa territory for more than eight years commenced at Maketu. But with several of the Rotorua tribes opposed to the Court's jurisdiction claiming interests in the coastal lands under investigation, this was beset by almost continual disturbances. In May it was claimed that:

> The Ngatiwhakaue Committee from Rotorua, headed by Petera Te Pukuatua, – a *paid Government officer* – and Pererika Ngahuruhuru, and the Tuhourangi Putaiki have, combined, been doing all they can to frustrate the sitting of the Court.[52]

Opposition to the activities of the Native Land Court and Crown land purchase agents appeared to be becoming much more organised and unified, to the extent that a Maori-language newspaper was mooted. Typically, just as in Hawke's Bay, some attributed this to the influence of meddling Europeans. C.O. Davis, who had been acting on behalf of Auckland speculators since his dismissal from Crown service in 1876, was the target of allegations that he had been 'doing his best to unsettle the natives, urging them to repudiate all the old transactions with the Government as being "para" or rotten, and telling the natives that the Government only want to pass the land through the Court for the purpose of making a lot of money'. Te Arawa leaders were in no mood to stomach these 'defamatory remarks' which sought to 'degrade the image of the Maori people and their Committees', however, and informed the readers of *Te Wananga* in no uncertain terms that:

> the [alleged] fact that the Maori speaking Pakeha are the ones guiding or educating the Maori Committees is utter nonsense, as my tribe emerged to its present heights on its own accord since the landing of the Arawa canoe, to this date.[53]

Further fuel was to be added to allegations that it was Europeans who were behind Te Arawa's actions by the events of the following months, however. Tensions at Maketu had nearly reached breaking point by early June, when an armed party of Ngati Whakaue travelled to the coast, reportedly to forcibly occupy disputed land which it did not wish to have taken through the Court. Te Keepa Te Rangipuawhe of Tuhourangi, with the assistance of other leading chiefs and Robert Graham, an Auckland merchant, intervened to bring the conflict to a peaceful resolution.[54]

Graham's motive for this intervention remains unclear, but in October he visited Ohinemutu, and held meetings with Ngati Whakaue, who invited him to stay in the district.[55] Subsequently, notices appeared warning all Europeans to 'henceforth cease paying money to any native, or hapu, or tribe on… [unadjudicated] lands, lest you may afterwards blame the Arawa Committee for your troubles'.[56] This appears to have been a forerunner to plans to revive the Rotorua 'Committee of Management', which had been dormant for some months, under the new label of 'Te Komiti Nui o Rotorua'. Aporo Tipi Tipi later recalled that 'On the 7th December [1878] the Rotorua Committee assembled together; the Rotorua people met Mr. Graham & they established the Great Committee of Rotorua'. Graham presented the Komiti Nui with a special flag to be flown whenever it sat, along with a bell to call its members together and a lamp; an official seal (featuring tree-ferns and the kotuku) was also later designed.[57]

At the initial meeting of the Komiti Nui several of its members explained why they supported the new body. Paora Te Amohau said that 'he had been loyal to the Government, but the

Government had not been considerate to them in regard to land transactions'. Graham and the Komiti, he believed, would 'help them to overcome the various evils about which they complained'. Henare Te Pukuatua thought that 'the committee of Rotorua would be able to settle the question of leases and sales, and also make by-laws and rules for the maintenance of order among themselves'. Graham, in reply, told the meeting that the Komiti 'had been formed for the purpose of advancing their social and moral condition; in fact, it was a system of local self-government they were in search of, and he would assist them to carry it out'.[58]

Whereas the earlier 'Committee of Management' appears to have been essentially a Ngati Whakaue body, the Komiti Nui claimed a wider jurisdiction, though without ever supplanting iwi bodies such as the Putaiki of Tuhourangi. This was evident from the fact that the day after the initial meeting at Tamatekapua, Graham visited the Ngati Rangiwewehi settlement of Te Awahou, where Wi Maihi Te Rangikaheke told him that 'they were now about to join the committee of Rotorua, because they thought it would do good'. Ngati Rangiwewehi later complained that the Native Land Court had overturned a ruling of the Komiti Nui in failing to award a particular piece of land to them.[59] In fact, it may well have been the constant threat of conflict between various sections of Te Arawa over disputed sections of land, largely arising from the actions of Crown and private land agents, and arguments over how these could best be resolved, which provided the spur to create a more broadly-based forum for settling disputed titles. Early in 1879 it was reported that:

> The Rotorua committee has completed its first session, and notices have been issued to call in all claims to land in the district before April 1st, when the committee will again sit. Neither the Land Court nor surveys are to be countenanced in the district at present. Mr. Robert Graham's claims have been recognised by the Maori committee of Rotorua. Mr. Dargaville's claim at Rotomahana is upheld by the individual claimants, though opposed by the tribe of Tuhourangi.[60]

Graham had been gifted a piece of land at Te Koutu by members of the Komiti Nui. Joseph Dargaville, a wealthy businessman, had visited the district in December and had apparently been successful in negotiating the lease of a few acres at Te Wairoa, where he proposed to establish a sanatorium.[61] By February, however, it was reported that those in favour of Dargaville's claim were opposed by the Putaiki and represented only one section of the owners, and in the face of this Tuhourangi refused to recognise his claims, which were quietly abandoned.[62]

By April 1879 the Komiti Nui was in full business, and the *New Zealand Herald*, commenting on developments in the region, informed its readers that:

> The Arawas have always been eager to preserve their lands, and have endeavoured to bring some kind of tribal organisation to bear to prevent individuals entering into negotiations for sale. The sittings of the Native Lands Court at Maketu have been attended with a great deal of disturbance, and the action of the Court has caused much ill-feeling between the different sections of the tribe. The committee of Rotorua has been established with the consent of the chief men of the tribe, and assumes apparently a charge over the Arawa lands, ignoring the Lands Court and assuming Home Rule to a very decided extent.

The Komiti had 'gone very thoroughly to business', the report added, issuing a series of notices in the style of those which appeared in the *New Zealand Gazette*. It was about to:

> investigate the titles to a number of blocks of land, and its decisions as to ownership are to be final. If the committee confines itself to this, and does not attempt to prevent sales of land, it may do good, as it will bring an amount of knowledge and also of public feeling to bear in the investigation of title which is beyond the power of the Native Lands Court.[63]

Beneath this report was appended a translation of one of the Komiti's notices, which provides further insight into the extent of the jurisdiction it claimed:

This notification is for the purpose of informing all persons, either European or native, residing in or about Arawa country:– 1. Do you not sell, or lease, or ask for money, or arrange for surveys for any lands which are under the *(mana)* authority of the Great Committee of Rotorua. 2. Europeans are cautioned not to give money or make arrangements as regards surveys for the lands which are under the *(mana)* authority of the Great Committee of Rotorua. 3. These are the blocks of land referred to: Rotorua and its surrounding lands, Horohoro and adjoining lands, Tumunui and adjoining lands, Paeroa and adjoining lands, and all the lands remaining at Maketu that have not been already sold or leased. 4. The words of the Committee of Rotorua have gone forth during the past month, and are proclaimed or declared again now. 5. Titles of land must be first investigated, and when such land or lands have been awarded to the person or persons claiming the same, the Committee of Rotorua will consider the matter over. 6. If you are wishful to survey or lease lands, it must be done under the *(mana)* authority of the Great Committee of Rotorua – that is, the surveying and leasing of lands, whether the blocks of land are large or small...

From Pererika Ngahuruhuru, Chairman of the Great Committee of Rotorua.

The annual report of the Tauranga Resident Magistrate provided further information about the constitution and aims of the Komiti Nui. H.W. Brabant, writing at the end of May 1879, noted that:

The paramount subject of interest to the Arawa tribes has been the establishment of the 'Great Committee of Rotorua', as they term it. It consists of about sixty men, selected from the several hapus, having for its object the investigation of Native land titles, their prominent ideas being that, if the committee hold a preliminary inquiry before a case comes into the Native Land Court, (1) money will not be wasted in overlapping surveys; (2) litigious claimants will not be able to oblige the owners to pay for surveys against their will; (3) they think the committee will have the confidence of the Natives, and could settle intricate claims better than the Court.

> They do not ask that the Court should be abolished, but merely that the committee should send up claims for confirmation.[64]

Clearly if the Komiti Nui was not advocating the abolition of the Native Land Court, it was at least seeking to restrict its powers within Te Arawa territory to the ratification of its own decisions, at the same time trying to stamp out some of the worst features of the Court system, such as applications for investigations made without the full consent of all owners, and costly and contested surveys. Brabant added that it was the opinion of many Europeans as well as of Maori that 'a Native committee would be the best able to deal with Native claims', and that if the Komiti Nui 'could carry out what they propose they would deserve the thanks of the Government and the tribes, for nowhere are land titles so complicated as in this district'. Unfortunately, Brabant reported, 'up to the present time the "great committee" have been chiefly conspicuous for quarrels amongst themselves'. Despite this, the Resident Magistrate stated that:

> they have amongst them chiefs who are really anxious for the good of their people, and they have appointed July next for a protracted sitting, when it is to be hoped that their proceedings may be more profitable than has hitherto been the case.

Brabant's apparent enthusiasm for the Komiti Nui does not seem to have been shared by his superiors in Wellington. In April, J.E. Dalton, a local settler, had wired the Under-Secretary for Native Land Purchase to ask whether the government would 'acknowledge the right [of the] Committee nui o Rotorua to make awards in this district & will govt. legalise their action'.[65] Dalton was merely requested to provide further details on the Great Committee. Yet neither his nor Brabant's subsequent reports seem to have impressed officials in Wellington, and the Komiti Nui, along with the Putaiki and other Arawa bodies attempting to control their own lands, never received the official recognition so essential to their longer-term survival. In February 1881, at the opening of a Native Land Court sitting at Ohinemutu, it was reported that 'The Rotorua Committee tried to have their standing recognised, but the Court could not do so'.⁶⁶ As noted previously, this led to complaints that the Native Land Court had ignored the decisions of the Komiti Nui.

Without official recognition, such bodies could continue to be undermined by Crown and private agents who persisted in dealing with individuals, by legislation allowing any Maori to apply to the Native Land Court for the investigation of title regardless of the wishes of the rest of the tribe, and by the absence of any legislation requiring the Court to heed decisions reached in such forums. Comments as to the ineffectual nature of the Komiti Nui's investigations of title thus need to be treated with a grain of salt, given the Crown's reluctance to provide any support or encouragement.

Moreover, it would seem that part of the reason for this reluctance lay not so much in doubts as to the efficacy of such committees' investigations of title, but in the fact that tribal entities such as the Komiti Nui and the Putaiki went against the thrust towards individualisation, and thereby provided Maori communities with some measure of tribal control over the process by which their lands might be alienated and made available for European settlement. Henry Mitchell, writing to the government in July 1879, made it clear that this was his main objection to these bodies (whilst at the same time he distorted their avowed aims to include facilitating the alienation of their lands) in stating that:

> the 'Putaiki' & Native Komitis have had unlimited sway for several years past. The Government have given these bodies every encouragement & opportunity to follow up the policy they profess of settling the titles to the lands &c. before parting with them by lease or sale, but the leniency shown seems only to have added to their self importance without in the least expediting the settlement of the land titles or furthering the progress of the district.⁶⁷

Contrary to Mitchell's statement, the government had scarcely given such bodies 'every encouragement'. The Putaiki had been informed as early as 1873 that the government could not recognise the boundaries of the area it proclaimed jurisdiction over without a prior sitting of the Native Land Court. Yet Tuhourangi had established the Putaiki precisely in order to protect their lands from the Native Land Court and the alienation of individual bits of the tribal patrimony which almost always followed in its wake.

Moreover, events over subsequent months suggested that there may well have been a deliberate campaign to undermine the Komiti Nui. Mitchell informed his superiors in Wellington that 'measures' were being adopted which would 'neutralize' the actions of this 'troublesome' body.[68] Disaffection with the government's land purchase operations in the Rotorua district again came to the fore in April 1879, when it was announced that Robert Graham was to be prosecuted for occupying Te Koutu, which along with most of the Rotorua region had been proclaimed as under negotiation by the Crown. The *New Zealand Herald* suggested that the government might well have considered that 'his recent proceedings in assisting to establish the "Committee of Rotorua" have interfered with and obstructed their land purchase operations in the district'. 'These proclamations', the paper added:

> there is no disguising, are virtually confiscations...The lands of the natives were guaranteed to them by the Treaty of Waitangi. and the question may be raised whether the Assembly can so deal with the private property of large bodies of the Queen's subjects. The Crown had, it is true, a pre-emptive right, but having parted with that, it is questionable whether that right can be resumed, or virtually resumed by these proclamations.[69]

Te Arawa also viewed these proclamations as akin to confiscation, informing readers of the *Herald* in June that the government 'was conscious of its wrong-doing when it paid [advance] money to Maoris who were mere strangers' against the wishes of the true owners, and had consequently in 1876 abandoned its claims to the land given to Graham. Te Arawa added:

> In the face of these clear understandings, on what grounds are we, the genuine owners of Te Koutou [*sic*] prosecuted? Mr Robert

Graham has nothing to do with this subject, for he was placed by us on our own lands. What, then, have we done amiss that the law should recklessly rush upon us to inflict punishment?[70]

The authors of this letter had sought to know to whom they and 'all the Arawas' should send petitions, and were informed by the editor in response that Parliament was the appropriate place to send their appeals. Yet members of the Komiti Nui apparently decided on a more direct approach, and in September Eruera Te Uremutu and others were deputed by the Komiti to travel to Auckland to lay their concerns before the Premier, Sir George Grey. The matters 'giving pain to all the tribes of Rotorua' which Te Uremutu raised with Grey, were, he stated:

> a protest against the trouble that is being brought about by the Government of Sir George Grey, and, secondly, to abrogate the Acts, which weigh heavily on the Rotorua tribes. Point No.1: The tying up of the lands of Rotorua, of Paeroa, and many other places by paying £100 under the direction of one of the agents of the Government, whose name is Mitchell. Point No.2: The desire of all the tribes to have Mitchell removed from Rotorua to some other district, because he is strenuously endeavouring to blind the eyes of the Maoris by his dishonourable ways.

According to the chief's account of the meeting, as reported in the *Herald*, he had told Grey:

> This is the sentence of the Great Committee of Rotorua[:] Your agent, Mitchell, has tied up Rotorua by a money advance. The money was advanced to four persons – namely, to Rotohiko, to Te Amohau, to Henare, and to Ngahuruhuru'. Sir George Grey replied, 'I am glad. My heart approves of that course. All private Europeans will be driven away, and all arrangements will be left in the hands of the Government in regard to lands. You, Maoris, will be benefited. The lands will be surveyed and put up to auction, and the proceeds handed over to the natives'. 'Then', said I, 'harken now. The Great Committee of Rotorua will not agree to Government arrangements. But all must be left to the sole management of the chiefs, and to the Great Committee of Rotorua in respect to all lands. Let there be no

> unauthorised interference on the part of the Government relative to Rotorua lands. O father! disallow at once the tying up of the Rotorua and all other lands by advances of cash'.[71]

Grey reportedly replied that there was no difficulty with this request. The matter rested with Te Arawa, and if they wished to abrogate any arrangements previously entered into they were free to do so. And in response to the Komiti Nui's request that Mitchell – with whom they were 'becoming intensely angry' as a result of his 'works of confusion' – should be removed from the district, Grey informed the deputation that this would be done soon, as the government planned to 'speedily cease to employ land purchase agents'. Returning home well-contented with the apparent success of the mission, Te Uremutu wrote from Rotorua a few days later that 'Assurances given by Sir George Grey that all Government land agents will retire, and restrictions on land be removed caused great satisfaction'. He added that the Komiti Nui had decided to lay out a township 'in the vicinity of the Hot Springs', and that a deputation would shortly visit Wellington to formally seek the removal of all restrictions on their lands. Yet the problems still confronting the Komiti Nui were apparent from the fact that all four men reported to have accepted deposits for land from Mitchell were leading chiefs of Ngati Whakaue, while Ngahuruhuru was chairman of the Komiti. Te Uremutu stated that:

> The committee is to arraign before its tribunal the four persons who lately received money from Government agents on Rotorua lands, the transactions having been vehemently repudiated by all the tribes. The chairman of the great committee is to be punished on account of the action taken by him re Government land agents...Agents of Government will be dispensed with.[72]

The Komiti Nui's indignant response to the prosecution of Graham, 'placed by us on our own lands', its earlier notice that applications for survey or lease would be considered by the Komiti, and its stated intention to lay out a township in the area, make it clear enough that it was not opposed in principle to European settlement of the region, provided this was done on its own terms and in its own time-frame. It might seem reasonable enough for a 'corporate' body, representing the owners of private property guaranteed to them by treaty, to assume that it had the right to decide for itself, subject to the approval of the confederate tribes it represented, how this property would be administered. Yet insofar as the Crown was concerned, it seems, controlled settlement of the region on terms dictated by Maori was not good enough, and government officials continued to search for a foothold which would allow them to dictate the terms of Rotorua's 'opening up' to Pakeha colonisation.

Mitchell's reference to 'measures...being adopted which will neutralize probably the actions of this body', combined with the tamana money received by the chairman of the Komiti Nui, strongly suggest that the land purchase officer may well have targeted members of the Komiti for advance payments as a means of undermining its authority. In the absence of any likelihood of a breakthrough in the negotiations, such payments at least allowed the Crown to keep a foot in the door. As Mitchell would well have understood, the Komiti's ban on individuals accepting payments for land would become increasingly difficult to enforce if Rotorua Maori saw its own members accepting them. And if the Komiti's mana and standing amongst the Rotorua tribes could be destroyed, there was always the prospect that he might induce enough individuals to accept payments to be in a position to go to the Land Court and complete his transactions on behalf of the government.

Whatever his punishment, though, Ngahuruhuru remained chairman of the Komiti Nui, which, possibly because of the swift action taken against him, does not appear to have lost any of its influence among the Arawa tribes. Despite Grey's reported promises, government land purchase agents were not withdrawn from the district and the proclamations over Te Arawa lands were not lifted, even after the Grey government's replacement in October 1879 by a ministry dominated by advocates of 'free trade' in Maori lands.

Instead, matters continued much as they had done, with the Komiti Nui still holding sway over the lands of Ngati Whakaue and other sections of Te Arawa at Rotorua, and Tuhourangi's Putaiki doing likewise at Rotomahana and Tarawera. Regular investigations of title continued to be undertaken by the Komiti, timed to cause the least possible disruption for local Maori. In August 1879, for example, it was reported that the Komiti's investigations were to be adjourned for the planting season – quite a contrast to the regular reports of native officers in other districts concerning Maori neglecting their crops because of their attendance at Native Land Court sittings.[73] With the Komiti convening locally to hear cases and timing its sittings to suit the claimants, it could afford to go thoroughly into each case, especially as there were no European lawyers involved in proceedings. In May 1880 Brabant reported that 'The "Great Native Committee" still sits at Ohinemutu, to hear land claims, but they get through but little business'.[74] The *Bay of Plenty Times*' correspondent though, noted that although the Komiti had decided only one case in ten days, 'The fairness with which the investigation is conducted gives universal satisfaction'.[75] Members of the Komiti were apparently considering asking for a Judge of the Native Land Court to come and reside permanently with them 'for the purpose of confirming their decisions regarding land titles',[76] and the *Herald*'s correspondent believed that the respect and satisfaction with which claimants accepted the Komiti Nui's decisions would 'greatly simplify and facilitate the working of the Native Lands Court'.[77] By June 1880 at least twenty blocks of land had been ruled on by the Komiti, and in August it was reported that:

> The Committee have worked well these last two months, and if there were no obstruction from the Government we might now open up this place for settlement; but the Government will not complete their purchases, and the colony is at a very considerable loss by the increased value the natives put year by year on their lands.[78]

The government's failure to complete its negotiations in the Rotorua district had not been through want of effort. In June 1880 it was decided to dispense with the services of Henry

Mitchell from the end of July; Brabant was now to have sole charge of all negotiations in the Bay of Plenty and Taupo regions.[79] For almost a decade the government had been attempting to acquire as much of the Rotorua district as possible. But the tried and tested method of making advance payments on a large area, and having the lands surveyed and passed through the Native Land Court, had signally failed at Rotorua. Instead, agents caught advancing money, and surveyors attempting to work surreptitiously, had been confronted by well-organised and determined opponents who demanded the right to control surveys, alienations and investigations of title themselves, free from interference by outsiders.

Yet with the Rotorua district's great tourist potential now well and truly confirmed, the government was coming under immense pressure to find some way of making lands there available for European settlement. In the late 1870s the Komiti Nui was effectively the government at Rotorua, just as Tuhourangi's Putaiki was at Tarawera – two districts where virtually no land had been alienated and into which the Native Land Court had yet to fully penetrate. But if Te Arawa considered that they had a right to decide themselves how their own lands would be administered, to most settlers this was akin to a 'state of confusion and anarchy' which was inimical to the prosperity of the colony.[80] As the *Bay of Plenty Times* put it in urging the government to 'spare no effort' to 'open up' the district to European occupation: 'To acquire the fee simple of the country should be the principal object, and, failing that, to obtain such leasing terms as would warrant the conversion of what is in reality a wilderness, to a fitting abode of civilised man'.[81] Quizzed as to what the government was doing to expedite this goal, John Bryce, the Native Minister, informed Parliament in June 1880 that:

> it had been admitted by successive Governments that it was very desirable that this part of the country should be acquired and retained as a permanent public reserve. But there was this difficulty in the matter: that the Native owners did not want to part with it. Several Governments had made approaches to them with the object

of inducing them to part with it for public purposes, but, so far, these efforts had not been very successful. To this extent, however, the Government had succeeded: that the Maoris had been induced to accept advances – not to a large amount – and, in consequence, the land was proclaimed as being under negotiation, thereby preventing private persons from seeking to acquire it.[82]

The Komiti Nui's announcement that it was planning to lay out a township in the vicinity of the hot springs provided a rare opportunity for the government to attempt to break this deadlock, and in November 1880 Bryce asked Chief Judge Fenton of the Native Land Court to visit Rotorua to follow up this proposal and endeavour to come to some arrangement with Te Arawa.[83] Fenton was soon at Rotorua and spent nearly a fortnight in the district, talking with Ngati Whakaue and neighbouring tribes about the proposals for a township. Yet the Chief Judge later reported that on his arrival:

> I found in existence at Ohinemutu a regularly organised local body with Chairman Secretary and officers. It was constituted as a Land League for the prime object of preventing alienations to the Crown, and in a secondary degree of obstructing or assisting as the case might be, private persons. But it subsequently assumed other powers and duties, and had acquired a position of some importance, being accepted by the tribe...with little more than its own influence and strength to enforce its decrees.[84]

Fenton soon discovered that he could achieve little at Rotorua without the support of the Komiti Nui, particularly as the site selected for a township, on the shores of Lake Rotorua, was predominantly owned by Ngati Whakaue, who were strong supporters of the Komiti. By 25 November it had been agreed that 99-year leases for a township site would be publicly auctioned by the Crown on behalf of the land's owners once these had been determined by the Native Land Court. Yet private correspondence between Fenton and members of the Komiti, along with subsequent events, strongly suggests that this agreement was understood to be conditional on the Court sitting merely to confirm previous investigations of title by the Komiti with respect to the ownership of the township block, Pukeroa-Oruawhata. On 22 November, for example, Rotohiko Haupapa (who had replaced Ngahuruhuru as chairman) and other prominent chiefs wrote to Fenton that 'The Maori [*sic*] Land Court will not adjudicate on lands which are associated with the Superior Committee of Rotorua'.[85] On the following day Haupapa wrote to Fenton along similar lines, stating that 'It is important that the Superior Committee of Rotorua adjudicate on the lands', and adding that the government should 'ask the Superior Committee of Rotorua about the surveying of the land'.[86] Fenton had already secured the agreement of several chiefs to the proposed township, but Haupapa, again emphasising the authority of the Komiti Nui, informed him that 'this agreement of the Chiefs to you will not be recognised', since only 'the Superior Committee of Rotorua has the mandate to agree to build a town at Rotorua'.[87]

Several members of the Komiti Nui signed the agreement on 25 November. Haupapa does not appear to have been among these signatories, but in a later letter to Fenton referred to the agreement as 'being carried out by you and the Committee'.[88] Presumably, then, members of the Komiti would not, in the light of Haupapa's prior warnings (and later endorsement of the agreement), have signed unless Fenton had given them some kind of verbal reassurance that the Native Land Court's investigation of title for the block would be merely for the purposes of rubber-stamping the Komiti's own decision with respect to it. And curiously, a draft clause suggesting that the Komiti would be incapable of undertaking such an investigation to the satisfaction of all parties is marked 'not in agreement'. Fenton's official report of his proceedings at Rotorua noted in relation to the Komiti Nui that he had:

> stressed this body and recognised it in the contract, relying upon it to do several things which it would be very difficult for the Land Court to do. I am not certain whether the 'Committee' will stand the strain, and rather fear that now thorough [?] and difficult work has to be done, the people will find that their own devices and energies will not suffice.[89]

The Komiti Nui had already done several things that the Land Court could not, investigating titles to lands at Rotorua, for example, without apparently costing Maori a great fortune – mainly in the very same lands – as a result. Yet once the Land Court got a foothold in the district and began seriously undermining the authority of the Komiti Nui, it indeed could not 'stand the strain'.

When the Native Land Court opened for its first sitting in January 1881, it was reported that 'The Rotorua Committee tried to have their standing recognised, but the Court could not do so'.[90] This was the beginning of the end, insofar as tribal control over Arawa lands was concerned, and within months many of the familiar scenes associated with the Land Court were beginning to be reported from Rotorua. In June 1881, for example, it was reported that 'On account of the natives indulging too freely in alcoholic liquor at the opening of the Land Court, the hotels are closed from 10 a.m. to 4 p.m., so that the business of the Court may be transacted'.[91] The Pukeroa-Oruawhata case had by then been dragging on intermittently for the best part of six months, and Arawa leaders wired Fenton asking for money with which to buy food for those attending.[92] Judgement was finally given at the end of the month with all but 45 acres of the block being awarded to Ngati Whakaue. In marked contrast to its severe criticism of the Komiti for its allegedly slow rate of progress in investigating titles, the local press was notably mute about the fact that it had taken the Native Land Court six months to decide the ownership of one relatively small block, or that the Komiti's investigations, in marked contrast with those of the Court, had not brought accompanying reports of food shortages and alcohol problems.

The Court's decision with respect to the township block had also quite clearly ignored the earlier findings of the Komiti with respect to the land, prompting several women of Ngati Rangiwewehi, 'Under pressure of pain for lost land', to inform Fenton that they did not understand why the Court had ignored their tribe's rights to the block, since:

> During January last the 'Komiti Nui o Rotorua' adjudicated upon those pieces. They were investigated before the four judges of that Komiti, and we appeared to state our claims before that tribunal, and some of those pieces were awarded to us by reason of our claims under maori custom.[93]

The Court's judgement on the township block had left it to Ngati Whakaue to submit their own list of owners. Gilbert Mair reported, however, that it was the Komiti Nui which was undertaking responsibility for this.[94] And whereas the government was anxious that only ten owners should be put on the title as trustees for the rest of the tribe, the list submitted contained some 800 names, including many who did not belong to Ngati Whakaue.[95] Fenton believed that Ngati Whakaue were 'putting in names for aroha';[96] more likely, though, they were endeavouring to include the names of those found to be owners by the Komiti Nui. On 7 July Fenton warned Petera Te Pukuatua, a Ngati Whakaue member of the Komiti Nui, that 'The Komiti should not return to things that have once been settled,'[97] ignoring the fact that it was the Native Land Court that was returning to matters already settled by the Komiti. Despite this, Judge Symonds was instructed by Fenton to examine every name and 'by no means admit any but Ngatiwhakaue'.[98]

Dissatisfaction with the Court's refusal to abide by the decisions of the Komiti (something Te Arawa almost certainly expected in agreeing to allow the Court to adjudicate on Rotorua lands for the first time) probably contributed to growing opposition to the township scheme. Just two weeks after the township block decision was handed down it was reported that Te Arawa were no longer as 'enamoured of [the] scheme' as they had been before the land was surveyed and brought before the Court, and that they were attempting to 'wriggle out of' the agreement signed with Fenton.[99] In the wake of the Court's refusal to accept their list of owners, Ngati Whakaue were reportedly 'much divided' on the question of who should be included,[100] and the conflict generated by this seems to have also affected the Komiti Nui. In August 1881 Henare Te Pukuatua informed the Chief

Judge that the Komiti had been undergoing some restructuring, apparently at Fenton's suggestion:

> Petera Te Pukuatua and I and the tribe at large have decided to reduce the number of the members of the Great Committee of Rotorua, and twelve members have been fixed upon by vote. Rotohiko Haupapa has been chosen Chairman of the Great Committee of Rotorua as it is at present constituted. It has now been arranged in accordance to your wishes which you expressed to me at Maketu, and we the Maori Chiefs, and some European gentlemen also have seen how well that Committee works – each person's motion is handed in to the Committee to be considered, and are settled in a very short time.[101]

This restructuring was apparently not completed without considerable friction, however, probably reflecting divisions over whether the Komiti should stand by its original decision with respect to Pukeroa-Oruawhata or abide by the Land Court's ruling that only Ngati Whakaue would be admitted as owners. At the end of August two individuals, Minehera and Tupara, appeared in the Resident Magistrate's Court charged with using abusive and threatening language to Henare Te Pukuatua and others during the elections for the new Komiti earlier that month. Both had accused Te Pukuatua of improperly conducting the elections and objected to the new mode of voting, 'which was by ballot, after the customs of the Europeans'. Te Pukuatua admitted that he had kicked Tupara in the chest after being taunted with various curses, and after some negotiation it was agreed that the charges would be dismissed once a written apology had been received.[102]

Clearly the Komiti Nui was beginning to succumb to the pressures brought about by the Native Land Court's introduction to Rotorua. As Rotorua Maori soon discovered, once the Court had established itself in the district, it was virtually impossible to get rid of it. In May 1881 Brabant had reported that:

> At Ohinemutu the principal event during the year has been the Natives giving their consent to Judge Fenton's scheme for laying out

and selling a township there. They appear to have gone heartily into the project, and the Court is now sitting to investigate title to the proposed township. The importance of this step will be seen when it is remembered that for years the Natives have persistently opposed the sitting of a Land Court in the Lake country; probably it is the thin end of the wedge which will eventually open their lands to European settlement and enterprise.[103]

The Court's decision in June had, as we have seen, turned Te Arawa against the scheme, but it was already too late, and in May 1882 Brabant was able to report that his expectations had been fulfilled:

> During the last two years a complete change has come over the feelings of the Arawas in relation to their lands; formerly they would allow no Land Court to sit within their district, and were continually occupying themselves with schemes for settling the titles themselves. Now, however, they wish to put all their lands through, and it appears likely that the sitting of the Court, which is now proceeding at Ohinemutu, may be continued for many months.[104]

Whether a 'complete change' had indeed come over Te Arawa with respect to their lands is a moot point. One thing was certain, however: they could no longer avoid the Native Land Court, whatever their attitudes towards it. The initial investigation of title to Pukeroa-Oruawhata had compelled Ngati Whakaue and other sections of the tribe to enter the arena of the Court in order to advance their claims to the block, more than likely under the impression that it would merely confirm the earlier findings of the Komiti Nui. Once the land had been surveyed and the block was before the Court for investigation they could hardly simply withdraw their claims when it became apparent that this was not the case, since to do so would more than likely have resulted in the land being awarded to rival claimants. It may have been possible to maintain some kind of tenuous cohesion between rival sections of Te Arawa when the Native Land Court was on their doorstep and threatening to come in, but once it was inside it was each for themselves, with virtually no prospect of resurrecting this kind of united opposition to its operations for any length of time. As Richard Boast says, 'A long and tenacious resistance to the Court on the part of the Arawa tribes collapsed completely'.[105] Te Arawa's 'schemes for settling the titles themselves' had been rejected by the Court from the outset of its first substantial sitting in the district, and the next two decades were marked by almost continuous Land Court hearings which resulted in native title to all but a negligible portion of the Rotorua district being extinguished, and less than half of it remaining in Maori ownership by shortly after the turn of the century.[106]

Te Arawa had not given up their various 'schemes' entirely, however. In 1882 the Premier, John Hall, wired Fenton from Rotorua, where he was inspecting preparations for the township, that a delegation from the Komiti Nui had requested that the government should recognise and vest some authority in the Komiti.[107] Hall believed that the Komiti might be a useful means of enforcing regulations amongst the Maori community and might also help to guarantee undisturbed occupation for the settlers of Rotorua. This was an attitude typical of that of many nineteenth-century politicians. Maori committees were considered desirable to the extent that they might usefully assist in implementing government policies or in expediting the work of the Native Land Court at negligible expense, but as substitutes for either local government or the Land Court they were entirely unthinkable. Whatever came out of these discussions, this did not include any formal recognition of the authority of the Komiti Nui.

Yet with the Land Court now a fact of life at Rotorua, both the Komiti Nui and the Putaiki appear to have engaged in tasks such as drawing up lists of owners and endeavouring to reach out-of-court settlements over disputed blocks. Henry Morton, who visited the Tuhourangi settlement of Te Wairoa in about 1883, recalled in his journal that:

> At the time of my visiting they were holding a 'committee' meeting in the native schoolroom, to individualise the titles to various blocks of land in the neighbourhood. This is of course encouraged by

125

Government, who of course send them supplies while the meeting lasts. But it saves a good deal of time when the claims come before the Native Land Court. I was much pleased with the good order which prevails during the sittings of the committee, and the business-like way in which the proceedings were conducted. Two or three secretaries kept very accurate minutes of their proceedings, and the various claimants appeared to have full opportunity to state their case. The three or four presidents were, I presume, chosen by themselves from tribes not interested. Some decisions were given, which caused some violent declarations and harangues amongst the losing party assembled outside, but it appeared to be accepted as inevitable.[108]

Early in July 1883 the *New Zealand Herald* reported that a meeting of the Ngati Whakaue tribe had 'resolved to re-establish the Great Committee of Rotorua, chiefly for the purposes of watching the movements of the Government, and checking any undue pressure likely to affect their interests' in the district.[109] The *Bay of Plenty Times* also noted this development, and added that:

> The natives recognise the authority of the Council to adjudicate upon any lands within their district...All judgements, if not appealed against, on lands passed by this Council, or by a Court constituted under its authority, are given in to the Native Lands Court whenever it sits here, and, having been read out and no objections made, the Native Lands Court immediately gives effect to them. But since its constitution the Council has gradually increased its powers, and may now be said to have the whole control of affairs affecting the natives within this district.[110]

The Komiti Nui had indeed once had 'the whole control' of all affairs within the rohe of those tribes who paid allegiance to it. Now, faced with the Land Court and government efforts to convert advance payments into clear title, it was reduced to fighting a rearguard action. The Land Court might give effect to its decisions, if these were not disputed, where convenient, but it was under no obligation to do so, and as was seen in the case of Pukeroa-Oruawhata clearly did not in some instances.

And although the Komiti Nui and the Putaiki might dispute the validity of the advance payments made by Davis and Mitchell in the 1870s, it was the government which now had the whip hand in deciding what would be done about these. On this question the government's stance was firm: advance payments were to remain over the lands and could not be returned or repudiated. In 1881, for example, Wi Maihi Te Rangikaheke of Ngati Rangiwewehi apparently sought to return payments made to his people in respect of lands west of Rotorua. Brabant was instructed to inform the chief that:

> govt. desire to complete the purchase of all land lying between Rotorua & Patetere therefore his proposal to pay back the advances cannot be sanctioned.[111]

Prior to the advent of the Native Land Court at Rotorua the Crown's prospects of completing any purchases in the district had been extremely limited because of opposition from bodies such as the Komiti Nui and the Putaiki (and other committees of Te Arawa attempting to control their own lands[112]). Now it could simply bypass these bodies and apply to the Land Court to determine its interests in any block, or acquire piecemeal the shares of each individual owner once these had been passed by the Court, without the need to deal with tribal entities. The Komiti Nui and Putaiki had effectively been marginalised and eventually faded from the scene, to be replaced by an official yet thoroughly ineffectual committee, which was intended to be little more than window dressing for what Maori saw as an increasingly autocratic and unjust Native Land Court system.

# 6. Autonomy Achieved? The Background to the Native Committees Act 1883

Te Arawa's committees of the 1870s were in some senses exceptional. In the Rotorua district Maori were striving during this decade to retain their autonomy, through structures aimed at resisting uncontrolled land sales and the activities of agencies such as the Land Court which were likely to expedite these. Tribes in almost all other districts outside the King Country and Te Urewera had already experienced the full impact of land alienations and the Land Court, however, and – just as Rotorua Maori did from 1881 onwards – were seeking to reassert their autonomy. Yet whether the aim was to defend, or to fight a rearguard action against the loss of autonomy, the fundamental problem for Maori committees remained the same: the lack of any legal authority to enforce their decisions. Te Arawa in the 1870s doubtless realised that they could not keep the Land Court away forever. Hence the willingness of the Komiti Nui to work through the Court, by sending quarterly reports to the Chief Judge and making it clear that they did not seek its abolition but merely desired that they should be permitted to hold preliminary investigations, with the Court sitting to confirm their decisions. And conversely, pragmatic Maori leaders in districts where the Court was already in full swing realised that the government would not simply send the Court away on request, and therefore also urged that legal powers be given to committees to undertake much of its work.

This agitation for committees to be given legal powers was fought on many fronts. Sporadic petitions on the subject were forwarded to Parliament, occasionally even receiving favourable recommendations from the Native Affairs Committee. In 1872 and again in 1876, for example, the Committee reported favourably on petitions requesting that Maori be given the right to elect their own councils or committees.[1] By the late 1870s a steady stream of petitions was being received on this subject. Combined with reports from native officers all over the country that Maori were establishing their own informal committees, this provided strong grounds for arguing, just as Waterhouse had in 1872 and Fox a decade earlier, that the best way to respond to this rising tide of Maori demands was by directing and incorporating it into the system; as one member of Parliament patronisingly put it in 1882, thereby 'giving the Natives something to employ their minds – something that would lead them gradually to a true appreciation of the benefits of law and order'.[2]

Yet Maori were seeking more than merely something to 'amuse themselves with, to soothe their dying couch and distract their attention'.[3] *Te Wananga*, the Repudiation movement's newspaper published between 1874 and 1878, was a strong supporter of the committees movement and, especially under the editorship of John White, the former Whanganui Resident Magistrate, regularly printed letters from committees reporting on successful hearings in their districts, accounts of large intertribal hui at which resolutions were passed in favour of committees, and editorials pointing to the injustice and inefficiency of the system of land title adjudication conducted by the Land Court. Whereas Maori who informed the government-sponsored Maori-language newspaper, *Te Waka Maori*, of the election of committees in their districts were gently reminded to 'be careful not to encroach upon the duties of the Magistrates, lest, with the best intentions, they get themselves into trouble', and that 'The Legislature only has power to make laws binding on the people generally',[4] *Te Wananga* pointed to such committees as examples of how land titles could be settled in a much more just and efficient, and less costly manner. The paper's readers were urged to petition Parliament on the subject, and detailed proposals for a remodelled Land Court of chiefs were regularly advanced. As one editorial in 1877 stated:

> For years the natives have been labouring under heavy wrongs in relation to the determination of their rights in land. They have had to submit to the operation of laws which they had no part in making, the working of which they did not understand, and the effects of which overwhelmed them with dismay. When at the Treaty of Waitangi the Queen assured to the Maori tribes their lands...it was of course understood by all parties that the title of the natives would be certain – at any rate as certain as before. But the Native Land Courts have rudely dispelled this hope. These tribunals – which to the Maoris seem fearfully and wonderfully made – objects at once of surprise and terror – of fascination and despair – composed really of Europeans, although a nominal Maori element is drawn in to give a semblance of justice, proceed calmly on their way, sweeping aside as they go the traditions, the customs, and the Maori laws of descent and ownership with unsparing hands.[5]

*Te Wananga* consistently argued that allowing Maori to determine land titles themselves would not impede European settlement of Maori-owned districts, but might indeed advance this, asserting that:

> if the Maori chiefs are permitted to take a more important part in settling their own land questions, there will be less cost to the public and more justice to the Natives; and what is of more consequence to the colonist, land that is now kept back from being brought under European tenure would quickly be submitted to that process in a Court possessing Native confidence.[6]

This was one thing the Native Land Court had never earned from Maori. For more than 600 years, the paper argued, the question of a particular tribe's entitlement to land had been a matter of life and death. Yet because of the ignorance of the Land Court's Judges as to the many and complex rules which guided Maori custom on this question, stories 'cunningly concocted and supported by evidence partly true and partly false' had frequently won out in the Court over the claims of those to whom the land ought to have been awarded according to Maori laws of land tenure. For although the legislation establishing the Native Land Court had been quite clear in specifying that titles were to be tried and determined in accordance with Maori custom, *Te Wananga* asserted that:

> there is not one European now, nor ever has been in New Zealand, who is sufficiently educated in the manners and customs of the New Zealander to entitle him to act as a judge to try and to give a righteous and just decision in, or a title to land claimed by the Maori. We also assert that those who may be conversant with the history, traditions, and customs of the Maori tribes of one part of New Zealand, admit that such knowledge does not suffice them to understand the claims to land put forward by the tribes of other parts of New Zealand.[7]

White was perhaps the leading Pakeha ethnographer of Maori society in the nineteenth century. He went on to produce a massive six-volume work, *The Ancient History of the Maori*, and would certainly have been aware of the variations in tribal custom from one part of the country to another, most of which were ignored by the Court in its search for a simple set of rules for determining titles.

Yet even with its simplistic notions of the bases of Maori titles, White pointed out that the Court frequently still failed to perform the task assigned to it:

> We have been in the Native Lands Court, and have seen in many instances, how the claims are laid before that Court. We have noticed that in some instances when a long and at times a difficult question has been under consideration, that it has been intimated that the Maoris should give the names of those who are to be included in the Crown Grant of the block that was under consideration, and acting under such hint names have been given, and the settlement of land disputes so made, have in most instances been those which have not been disputed by the Maoris. But we must notice the course of action between the Court's investigation of the disputes and the names being given. The disputants under the chiefs of the two contending Hapus have held a meeting, at which they have come to an understanding, that each should give the other some vantage ground, and thereby allow names from each party to be included in the Crown Grant, to be given by the Court.

In these circumstances, *Te Wananga* asked, 'if such is the action taken by the Maori, even when a costly and not satisfactory Native Land Court is playing the farce of settling land claims, whether the Maori is not the principal judge who decides the case'.[8] The Native Land Court had 'caused a vast and useless expense to the colony, and sown the seed of a terrible harvest of litigation'.[9] The alternative was to return to the kind of system suggested by the Judges of the Supreme Court in 1861, and shown to work successfully at Kaipara in 1864: allowing Maori to investigate and decide on land titles themselves, with an officer of the Crown present to set the seal on their decisions. This was what many Maori leaders had requested when first consulted on the land laws in 1871, and had been consistently advocated since.

*Te Wananga*'s role in encouraging the formation of committees and informing disparate Maori communities around the country of their work should not be underestimated. The lively correspondence in its pages on Tuhourangi's Putaiki suggests that some tribes consciously set about encouraging a committees movement in tandem with the repudiationists, and the regular reports which it printed of large intertribal gatherings at which committees were advocated as an alternative to the Native Land Court suggest that this was partly successful, at least among those tribes who sympathised with the Repudiation movement's aims and objectives. Yet despite this, the real push for committees to be given legal status came after *Te Wananga*'s demise, and was boosted mainly by the interest which the northern tribes, who had never been involved with the Repudiation movement, began to show in the subject.

In 1879 the Ngati Whatua chief Paora Tuhaere convened the first Maori Parliament at Orakei, as a successor to the Kohimarama Conference of 1860, which the government had failed to make an annual event as it had originally promised. Confiscations and the Native Land Court were condemned at the nine-day gathering attended by more than 300 tribal leaders from the north, and calls were made for Maori committees to be given powers to administer Maori-owned lands.[10] Tuhaere's Parliament met again at Orakei in 1880 and 1881, and at Kaipara in 1884, with each meeting passing resolutions seeking to curtail the powers of the Court and transfer these to Maori committees.

Meanwhile, similar developments were occurring amongst the Ngapuhi tribe, who had rapidly come to regret their initial enthusiasm for the Native Land Court. By the mid-1870s unofficial committees were reportedly much 'in fashion' in the Tai Tokerau district, encouraged by energetic young figures such as Hirini Taiwhanga and Hone Mohi Tawhai, both of whom had become disillusioned with the Court after earlier being heavily involved in its proceedings.[11] In 1881 a large meeting house called Tiriti o Waitangi was opened at the site where the Treaty had been signed in 1840. Regular political gatherings were held there to discuss matters of concern to northern Maori, not the least of which were the operations of the Native Land Court. Concurrently, it seems, committees established under the label of 'Te Komiti o Te Tiriti o Waitangi' appointed their own police and engaged in a wide range of judicial and social functions, including investigations into land titles.[12]

In fact, by the late 1870s committees appear to have become the rule rather than the exception in most Maori communities.[13] Captain T.W. Porter noted that a 'powerful lever' among East Coast Maori was:

> the general desire to institute some system of self-government; and committees or bodies somewhat analogous with the old runangas have been established, and have exerted a strong influence upon the state of the Natives, both in habits and in land matters.[14]

Porter believed that 'it would be wise to encourage to a limited extent', this movement, 'particularly in connection with land disputes', but added the warning that 'The committees, as now formed, although evincing a laudable self-reliance, have threatened to become dangerous by the wrongful assumption of unauthorized powers'. Like many Crown officials in the nineteenth century, Porter seems to have considered Maori committees useful to the extent that they might assist the work of the Native Land Court, but was reluctant to see them assume any authority which might undermine the Court's functions or standings.

There were, however, some notable exceptions to this relatively pragmatic approach towards unofficial committees by Crown agents. In 1880 George Kelly of the Mangonui Resident Magistrate's office informed his superiors in Wellington of the emergence of a movement amongst the Muriwhenua people 'to reestablish the "Mana Maori", the Maori rule or authority'.[15] Kelly reported that large meetings of Maori had recently been convened at which various 'by-laws' had been passed, and that each kainga had appointed a committee known as 'The Twelve' to adjudicate on all civil and criminal cases and settling land titles, a boycott of Pakeha courts being also in force. His response to news of this development was, to put it mildly, heavy-handed. Kelly wrote immediately to several of those involved, warning them in no uncertain terms of the dire consequences they risked bringing on themselves:

> Friend. It having been reported to me that you with others have taken upon yourselves to hold Courts, and decide cases contrary to the law; I refer to the establishment among you of the 'Twelve'. I am given to understand that you take upon yourselves to appoint yourselves Magistrates, hold Courts, hear cases, and inflict penalties. This is a very serious offence punishable by fine and imprisonment through the Supreme Court, and would be very seriously dealt with if brought before the court.
>
> ...I wish therefore to caution you against interfering in any way with the present law for administration of Justice. As I am fully determined to prosecute any person I find presuming by such action to bring the Government Law into contempt.[16]

A year later Kelly could congratulate himself, in his annual report to the Native Department, for having 'succeeded in stamping...out entirely' this 'attempt on the part of the Natives... to inaugurate a new system of self-government'.[17] Muriwhenua Maori certainly did not give up their efforts to administer their own affairs, however and Kelly's intimidation, bordering on persecution, of the northern tribes if anything pushed them increasingly towards the new tactic of kotahitanga, a union of the tribes to achieve the same widely-shared aspiration.

Clearly the 'unauthorized powers' which most of these committees were seeking to assert were intended to counter the Native Land Court's work of individualising land titles and retain some sort of tribal control over their lands. Individualisation was the key to alienation, and Maori sought to retain a tribal veto over land dealings without which their individual interests could be acquired piecemeal. As an 1879 petition from Poverty Bay explained:

> When...[our] lands were adjudicated upon by the Native Lands Court there were several Europeans following the Maoris about endeavouring to induce them to sell.
>
> A number of these Europeans secretly bought up individual shares and before the other owners of the land were aware of it, deeds of mortgage, lease, or sale were completed in connection therewith.
>
> Grave troubles have been growing up from these underhand dealings, and it is not right that they should be allowed to continue.
>
> We your petitioners pray that you should make some law establishing a Maori Committee in each district who must first sanction any sale, lease, or mortgage. Then if individuals were not allowed to sell separately these troubles would cease to spring up between the two races.[18]

Allowing Maori committees to investigate titles may not have quashed the kind of 'underhand dealings' complained of if the title to be awarded continued to be an individualised one, but given that the high costs involved in attending lengthy Land Court sittings often saw Maori fall into debt to Europeans anxious to 'induce them to sell', it certainly would have helped to overcome this problem. And given that rival Europeans often fomented divisions among claimants by advancing money and supplies to contesting parties, a less adversarial forum for determining titles, based on local custom and conducted locally on the lands concerned, may well have helped to preserve some measure of tribal cohesion and allowed a considered decision to be made as to how the lands would be dealt with once investigated.

It was with a view to settling these internal disputes, which though often grounded in traditional rivalries had been greatly exacerbated by the Native Land Court system, that many Maori communities sought the right to determine land titles themselves. While this often happened on an informal basis, with Judges approving out-of-court settlements reached by claimants, it was not always the case. Instead, 'cunningly concocted stories' could win out over the more valid but less carefully constructed claims of the real owners, with almost irreparable damage done to intertribal relations in many districts as a result of the lies and distortion of custom necessitated by this costly and protracted method of determining native title. As one petition put it in requesting that the government 'vest all the Maori Committees of the Ngatiporou with authority' to investigate titles themselves:

> this would be the means of overcoming many of the intertribal troubles concerning the lands held both by conquest & through ancestry. It would be far better that a Native Committee should in the first instance investigate the titles to land as they are the best judges, and then they could send it on to be dealt with by the Native Land Court. This would hasten it considerably, & the present tedious proceedings shortened very much. Again, these preliminary investigations would not cost the Colony much as the people would have to defray the cost themselves.[19]

The government's typical response to such petitions and requests was to state that the Native Land Court was the committee appointed by law, and that there was no statute by which such Maori committees could be granted legal standing.[20]

In 1880 Hone Mohi Tawhai, the member of Parliament for Northern Maori, with the support of Henare Tomoana, the Eastern Maori representative, and Wi Te Wheoro of Western Maori, set about rectifying the latter situation. John Bryce, the Native Minister, was presented with a draft bill providing for the election of committees throughout the country. These committees were 'to have authority to enquire into disputes arising in the district in connection with the surveying of land, applications for the investigation of title to lands, and the sale of lands upon the application of the persons interested in the land under dispute'.[21]

Reporting triumphantly on a tour of his constituency, during which he had explained the provisions of the draft bill to his own people, Tawhai informed the Native Minister that the Ngati Whatua, Ngapuhi and Te Rarawa tribes were 'very much pleased' with the proposed measure.[22] Bryce promised to have the bill printed and 'properly drawn out and translated before [the] next session', without actually committing the government to supporting it.[23] But in January 1881 Bryce resigned as minister over his handling of the Parihaka affair, and the 'properly drawn out' bill printed that year under the name of Tomoana contained important changes from the draft legislation forwarded to the Native Office by Tawhai. Under the latter, the committees were to have control over surveys, sales, and investigations of title. The bill as printed, however, contained no reference to surveys or sales, although the committees were to be empowered to try disputes up to a value of £50, and have powers to pass by-laws 'for the better suppression of intemperance, and the regulation of social order'. And although the Native Land Court was to 'take judicial notice' of the committees' decisions with respect to title investigations, this was subject to the important proviso that the Court was first to satisfy itself that 'the parties agreed to submit any such case to the decision of the Committee'.[24]

Rumours about the proposed measure prompted some Maori communities to request legal standing for their own committees, after hearing 'that the Government have given this authority to all the Native Committees in New Zealand'.[25] William Rolleston, who succeeded Bryce as Native Minister, instructed his Under-Secretary to reply that while the matter was one for Parliament to deal with the government was giving the question some consideration.[26] Privately, though, Chief Judge Fenton advised that it would be a 'waste of time to think seriously of this device',[27] and in July, Tomoana, apparently dissatisfied with the government's obvious lack of interest, introduced the Native Committees Empowering Bill himself.[28] But by the time the bill came up for its second reading on 15 September the parliamentary session was almost at an end. Tomoana complained that 'his Bill had occupied every number of the Orders of the Day on the Paper. It had been down to the very lowest number; it had travelled upwards and been sent down again'. Now that it was too late to pass the bill before the end of the session, Tomoana informed the Assembly that he was prepared to introduce it again in the next Parliament, after taking the opportunity to state that:

> it was desired by all the Natives in the colony. When former Governments were in power the Native tribes were in the habit of sending petitions to them to bring into force such a measure as this. Being of opinion that the Government had control over all the affairs of the colony – over all the land and everything else – the Natives considered it wise to apply to the Government to give them some sort of power by which they could carry on a system of local government amongst themselves...Each year the Natives had petitioned the Parliament for an Act such as this, by which they could control their own local affairs.[29]

Tomoana's bill received a pro forma second reading without debate, but was discharged a week later when the session ended. Bryce resumed office as Native Minister the following month, and in January 1882 instructed his Under-Secretary to bring all the relevant papers on the proposed legislation before him, adding that he 'may possibly make something out of them'.[30] But by May Bryce had apparently had a change of heart on the subject, writing that Tomoana's bill would 'probably not be found necessary' since it was 'something quite different to what was once discussed between the Maori members and myself'.[31] In fact, when the bill was again brought forward for its second reading in July Bryce urged members to vote against it, taking particular exception to the 'most inadvisable' clause which specified that the Native Land Court was to take judicial notice of the decisions of the committees.[32] Tomoana, though, informed the House that since the introduction of the bill the previous year he and the other Maori members had been inundated with letters from tribes around the country urging that they should endeavour to pass such a measure. Maori committees were no new thing, he added; they were already in existence throughout the country and dealing with disputes as they arose, 'whether they were personal matters or in reference to titles to land; but their decisions could not be enforced', and it was for this reason that he had introduced the bill.[33]

Predictably enough, Tomoana's bill was warmly endorsed by the other Maori MPs. More surprising, in view of the generally contemptuous and patronising attitudes which settler politicians adopted towards the proposals of their Maori colleagues, was the considerable level of support which it received from European members. Though some patronisingly supported the measure on the grounds that it was harmless enough and would give Maori something 'to employ their minds', others argued that the committees might well help to expedite the work of the Native Land Court, whilst at the same time encouraging and involving Maori in the administration of British law in districts where this was still fully to make its influence felt. Richard Turnbull, for example, believed that:

> It would gradually imbue them with respect and reverence for Courts of justice. It was a Bill in every way calculated to meet the requirements of a race in a process of transition from what he might call a state of nature to a state of civilization...The Natives showed a desire to encourage the supremacy of the law, which the House should endeavour to gratify...He thought the Bill would not interfere with the functions of the Native Land Court, but would assist it, as the Committees would take the responsibility of finding out who were the persons entitled to land, and would, in fact, do a great deal of preliminary work for the Court.[34]

Frederick Moss, concurring in this view, added that the fact that the committees could only investigate disputes with the agreement of both parties meant that they would really occupy the position of arbitrators. The Native Land Court would still exercise its present functions, and might be assisted greatly by the work of the committees in resolving difficult land disputes. Thomas Weston believed that it would be 'much better to sanction the creation of such a tribunal than to see disaffection prevailing in the Native districts',[35] while William Swanson thought that it should be given a trial. 'It could not do much harm' and could always be repealed next year if found to be unsatisfactory.[36] Major Harris, reiterating this view, thought that it would be well to 'give the Natives an opportunity of seeing what they could do if they had a little self-government'. There were only four Maori MPs in the House. They could not do any harm, being so completely outnumbered, 'and in Committee the Europeans could do as they liked; so that he thought it was quite safe to let the four Natives bring in their Bill'.[37] Thus for a variety of pragmatic and patronising reasons, and despite the objections of those who considered it a grave matter to pass such 'exceptional' legislation, the bill passed its second reading comfortably enough, by a majority of fourteen votes.

But when the bill came back before the House in August, Bryce was even more vehement in his criticism, informing Parliament that he 'could not conscientiously bring this Bill into operation', adding that:

> This Bill runs counter...to everything I have professed with regard to Native affairs ever since I took an interest in them. I am quite aware of the truth of what has been urged, that there are many laws which have a different application to Maoris and to Europeans; but I for one have always professed that I would keep steadily before my mind's eye the idea of assimilating the treatment of the Maoris to the treatment of the Europeans, and I have always aimed at giving effect to that. Now, at any rate this Bill does not do that.[38]

Tawhai countered this by asking Bryce why he did not in that case object to being called 'Native Minister', adding that if he objected to the bill on the grounds that it would put too much power in the hands of Maori, 'we must also consider what the Treaty of Waitangi says – namely, that the Maoris were to have as many powers and privileges as are given to British subjects'.[39] John Buchanan, the member for Napier, also questioned the Minister's apparent objections to such 'exceptional' legislation, referring to the Native Reserves Bill then before the House, which proposed giving the Public Trustee extensive powers in the administration of Maori lands.[40] It was in his view nothing but 'folly and nonsense' to suggest that Maori received equal treatment under the laws of the land. Hori Taiaroa, the member for Southern Maori, also considered it 'not fair that you should confine to yourselves – that is to say, to the Europeans – the sole management of affairs affecting the Native race'.[41] The grievances under which the Maori race suffered were, he added, 'caused by no other House but this'. Others, too, argued once again that the bill would not do away with the Land Court but might well improve its operations, and that the committees would only have the power to arbitrate in cases where both parties agreed to submit to their decisions. Cecil De Lautour added that:

> Social order is not to be promoted among the Natives by compelling them to go into all our semi-civilized European towns to be demoralized by publicans and those who haunt their bars. It is not in that way you are to reclaim the Native race, and teach them to amalgamate with what is most worthy in ours. That is really what our present system does...I have never known two Natives seeking justice as between themselves in one of our Courts. The reason is plain – they could not get it. Our Courts are simple, no doubt, but no Court of ours is able to mete out justice between two Natives themselves. Our Court does not understand their witnesses, or their customs and habits, or the plaintiff or defendant, and has really to depend upon others. No justice would really be meted out in such cases. In point of fact these Arbitration Courts exist informally and unauthorized at the present time. Nothing is more common than for the Natives to enforce rules in their own districts. Year by year, as our civilization encroaches upon theirs – and I am not sure that theirs is not on a level with ours in many respects – their power of maintaining order by voluntary regard to their leaders is weakened...I see no harm in encouraging the Natives under such circumstances to come to our Courts to ask them to enforce the decrees of their own Native tribunals.[42]

De Lautour added that even though the details of the bill had been criticised, he had undertaken to take charge of it from Tomoana and would be prepared to defend it clause by clause when it was considered in Committee.

Despite this continuing strong support for the bill from many European members, others saw an even more fundamental reason for opposing it: Maori were, in their view, simply incapable of administering their own affairs. As Colonel Trimble, the member for Taranaki and Chairman of the Native Affairs Committee (and later a Judge of the Native Land Court), put it:

> The question really comes to this: Are the Maori people of this colony fit to conduct their own affairs? I ask, has there ever occurred this session, or during any other session, an occasion when the Native members have thrown one scintilla of light upon any question in relation to Maori matters? We know perfectly well that nothing of the kind has ever occurred…It is humiliating to think that honorable gentlemen should go before the country and pretend that these Maori gentlemen are fit to conduct their affairs apart from the ordinary laws of the land…The Judges of the Native Land Court are appointed because they are considered to be experts not only in the Maori language, but also in Maori customs and ideas. What is the position of this Court in future? The Native Land Court, it says,…shall take judicial notice of a decision of the Committee…That is to say, the Committee is to have positively more power in the administration of justice than the Court of the colony…[I]f this Bill is passed in anything like the form in which we have it before us now, you will deal a death-blow to Maori civilization, and raise up a war of races in the North Island which years hence you will deeply regret.[43]

Tomoana stated that he would not deign to reply to Trimble's remarks about the Maori members, but when the motion for committal was put it was defeated by two votes. Bryce's countermotion that the bill be further considered in six months was lost on the casting vote of the Speaker, effectively leaving it in limbo.[44] Even so, such a close vote suggested that if the bill came forward for attention again, with the right amendments, it would stand a good chance of success.

There were other factors working in favour of a modified version of the Maori MPs' bill eventually gaining acceptance in Parliament. The sorry saga of Parihaka, which had been invaded and occupied by Armed Constabulary troops, headed by Bryce, in November 1881, had brought race relations in the colony to their lowest point since the end of the wars. These actions were universally condemned by Maori throughout the country, and once more drew London's attention to the treatment Maori received from the colonial administration. In mid-1882 Hirini Taiwhanga, accompanied by two other Ngapuhi chiefs, travelled to England in the hope of presenting a petition to the Queen laying out the grievances of the Maori people. In outlining the history of Maori-Pakeha contacts since 1840, the petitioners laid much of the blame for the conflicts that had occurred on the colonial administration, stating, for example, that 'the Maoris throughout the Island were unaware as to the reason why war had been made on the Waikato' tribes, who had merely 'formed a land league, in accordance with the Treaty of Waitangi, to preserve their native authority over the land, which principle is embodied in the treaty'. The subsequent land confiscations and the more recent imprisonment of Te Whiti and his followers were also condemned, along with:

> The making of unauthorized laws relating to Maori lands – namely, the Land Acts of 1862, 1865, 1873, 1880 – which Acts were not assented to by the Native Chiefs in all parts of the Island. Nor is there any basis in the Treaty of Waitangi for these laws, which continuously bring upon our lands and upon our persons great wrongs.[45]

'Wrongfully confiscated' lands should be returned, the petitioners requested, and a 'Royal English Commission' appointed 'to abrogate the evil laws affecting the Maori people,' with a Maori Parliament also sought in order to 'hold in check the European authorities who are endeavouring to set aside the Treaty of Waitangi'.

Taiwhanga and his party were denied the opportunity to present their petition to the Queen, but did gain an audience with the Secretary of State for the Colonies, the Earl of Kimberley, who informed them that the matters raised in it were for the New Zealand government to deal with.[46] Yet despite the failure of Taiwhanga's mission to London, the colonial government remained alive to the potential for embarrassment it and suppressed documents relating to the arrest of Te Whiti could cause in English circles, and by the time the deputation left London in September, the Premier, Frederick Whitaker, was busily engaged in a campaign to discredit the petitioners, soliciting information on them from officials in the north.[47] Whitaker denied that the petition was at all representative of Maori opinion, pointed out that many of the grievances complained of related to the period when Native affairs were the responsibility of the Governor, and asserted that the legislation of the colony had been 'more than just' with respect to its impact on Maori. He added that:

> The special legislation referred to in the memorial as 'unauthorized laws relating to Maori lands...not assented to by the Native Chiefs in all parts of the Island', and as having no 'basis in the Treaty of Waitangi', is not restrictive but enabling. The object of the Native Land Acts enumerated was to provide a special tribunal for the determination of Native title; to relieve the Maori owners from the monopoly held by the Government; and to enable them to sell their lands to whomsoever they pleased. In no way are the provisions of the Acts compulsory. The Maoris were and are at liberty to avail themselves of the powers conferred, or to abstain from doing so, at their pleasure.[48]

By April 1883 northern Maori had formally been informed that their petition had been dismissed, but Taiwhanga was already busily engaged in seeking the support of other tribes for a new one. This petition explicitly sought 'To entirely abolish the Native Land Court' and asked for 'claims to land [to] be adjudicated upon in accordance with the Treaty of Waitangi', but it was abandoned after failing to gain the broad support hoped for, partly as a result of adverse publicity about its instigator's private life unearthed by the colonial press at the time of the first petition.[49]

In July 1883 the four Maori MPs sent their own appeal to England, protesting to the Secretary of the influential Aborigines

Protection Society about the breaking of the 'bond of Waitangi' by the colonial government, 'which being a party to a suit in the question of lands, acts also as its judge'. Te Wheoro, Tawhai, Tomoana and Taiaroa informed the Society on behalf of their constituents that:

> We merely desire to get the control of our lands into the hands of an elective body of Maoris.
>
> At present our lands are dealt with by the Native Land Courts, which are presided over by Judges appointed by Government to decide questions of native title. The decisions of these judges are very often unjust. Tribal lands are often declared to be the property of individual Maoris. The land [often takes] years going through the Court. Maoris who have no right to land often have it awarded to them through false swearing. European lawyers are allowed to practise in the Courts, and they and numerous officials usually swallow up the proceeds from the sale of the land.

Te Wheoro and the others added that 'the Native [Land] Courts should be done away with, and the land vested in an elective body of Maoris, who would be better able to decide questions of title than European judges'. 'Every year', they stated:

> laws are made taking the control of land more out of our hands, and vesting it in the Minister for Native Affairs, and our voices, being but four, are powerless against eighty-seven representing the European portion of the population in the New Zealand Parliament.[50]

This letter was referred to the Secretary of State by the Secretary of the Aborigines Protection Society, who added his regret that the Maori representatives in the New Zealand Parliament were 'apparently...unable to obtain from the Colonial Government' the 'reasonable concessions' to Maori feeling they had requested.[51] But when the letter was referred back to the New Zealand government for comment, Bryce's reply in January 1884 was highly dismissive. The Native Minister alleged that the letter did not reflect the four Maori members' true sentiments but had emanated from 'some tenth rate politician in New Zealand, with probably a petty grievance against the Government'. Bryce defended the operations of the Native Land Court, and commented that:

> As for the suggestion that Maori title should be determined by a body of Maoris, the idea is utterly impracticable; decisions would be very rarely arrived at, and scarcely ever accepted. The determination of Native title would become entirely hopeless, and as the old men who could give evidence died off, the confusion, sufficiently great at the best, would become worse confounded. Moreover the dissatisfaction of the Natives interested would certainly be profound partly with the inevitable delay, but principally with the suspected partiality; for however great may be the distrust felt by some of the Maoris of European management and decisions the distrust entertained of their own countrymen is much stronger.[52]

It was self-evident, Bryce considered, that 'the Maoris must cast in their lot with the Europeans, accepting their institutions and laws', since 'Any other course would assuredly result in disaster to the Native race'. In a private memorandum to the Governor written the following month, Bryce was even more contemptuous of increasing Maori demands for elected committees rather than the Land Court to determine native title and for Maori self-government generally, commenting that:

> An attempt to carry out the first idea would simply result in hopeless confusion. Title would never be discovered by such means. It can only be advocated by those who are ignorant of the subject, or who have a confused desire to revert to Maori customs, or by Natives who having no title themselves wish to postpone indefinitely its determination.
>
> The second idea, that of providing a system of local government for the Maoris is an absurdity...Looking at the large and increasing European population and the small number of Maoris it is very evident that the best hope of the Native race is to frankly accept European institutions and laws.[53]

Yet however dismissive Bryce may have been of Maori aspirations to manage their own lands and local affairs, the fact was that committees continued to function in many parts of the country, with or without official recognition. In fact, just as in 1872, news of Tomoana's bill seems to have spurred some Maori communities to elect their own committees based on the model it provided. Maunsell reported from Greytown in June 1883, for example, that:

> Lately Maoris have elected a Committee of twelve members. Their duty is to inquire into and decide all questions relating to land titles and matters concerning their social being. They looked forward to the passing of the Maori Committees Bill, introduced during last session. Being disappointed by the rejection of such Bill, they have agreed to abide by the decisions of a Committee constituted without Act of Parliament, and to adopt the European mode of conducting its deliberations, appointment of officers, and so forth.[54]

Clearly many Maori were willing to accept 'European institutions and laws' provided this did not mean Europeans also controlling and managing their affairs.

In the light of the overwhelming Maori support for committees, the apparent willingness of many politicians to consider legislation recognising these, and the severe criticism which the Government's handling of Maori affairs had been subjected to, both at home and abroad, in the wake of events at Parihaka, Bryce – despite his obvious opposition to the 'absurdity' of allowing Maori to control their own affairs – could not afford to simply do nothing. Hence during the 1883 session of Parliament the government sponsored a much-modified version of the Native Committees Bill which provided the shell, if not the substance, of local self-government for Maori.

Bryce's willingness to consider legislating for committees at all was probably prompted by the delicate state of negotiations over the construction of a main trunk railway through the central North Island. In June 1883 the 'Rohe Potae' petition signed by more than 400 Maori was presented to Parliament. Members of the Ngati Maniapoto, Ngati Raukawa, Ngati Tuwharetoa and Whanganui tribes informed the Assembly that the matters that had caused them anxiety had 'principally emanated from you, the Europeans, in the form of legislation':

> We have carefully watched the tendency of the laws which you have enacted from the beginning up to the present day; they all tend to deprive us of the privileges secured to us by the second and third articles of the Treaty of Waitangi, which confirmed to us the exclusive and undisturbed possession of our lands.
>
> We do not see any good in any of the laws which you have enacted affecting our lands, when they are brought into operation, in adjudicating upon lands before the Native Land Court at Cambridge and other places; and the practices carried on at the Land Courts have become a source of anxiety to us and a burden upon us.[55]

Through their 'ignorance' of the laws, and 'beset on every side by outrageous practices', the petitioners stated, they had fallen prey to the activities of lawyers and land agents:

> In our perplexity to devise some means by which we could extricate our lands from the disasters pointed out, we ask, is there not a law by which we could suppress these evils? and we are told that the only remedy is to go to the Court ourselves.

The petitioners were 'not oblivious of the advantages to be derived from roads, railways, and other desirable works of the Europeans', but they could live without these things, whereas they 'could not live without our lands'. For these reasons, they asked the House to give effect to the following

> 1. It is our wish that we may be relieved from the entanglements incidental to employing the Native Land Court to determine our titles to the land, also to prevent fraud, drunkenness, demoralization, and all other objectionable results attending sittings of the Land Court.
>
> 2. That Parliament will pass a law to secure our lands to us and our descendants for ever, making them absolutely inalienable by sale.
>
> 3. That we may ourselves be allowed to fix the boundaries of the

four tribes before mentioned, the hapu boundaries in each tribe, and the proportionate claim of each individual within the boundaries set forth in this petition...

When these arrangements relating to land claims were completed, the petitioners added, 'let the Government appoint some persons vested with power to confirm our arrangements and decisions in accordance with law'. The tribes did not wish to keep their lands 'permanently locked up from Europeans, or to prevent leasing, or roads...or other public works,' but merely wished to see the 'present practices' of the Native Land Court 'abolished'.

As the Waitangi Tribunal has commented in its *Pouakani Report*, this was 'a plea for a more equitable system of land administration in which Maori had more control of their own affairs',[56] rather than an outright rejection of all things Pakeha. Certainly this seems to have been how the Native Affairs Committee viewed the petition. Early in August 1883 it reported that 'the complaints and fears expressed are too well-founded, and...the apparent desires of the petitioners are reasonable'.[57] The Committee recommended the petition for 'favourable consideration' when Bryce's Native Committees Bill, which had been given its first reading a few weeks after the Rohe Potae petition was presented to Parliament, was again brought before the House.[58]

It has already been seen that Tawhai's draft bill providing for committees to take control of surveys, sales, and title investigations contained, by the time it had been printed and 'properly drawn out' at government expense, no reference to either surveys or sales, and empowered the proposed committees to reach binding decisions with respect to land titles only with the consent of both parties (allowing those with weak cases to continue to spin cleverly concocted stories in the Native Land Court). Bryce's bill went one step further by providing that the committees could investigate questions of title to land merely 'for the information of the Court'. And while the provisions dealing with procedural matters such as the method of electing the committees and their constitution were virtually identical in both bills, the government-sponsored version contained other important omissions which would render the proposed committees practically impotent from the outset. They were to have no power to pass local by-laws, could not try cases of theft or assault, were debarred from investigating disputes over matters worth more than £20, could investigate cases involving less than this sum only with the consent of both parties, and had no power to levy fines. Thus the committees were effectively restricted to arbitrating on petty disputes and reporting on title investigations for the benefit of a Court which was under no obligation to take any notice, and more often than not failed to do so. It is little wonder, then, that Bryce dismissed Maori demands to investigate titles themselves as 'utterly impracticable' and their desire for local self-government as an 'absurdity' without even passing reference to the Native Committees Act 1883. He knew that the committees to be elected under the Act would be completely powerless and would not satisfy Maori aspirations for control of their own affairs.

Whether the Maori members of Parliament realised this initially seems doubtful. Tawhai and Taiaroa told Bryce that they all supported the bill and were anxious for him to introduce it as soon as possible 'in order that the views of Members regarding it may be ascertained'.[59] In surprising contrast to Tomoana's proposed legislation of the previous year, Bryce's bill passed through the House without debate,[60] the Native Minister merely explaining during its second reading that:

> its object was to supply a means to enable the Maoris to discuss matters of interest connected with their land, and to report the decisions they might arrive at to the Native Land Court, for the information of the Court. That was the principal object of the Bill...The establishment of these Committees was a thing that had long been desired by the Native population in some form; and he might say that so long ago as 1880 certain Native members of the House and himself prepared clauses which they thought might be embodied in a Bill. In the following year he was not a member of the Government and although he would have been willing enough

151

> at that time to assist the Natives in bringing in a Bill of this sort, based upon the clauses they had prepared, yet he did not like to force his good offices either upon the Natives or upon the Government, and therefore nothing was done during the session of 1881. Last year a Bill called the Native Committees Empowering Bill was introduced, which he felt bound to oppose, because he thought it went too far by giving the Committees a jurisdiction and power which were likely to cause disputes and conflicts between the races...However, the present Bill was based upon the clauses which were prepared by the Native members and himself in 1880, and he thought the Native members were themselves perfectly satisfied with the Bill...[61]

This account was highly misleading. There is no evidence to suggest that Bryce had been involved in drafting Tawhai's bill of 1880, which went even further than those presented to Parliament in 1881 and 1882 in providing for real powers to be given to the proposed committees, and to which his own bill bore few similarities. Indeed, perhaps the most telling change from the bill the Maori members had endeavoured to pass was that the word 'Empowering' had been dropped from the short title.

In fact, when the bill was debated in the Legislative Council several members queried the wisdom of setting up official committees which would be completely powerless to achieve anything. Sir George Whitmore, for example, stated in typically blunt fashion that he:

> hoped the Council would send this ridiculous Bill out of the Council as quickly as it came in. It was one of the most childish Bills ever introduced to Parliament. It could have no possible effect for good, and it must do an immense amount of harm. Last year a Native member in another place (Mr. Tomoana) brought in a Bill which would have been of unmixed advantage to the colony. He proposed that the Natives should form Committees to ascertain who were the proper owners of certain blocks of land, and practically speaking those Committees would have taken the place...of the Native Land Court, and that would have been a very good thing to do...The Government did not favour that proposal,

> but they now brought in a Bill themselves. Now, would honourable gentlemen read this Bill, and see what sort of rubbish it was they were asked to agree to? This was a Bill containing an immense mass of machinery, machinery quite as great as that provided for the election of members of the House of Representatives, or for the whole machinery of a County Council...Well, what was all this for? If two Natives had a dispute about a matter not exceeding £20, and they chose to sign saying that they wished to have the matter investigated by the Native Committee, they were to have power to decide it. That was all that came out of this immense mass of legislation.

Whitmore commented that 'the Bill was introduced to throw a little dust into the eyes of the Native members, but even they were quite awake to it now':

> It had taken them some time to get over the difficulty, as the title was the same as that of the Bill of last year, but now they understood that it gave them nothing but a sort of sop to keep their mouths shut. They were not at all pleased with it, and he would recommend the Government to withdraw it at once.[62]

The committees 'could do nothing', and 'had no power whatever', he pointed out, other than to 'express an opinion to the Land Court, which the Court might accept or reject as it thought fit'. This would lead to nothing but 'a succession of quarrels from end to end of the districts'. What was required, Whitmore believed, was for Maori to be given:

> a more potent voice in declaring who were the actual proprietors and successors in the case of Native land. At present they could do nothing. A clause was put into the Bill which meant nothing, and was not intended to mean anything. A whole series of clauses, for machinery purposes, was introduced, which gave no power at all, except the power of creating litigation.[63]

Daniel Pollen, the former Native Minister, believed that the real objection to the bill lay in the probability that it would prove inoperative. He understood it to have been introduced at the request of Wahanui, the Ngati Maniapoto chief, with whom the government was negotiating over the North Island main trunk railway line, but that the chief:

> had since expressed his dissatisfaction with the provisions of the Bill, and he (Dr. Pollen) found in a paper recently laid on the table that it was stated a large section of the Natives with Tawhiao in the King country also objected to the Bill.

In these circumstances, Pollen 'did not think there was the smallest possibility of any good coming from it'.[64]

Whitaker, the Premier, admitted that Wahanui and the King's supporters had expressed some dissatisfaction with parts of the bill but claimed that they had approved of most of it. Moreover, it was entirely up to Maori whether they wished to implement the bill's provisions:

> It did not compel them to do anything: it merely said, 'You have expressed a wish for such a power. If you desire it, here are the means for you to possess it, and the Government will assist you'.[65]

In contrast with Bryce, who stated that the bill was based on one drawn up in 1880, Whitaker asserted in response to Whitmore's criticisms that:

> With some few exceptions the present Bill was a copy of Mr. Tomoana's. The majority of the clauses were taken from that Bill...which, for the first half-dozen sections, was word for word the same as this Bill. There was some alteration as to the jurisdiction. Instead of making it so stringent, it was thought better to begin by degrees, and not make it too wide as to jurisdiction.

The first six sections of the bill were of course for the most part those dealing with procedural matters, such as the mode of elections, and Whitaker's euphemistic remark about altering the jurisdiction of the committees only confirmed what Whitmore had alleged: an elaborate mass of machinery was to be put in place to appoint committees which, at the end of the day, would be completely powerless and ultimately pointless except as a thinly-veiled sop to Maori aspirations to administer their lands and local affairs themselves. Even Whitaker came close to admitting this in commenting that the bill was 'a tentative measure', 'innocent in itself', and from which 'he did not think any harm could result'.[66] Indeed, unlike Whitmore, several members of the Council remarked that they intended to support the bill for the very reason that it was 'a harmless one', which 'could be withdrawn at any time', and might 'insure increased satisfaction on the part of the Natives with the working of the Native Land Courts'.[67] The latter was one thing that the bill would certainly not achieve, as Whitmore had pointed out, but it nevertheless passed into law in September 1883 as the Native Committees Act.[68]

*First Meeting of the Takitimu Council*
PHOTOGRAPH MUSEUM OF NEW ZEALAND TE PAPA TONGAREWA, B.007148

'Meeting of Great Chiefs, King Country'
PHOTOGRAPH MUSEUM OF NEW ZEALAND TE PAPA TONGAREWA, C.010017

*Tamatekapua Meeting House, Ohinemutu, Rotorua*
PHOTOGRAPH MUSEUM OF NEW ZEALAND TE PAPA TONGAREWA, C.010316

*Huriwhenua, Ranana, Whanganui River*
PHOTOGRAPH MUSEUM OF NEW ZEALAND TE PAPA TONGAREWA, C.010319

*Maori Committee Meeting at Wellington During Session, 1913*
PHOTOGRAPH MUSEUM OF NEW ZEALAND TE PAPA TONGAREWA, B.019453

*Aotea Maori Council*
AUCKLAND STAR COLLECTION, ALEXANDER TURNBULL LIBRARY, G- 3126-1/1 -

## 7. 'A Semblance of Authority': The Demise of the Official Native Committees

Considered either as a sop to Maori aspirations to administer their own affairs, or as a genuine attempt to meet these aspirations, the Native Committees Act of 1883 was a signal failure, as those historians who have considered the question have concluded. J.A. Williams, for example, judges that 'The Government had not really wanted the act at all', and that this was reflected both in the legislation itself and in its subsequent implementation. As he notes, Maori committees could have arbitrated on petty disputes or reported on land titles for the information of the Native Land Court with or without legal recognition, and once Maori realised that the Act was of no benefit to them, many communities preferred to continue on with their own informal committees, remaining independent of Government control.[1] Jane McRae's detailed case study from the Tai Tokerau district concludes that 'The failure of legislated-for Committees was preordained'. An 'ill-conceived' piece of legislation which paid no heed to Maori aspirations was, she argues, administered in an 'apathetic' manner, which both intimated and ensured failure.[2] Claudia Orange considers that the government's commitment to the legislation was at best 'half-hearted', and that the Act 'proved an unsatisfactory solution to Maori demands', partly because the government 'deliberately frustrated the Act's intent'.[3] C.L. Andrews sees the Act as 'an attempt both to meet...demands for local self-government and to control the Maori response by incorporating it in the European system of administration', but with the latter consideration prevailing, thereby ensuring continuing Maori discontent.[4] R.J. Martin argues that had the legislature intended the Act to be more than an expedient to deal with overwhelming Maori

163

requests for greater control over land matters, 'it would have ensured that the Committees were granted sufficient finance and vested with adequate authority and prestige, to make them workable'.[5] Alan Ward concludes that the official Committees 'did little to out-bid the mounting movement in Maori society to establish institutions of local self-government', partly because the districts covered by each Committee were so large that Maori could not place any confidence in them, and partly because Land Court Judges frequently took little notice of their land title investigations.[6] And the Waitangi Tribunal's *Pouakani Report* concluded that 'The Native Committees Act 1883 gave Maori no effective power to administer their lands'.[7]

In fact, Maori continued throughout the 1880s and 1890s to petition, lobby, and introduce bills aimed at gaining such powers, often without reference to the 1883 Act, which even Pakeha politicians were describing as a 'dead letter' as early as 1884.[8]

W.L. Rees and James Carroll, in their 1891 commission of inquiry into Maori land laws, were equally critical of the legislation, commenting that:

> The Native Committees Act is a hollow shell, the object of which it is difficult to see. It mocked and still mocks the Natives with a semblance of authority. They wish it to be turned into a living Act, giving them power to do something for themselves.[9]

Two years later, Rees, in an open letter to the Premier, R.J. Seddon, was even more outspoken in his criticism of the 1883 Act, commenting that the Committees established under it were 'at the best but an impotent and cruel farce'. No funding was provided for the Committees to carry out their work; their jurisdiction over minor disputes was rendered null and void by the necessity to first gain the agreement of both parties; and no machinery was provided for the summoning of witnesses, nor were any other methods of ordinary Courts procedure afforded the Committees when it came to their title investigations. Moreover, the fact that the Committees had power only to refer their reports to the Native Land Court had rendered the Act little more than a 'dead letter'; 'it is, and was', he asserted, 'a mere pretence', since:

> The Native Land Court, jealous of this new tribunal, and looking with disfavour upon the possible loss of any of its own power or prestige, treated the finding and the reports of the committees with contempt; they were immediately relegated to the waste paper basket. The Committees finding their reports thus disregarded, and themselves despised, discontinued their action. Indeed, the consequence was foreseen, and it happened according to expectation.

Rees added that:

> Voluntary committees, such as the great committee of the Ngatituwharetoa, partially accomplished the purposes of their existence, but existing without legal authority, and having no definite form, procedure, or purposes, they naturally fell into decay after a more or less chequered history.[10]

Yet if Maori eventually came to realise the completely ineffectual nature of the Committees established under the 1883 Act and opted instead for their own informal bodies, the initial response to the legislation was in many districts enthusiastic. Ngati Tuwharetoa, for example, had been investigating titles in the Taupo district through their own committee since at least 1878.[11] When news reached them of the Native Committees Act they convened a meeting at which a committee of twelve, headed by Te Heuheu Tukino, was elected. This wrote to the Native Minister a few days later asking that the government grant it legal standing in accordance with the Act.[12] It had, however, already been decided to establish Committees for 'large districts containing many interests',[13] and T.W. Lewis, the Native Under-Secretary, commented that Ngati Tuwharetoa would probably be 'aggrieved' at being included in the Rotorua district, adding that once the boundaries of the districts had been published in the *Kahiti* 'no doubt these and other natives will write on the subject'.[14] Te Arawa, too, had their own ideas on the issue, Wiremu Maihi Te Rangikaheke of Ngati Rangiwewehi informing Bryce in October 1883 that as there were four main divisions of the tribe, there should also be four Committees for them.[15] Bryce, though, had earlier instructed Lewis that he did 'not wish the districts to be too numerous – six or seven would be enough...for the North Island'.[16] Te Rangikaheke's request, like Ngati Tuwharetoa's tribal committee, was therefore 'out of the question', Lewis commenting that even one covering the entire Bay of Plenty and Rotorua districts would be too small for Bryce.[17] Two Committees were eventually appointed for the Bay of Plenty, the Rotorua one including not only all of Te Arawa, but also their old enemies Ngai Te Rangi and Ngati Ranginui, as well as Ngati Tuwharetoa, and stretching from Tauranga to Taupo. In fact, the Tauranga tribes' sole representative on the Committee later complained that he was looked upon 'as an outsider' by the other members,[18] and along with the rest of the Tauranga people lobbied for a separate Committee, as did Ngati Tuwharetoa, who pleaded (in a somehow aptly confused manner) that they did 'not wish to be mixed up with the Arawa Committee of Tauranga'.[19]

News that 'an influential Committee' had been elected at Tapapa in December 1883 met with the terse response from Bryce that 'This is premature'.[20] Despite this, the Native Department continued to receive reports of Maori electing their own Committees, queries as to their jurisdiction, and requests for the official recognition of Committees already appointed. Hauraki Maori, for example, informed the government that they were 'most anxious that our Committee should be invested with lawful authority to adjudicate on lands and offences'.[21]

They had, W.H. Taipari informed George Wilkinson, already decided at a meeting held in November on the apportionment of tribal representatives amongst the different sections of Marutuahu, but 'were in doubt about...the question of dealing with minor offences, as the Committee will not sit every day in each week'.[22] Bryce, obviously concerned by the tone of this inquiry, instructed his Under-Secretary that copies of the Act should be supplied to all Committees, 'and of course they must be confined to the powers conferred by the Act. They possibly think that the powers of the Committees will be more absolute than is really the case'.[23]

Native Department indifference to the implementation of the legislation probably contributed to many Maori initially labouring under this illusion. Inundated with requests for copies of the Act, the Native Office in 1884 stated that it had been translated into Maori 'but not generally circulated'. One request for copies was met with the reply that 'one or two can be spared' – hardly encouraging when the Committees each had twelve members. And when a discrepancy between the English and Maori versions was pointed out, officials were instructed to 'work to the English'.[24]

Nearly four months after the Act was passed, in January 1884, twelve Native Committee districts were finally proclaimed under it.[25] Fifteen months later, half of these Committees had still to be convened. Despite Hori Taiaroa's enthusiastic support for Tomoana's earlier bill, no committees were appointed for the South Island,[26] and those in the North all encompassed huge areas, in most cases millions of acres. With former enemies such as Ngati Porou and the Poverty Bay tribes of Rongowhakaata and Te Aitanga-a-Mahaki lumped together in one mammoth district, it is little wonder that the initial enthusiasm which had greeted news of the legislation was not sustained, particularly once Maori came to appreciate that the Committees had no real powers anyway. It was hardly surprising, therefore, that as Ward points out, 'committee activity throughout most of the 1880s consisted largely of squabbling between tribal groups for control of the committee elections and requests for more committees representative of smaller units'.[27] Indeed, even where tribal cohesion was relatively strong the sheer size of the districts worked to undermine the Committees' operations. H.W. Bishop, the Mangonui Resident Magistrate, reported in April 1885, for example, that:

> The Bay of Islands Native Committee held their first meeting here in January last; eleven out of the twelve members were present, the majority having travelled great distances in order to take part in the proceedings. Hone Mohi Tawhai, late member of the House of Representatives, was elected chairman, and as provided by law, he

> immediately took the oath of allegiance before me, subsequently administering the same himself to the other members of the Committee. I am not aware that the Committee has as yet done anything worthy of note, and I do not think very much interest is taken in its existence. The enormous district within its jurisdiction, and the great distance that some of its members will have to travel in order to attend meetings, must militate against its usefulness in some degree.[28]

This was, of course, not only a problem for members of the Committee, but also for those who wished to bring their land claims before it for investigation. At least when Maori travelled enormous distances to Native Land Court hearings they could be certain that the Court was empowered to award title to one or another of the claimants at the end of proceedings. Unfortunately, as will be seen, the Bay of Islands Committee, hampered by its lack of powers and undermined by Crown and private agents, found great difficulty in persuading Maori that they should travel great distances to bring their claims before it, notwithstanding the energetic and enthusiastic – and later, increasingly frustrated – leadership of Tawhai.

Bishop, in reporting a year earlier on the election of the Bay of Islands Committee, had noted that:

> Very little interest was taken in the result. As yet the matter is but little understood, and the Rarawas appear suspicious lest the Committee should abuse their power, while the Ngapuhis do not like the idea of their self-constituted tribunals being overshadowed by a body endowed by law with certain judicial powers. It is of course premature at the present time to express an opinion as to the ultimate results of the working of the Act.[29]

Yet in many districts the results were all too predictable. Brabant's report on the election of the Rotorua Committee in March 1884 would hardly have come as a surprise to Native Department officials who had previously received numerous applications for several Committees to be appointed for the district:

> The district for which the Committee was elected comprised those

of Tauranga, Maketu, Rotorua, and Taupo. Very few Natives voted, and very little interest was taken in the matter. This the Natives account for by saying that the district was too large, and what they want is a Committee for each tribe.[30]

Reports from other districts also indicated a mixed response to the Committee elections, with some tribes appearing eager to gain representation, and others remaining aloof. R.S. Bush reported from Opotiki in May 1884 that:

> On the 7th instant the election of a Native Committee for this district...took place at the courthouse, when fourteen candidates were nominated, a majority of whom belonged to the tribes residing between Raukokore and Torere. None of the other tribes appeared to take much interest in the proceedings, although a long notice had been given, and steps taken to make it generally known through the district.[31]

Robert Ward reported from Whanganui that some interest had been shown in the election, but not as much as he had expected.[32] G.T. Wilkinson, also writing in May 1884, reported that:

> During the month of March last I conducted the elections for Native Committees for the three districts of Kawhia, Waikato, and Thames, in accordance with the provisions of 'The Native Committees Act, 1883'. In each case the maximum number of members allowed by the Act was elected, namely, twelve. The Ngatimaniapoto Natives in this district profess to take a great interest in the working of the Act, and nearly all the members that were elected for the Kawhia District were nominated by them; and, although they took the precaution to choose members from different districts within the boundaries, still the fact that the Waikatos neither nominated, voted, nor in any way took part in the election will, I think, militate against its being a success at present. However, those who have been elected are anxious to be called together (as provided by the Act) and to commence work. Their great wish is to be allowed to decide upon, or rather hold, a preliminary investigation of their own claims to the large block that

is now being surveyed, upon which they would make a recommendation to the Native Land Court; but I am very dubious as to their being the proper tribunal to adjudicate, even in a preliminary form, on that block, especially as their opponents and counter-claimants, Waikato and Ngatihaua, would not be represented on the Committee.[33]

The Kawhia Committee, under the chairmanship of the youthful John Ormsby, was one of the most active in the country, partly because of the government's continuing anxiety to ensure the success of the North Island main trunk railway project and the convenience of having a recognised body with which to conduct continuing negotiations.[34] The aloofness of Waikato was, however, mirrored in Taranaki, where one fewer than the minimum six members were nominated. Robert Parris, the returning officer, informed his superiors in Wellington that:

> It would have been possible to have induced them to nominate a sufficient number to constitute a Committee under the provisions of the Act from the Taranaki and Atiawa tribes, but as they have no land left outside the Confiscation [boundaries], such a Committee would have been useless, as the Ngatiruanui, Ngatihine and Ngarauru tribes would never agree to submit any cases to them.[35]

No further efforts were made to elect a Committee for Taranaki; and Bryce, who had done more than any other individual in recent times to destroy what shreds of faith Taranaki Maori still had in the Crown in the wake of the confiscations, wrote without even a hint of irony that:

> The small amount of interest taken in the election of Maori Committees will render it necessary that I should consider whether the Native Committees Act of last session is likely to be of any real value.[36]

It was Bryce's reluctance to concede any powers to the Committees, his insistence that the districts covered by each should be as large as possible, his refusal to listen to sensible Maori suggestions and initiatives with respect to their boundaries, his unwillingness to grant them any source of funding, and his apparent lack of interest in ensuring their success that had all combined to ensure that the Act would prove to be of little real value. Indeed, as McRae says, its failure was preordained.

Bryce's replacement as Native Minister in August 1884 by the somewhat more sympathetic John Ballance might have been expected to augur well for the future of the Committees, and there were some noticeable advances, such as a greater willingness to grant requests for new Committees more reflective of tribal alliances.[37] Yet for all Ballance's willingness to listen to reasonable Maori demands, ultimately he remained too much of a paternalist when it came to Maori matters to heed calls for real control over their own lands and other affairs. In November 1884 the Ngati Maniapoto chief Wahanui, granted the rare privilege of addressing both Houses of Parliament, in both speeches emphasised the desire of his people to have full control over their own lands, in respect of which they wished to exclude the Native Land Court and instead administer them through their own official Committee, which should be 'empowered, so that all dealings and transactions within that proclaimed district should be left in the hands of that Committee'.[38] Ballance, in reply, considered that this 'movement' amongst Maori for the right to control their own lands was only just in its infancy, and was 'calculated to place in their hands the fullest privileges of self-government with respect to dealing with their own lands'. Maori 'from one end of the Island to the other', he stated with some exaggeration, 'seem very much inclined to take up the Bill which was passed two sessions ago for the appointment of Native Committees, and to come under the working of that measure'. Yet although admitting that the Native Land Court 'has not given satisfaction to the Native people', Ballance contended that 'no Court, however constituted' could be expected to do so, adding that:

> no European tribunal adjudicating in reference to the ownership of Native property can ever be entirely successful, because, according to Native custom, there never has been in the past individual right to property in the sense in which we understand it. The customs of

the Natives of this colony, like the customs of all primitive people, are socialistic and communistic. They hold land in common, and any Court which does not recognize their socialistic customs would fail to give satisfaction to the Natives.[39]

This was of course the point that many Maori had been endeavouring to make; that the Native Land Court system created an individual right in land where none had previously existed in Maori custom, even though the Court had ostensibly been set up to convert customary land rights into titles derived from the Crown. For Ballance and other nineteenth-century Europeans, individualisation of title was the key to Maori 'civilisation' and advancement. Yet few contemporary observers would have dared to suggest that the Anglican Church, like many other corporate landowning organisations, was somehow uncivilised or backward because title to its churches had yet to be divided among the parishioners.

Ballance, then, believed that 'large allowances' ought to be made for the difficult tasks the Court had to encounter. It was never going to please Maori entirely, because its task of individualising titles was so alien to Maori custom. Yet while considering there was a good deal to be said in favour of Maori committees determining titles, Ballance again raised the familiar bogey of partial committee members finding in favour of their kin. Therefore, he stated:

> the Court is an institution that must remain amongst us as long as Native title requires to be ascertained. As to the Native Committees...with slightly larger powers than they have, they might perform some very useful functions. They might act as a Court of first instance, allowing the Native Land Court to act as a Court of Appeal.[40]

Ballance signalled his intention to introduce legislation directed towards this aim. Yet while his short-lived Native Lands Administration Act of 1886 (discussed below) allowed the owners of a particular block, once determined by the Native Land Court, to have a greater say in its disposal, there was to be no legislative boost to the powers of the Committees elected under the 1883

Act during his three-year tenure as Native Minister.

The limitations facing the Committees began to be apparent to their members as soon as they were convened. The Thames Committee had been elected in March 1884, with more than 30 candidates nominated for just twelve positions, and two months later was the first in the country to be formally convened and have its members sworn in. Reporting on this first meeting, the *Thames Advertiser* noted that it 'possessed considerable importance in the eyes of the natives of the district, as being the first step towards the exercise of something resembling self-government'. The assembled members, it was reported, 'entered upon their duties with more zeal than usually characterises the average European executive'; their 'earnestness in selecting officers' was apparent from the fact that more than an hour's deliberation took place before Raika Whakarongotai was appointed Chairman, with the rest of the day being taken up in framing a set of regulations for the conduct of business.[41] Under the Act, however, all such rules were first to be inserted in the *Gazette* before coming into operation, and because no action was taken to give effect to the regulations forwarded by the Thames and other Committees until June 1886, when a set of regulations applicable to all Committees was gazetted, they were essentially operating in a vacuum for the first two years of their existence. In fact, in October 1884 the Thames Committee wrote to the Native Department that:

> The Committee wish to be informed of the nature of their duties, seeing that they have now met three times and have had nothing to do.

With the limitations of their role as a court of arbitration becoming all too apparent to them, the Committee members resolved that the Native Minister should be requested to pass regulations empowering them to issue summonses, observing that:

> if that section [of the Act] is not amended the Committee will not have any power, and further a dispute would not be submitted to

173

the Committee if one of the disputants felt that he would lose the case if it were submitted to the Committee.[42]

Despite this and similar requests from the Whanganui and other Committees for the right to issue summonses, no action was taken. By 1885, their requests ignored, the Thames Committee was issuing its own legally-unenforceable summonses but finding these too ignored by those served with them.[43] When the Committees' regulations were eventually gazetted in 1886 no power to issue summonses was included,[44] and the Rotorua Native Committee was still being reminded of this point as late as 1889, when it sought advice as to what could be done about those who refused to appear before it.[45]

Early in 1885 Ballance undertook an extensive tour of Maori communities throughout the North Island during which many of the difficulties confronting the Committees were brought to his attention. At Ranana, on the Whanganui River, for example, Paora Kurimate, the chairman of the local Committee, informed the Native Minister that they wished its jurisdiction to be confined to the Wanganui district only (the boundaries of which their own committee had made known to the government in 1880), and that they wanted it to have full control over investigations of title, surveys, leases and sales, as well as access to the river for steamers.[46] Ballance concurred with their first request, considering it 'absurd...that some of the members of this Committee are living at Otaki', and promised to amend the boundaries on his return to Wellington. This does not appear to have happened.[47]

On the question of the Committees undertaking investigations of title, Ballance informed Whanganui River Maori that:

> It may sometimes happen that the Committee, in ascertaining the title to land, may themselves – the members of the Committee – be interested in having the title ascertained in a given direction. It is right, therefore, that there should be appeal to a body above suspicion, who will have no interest in the question of title. Therefore, I think that, after the Committee has ascertained the

> title, there should always be an appeal to the Land Court; and then it will be necessary, of course, that the Court should give legal sanction to the decisions of the Committee. You ought therefore to recognize that the Land Court still remains to decide ultimately the question of title amongst you.[48]

Of course, if the Native Land Court remained the ultimate arbiter of native title it would be under no obligation to give legal sanction to any of the decisions of the Committees. Ballance was promising no more than the status quo, at the same time deflecting attention from the other demands by talking about his promised legislation to establish block committees.

A similar dialogue occurred at the Ngati Maniapoto settlement of Kihikihi, where John Ormsby, with the support of Wahanui, again asked that the Committees should have full power to determine titles, and to award the lands to hapu, who would each elect their own committee to administer them. Ormsby informed Ballance that:

> with regard to the forming of the Native Committees, that was not carried to such an extent as we wished. It was only a shadow when we came to take hold of it to work it – it was not substantial. I now ask that the Committees shall have some power given to enable them to force disputants to bring their cases before the Committee, and that the Committee should be placed in the position of the Native Land Court.[49]

They had, Ormsby added, 'never seen any good yet come out of the work of the Native Land Court'. Lands that passed through it invariably ended up in the hands of Europeans, when all that they wanted, Wahanui stated, was for the Court to leave them alone and for Europeans to 'refrain from interfering with the Maori lands, but leave the Natives to manage them themselves'.

Ballance again defended the role of the Native Land Court: it was intended to be an independent tribunal and although not perfect was, in his view, at least not susceptible to the dangers of partiality, as the Committees allegedly would be. Even so, Ballance believed that the Committees 'may render great service in administering the laws among the Native people', and announced his intention to introduce during the next session an amending bill which would allow them to adjudicate on disputes up to a certain amount without the consent of both parties, adding that:

> I think it is also desirable to give them some revenue, if they desire it, and I am considering the expediency of handing over to them the collection of the dog-tax, for instance. I think also that the Chairman should be paid a small sum for attending to the duties that may come upon the Committee. Then we propose to give them larger powers on preparing cases for the Native Land Court, so that all cases will come before the Native Committee in the first instance, and then go on to the Native Land Court, which will finally deal with the matter.[50]

There was to be no such amending legislation widening the jurisdiction of the Committees, however, nor was any independent source of revenue granted them. In February 1884 Bryce had instructed that no expense was to be incurred without specific authority from the Native Office, adding that the extent of any financial assistance given would depend on the circumstances.[51] An annual payment of £50 per annum to all Committee Chairmen was approved by Ballance following his tour of the North Island, but without clarification as to whether it was intended as payment for the Chairman's services or to cover the Committees' expenses widespread confusion resulted, which had not been settled by the time the grant was abolished as part of a general retrenchment of Native Department expenditure in 1887.[52] In any case, the total sum provided to cover the expenses of all twelve Committees, each with up to twelve members, was hardly great, being no more than the annual salary of an ordinary Native Land Court Judge, which was set by statute at £600 per annum.[53]

At Whatiwhatihoe, where Ballance met Tawhiao and his supporters in February 1885, the issue of Maori self-management of their lands and other affairs was again debated. Tawhiao asked the Minister why self-government was denied the Maori people, who wished merely to manage their own affairs. Ballance replied that there could be but one government in New Zealand, the Maori people having bound themselves to accept the Queen's laws when they signed the Treaty of Waitangi, but that:

> subject to that, we are prepared to extend to the Native people large powers of self-government by means of their Native Committees. We propose to give to those Committees larger powers, and to make them really represent the people.[54]

Te Wheoro, however, pointing to the manner in which the Native Land Court denied Maori control over their own lands, told Ballance that 'It would appear, when a block was going through the Native Land Court, as if the land was owned by the Court itself, and not by the litigants', adding that:

> I have been allowed no share in the management of matters for the Natives, and, although you may appoint me as a representative, everything that you instigated, and nothing that I recommended or instigated, was done. Your statement that all power was given by the Treaty of Waitangi to the Europeans is not correct. It was given to both of us. It was given to you, and to me, too. The reason I say it was given to me as well as to you is because it states in the Treaty of Waitangi that the Maori chiefs should be treated in the same way as the people of England, and given the same power. It was understood that the Maoris would be allowed to govern themselves in the same way that the Europeans are allowed to govern themselves...I am willing to accept the Queen as our head, and we shall be responsible to her for the management of our affairs in the same way as you are responsible to her. Give the government of the Maori race to the Maori chiefs. What harm is there in it? Has it ever been tried yet, to see whether evil will come of it or not?

Ballance indicated that he was prepared to countenance increased Maori representation in Parliament, but beyond that self-government for Maori would be confined to the official Native Committees.

An increase in the powers of the Committees was a familiar request from Maori at the other settlements visited by Ballance. The Thames Native Committee, for example, asked that it be allowed to undertake preliminary investigations of title, which might then be referred on to the Native Land Court for confirmation. Ballance agreed to this, and to additional requests for the Chairmen of the Committees to be permitted to frank letters on official matters, and for provision to be made for vacancies on the Committees to be filled by by-elections.[55] But while the promise to allow Committee Chairmen to frank mail was soon fulfilled, the filling of vacant positions had already been rejected on the grounds that 'It would not do to put the Country to the expense of an election each time a member resigned'.[56] With members resigning, dying or finding it impossible to attend Committee meetings owing to the huge distances they were required to travel, or because Land Court hearings were scheduled at the same time, it is little wonder that by 1889 the Rotorua Committee was seeking unsuccessfully to have the legal quorum reduced from six members to three.[57]

At Rotorua, Ngati Whakaue requested that their Committee should have the direction of surveys, Retireti Tapihana adding that:

> The members of the District Committee have been elected according to law by the people…; but they are quite aware that they have not sufficiently large powers to deal with all the subjects they wish.[58]

Ballance repeated his promises to increase the jurisdiction and powers of the Committees. At a separate meeting with the Tuhourangi tribe a day later he was informed that the people wished to have their own committee – apparently a successor to the Putaiki – legally constituted so that they could act under the direction of the Rotorua Native Committee. Te Keepa Te Rangipuawhe, the Chairman of the Rotorua Committee, told Ballance that the nineteen persons who formed the Tuhourangi committee had been elected by the 600 owners of the large Rotomahana-Parekarangi Block, most of which had been awarded them by the Native Land Court, but that the Court had refused to recognise their committee, on the grounds that a hundred owners had not endorsed the body. According to

Rangipuawhe, it had proved impossible to gain the consent of these absentee owners not because they objected to the committee but because they were scattered all over the country. Hori Taiawhio, endorsing these comments, stated that the committee had been properly elected, and added that:

> This Committee performs a great many works in the way of carrying out the work of the tribe – in keeping order. This Committee has heard a great many land disputes and other disputes; but they have no legal standing, and therefore we now ask that they may be recognized.[59]

Ballance informed Tuhourangi that while their committee had no legal standing its position was not contrary to the law. This was hardly encouraging, however, in the light of some of the examples of the committee's attempts to enforce order in the district which had been undermined by the absence of any legal authority. Tuhourangi, as guardians and owners of the Pink and White Terraces, Ballance was told, had endeavoured to stop tourists vandalising them by breaking off pieces as souvenirs or writing their names on them. Regulations had been printed in English and Maori and circulated, and offenders who were caught breaking them were fined. But while some agreed to pay, Rangipuawhe stated, others had refused on the grounds that the regulations did not carry the force of law, 'although we try to persuade the Europeans that they have'.

Ballance's failure to act on his promise to grant the official Committees increased powers, and the unwillingness of successive governments to recognise tribal committees such as that of Tuhourangi (especially when these endeavoured to bind Pakeha to their decisions), hardly indicated any great inclination on the part of the Crown to allow Maori substantive control over their own affairs. Indeed, rather than the mechanisms of self-government Ballance continually promised Maori the Committees set up under the 1883 Act would become, they remained instead the 'impotent and cruel farce' described by Rees in 1893.

The problem of Committee members having an interest in a case, which Ballance used to dismiss Maori arguments for the

Committees to take the place of the Native Land Court, was certainly a real one. In 1885, for example, Ratema Te Awekotuku and 'all Ngatirangiteorere' wrote to Ballance to inform him of their objections to the subdivision of a particular block being handed over to the Rotorua Committee, on the grounds that 'all the members of that Committee have claims to the land in question, either in their own names or in the names of the wives of some of them'.[60] Lewis, the Under-Secretary, informed Ballance that this was 'one of the cases of difficulty in the way of Native Committees investigating title to land...I fear the same objection will arise in most cases where the Committee assumes the function'.[61] Yet rather than looking for a solution to this problem, whether by requiring members personally interested in a case to stand down, with the remaining members being empowered to temporarily co-opt new members to assist in the adjudication,[62] or through a completely different type of committee structure of the kind proposed by Tuhaere, Te Wheoro and Hikairo as early as 1871, the government was content to ignore the problem, leaving the Native Land Court – which was not without its own biases when it came to interpreting Maori custom – with the real power to determine the ownership of Maori lands. The government was not truly interested in making the Committees more effective agents of self-government for Maori, especially at the expense of the Native Land Court, which had proven such an effective mechanism of Pakeha colonisation. Ballance might allow the Committees to frank mail and pay their Chairmen a nominal sum to cover expenses, but there was little genuine commitment on the part of the Crown to allowing the Committees real powers over Maori land.

That the Native Land Court remained in the driving seat was ironically revealed by the unsuccessful efforts to convene the first meeting of the Wairarapa Committee in May 1885 – half the members elected were absent at a Land Court hearing at Hastings. Nearly a year later the Committee had still to be sworn in, and E.S. Maunsell was reporting that 'no chairman has been appointed owing to the absence of two leading men who are engaged as Assessors under the Native Land Court'.[63]

Eventually fresh elections were held in December 1886, but there is no evidence that it met more regularly or was able to achieve anything of significance thereafter.

One Committee which did meet regularly, yet also remained plagued by its lack of any effective authority vis-à-vis the Native Land and Resident Magistrates Courts, was the Bay of Islands Committee, which met for the first time in January 1885, when Hone Mohi Tawhai was elected chairman. By April J.H. Greenway, a clerk in the Resident Magistrates Court at Russell, was describing the Committee as 'so far a failure', adding that:

> I am unaware of any business having been transacted beyond the election of a chairman; they seem to prefer their own Committees, probably from the fact of these not being elected under Government supervision, these Committees, however, having no legal status, appeals from them to the Resident Magistrate's Court are frequent, or rather many cases are brought, during the hearing of which it transpires that they had been investigated before the Committee, the decision of which the losing party had refused to abide by.[64]

Greenway believed that the day was 'not far distant when Native Committee tribunals will be a thing of the past'. Yet if the Crown's indifference to the fate of the official Committees made this something of a self-fulfilling prophecy, the work of the Bay of Islands Committee demonstrates that this occurred despite the best efforts of many Maori, who endeavoured to make a success of the 1883 Act but were ultimately thwarted in this by the lack of any effective authority. During the period when the Bay of Islands Committee was active, from 1885 to 1889, for example, the still-functioning Treaty of Waitangi Committee appears to have refrained from conducting title investigations, resuming this role only after the official Committee became defunct.[65] McRae notes that the Bay of Islands Committee 'succeeded in settling agreement for sale between tribal owners and a Pakeha purchaser the division of a block of land, and adjudicating in local disputes, for example, over the location of a school, ownership of horses, and trespass on fishing and shooting reserves'.[66] Its primary task of undertaking preliminary title investigations was, however, continually undermined and frustrated by government indifference, notwithstanding the enthusiastic efforts of Tawhai to persuade claimants to bring their cases before it.

Tawhai regularly sent the Native Minister suggestions as to how the Committees might be made to work more successfully, more often than not receiving a lukewarm response. In June 1885, for example, he suggested that the Native Committees should be sent copies of all relevant legislation concerning the Native Land Court, local bodies, public works, and so on, 'so that the proceedings of the Committee may be careful and not done in ignorance'.[67] This request appears to have been ignored. By the following month nine applications for investigation of title had been forwarded to the Native Office for insertion in the *Kahiti*.[68] No action was taken to publish these or similar notices received from the Rotorua Committee, on the grounds that 'pending legislation re Native Lands it is not desirable to publish the notices forwarded'.[69] Nearly two years had elapsed since the passage of the Native Committees Act, yet the Committees so far established under this Act were still prevented from even investigating titles 'for the information of the Court'. This might have been understandable had Ballance actually honoured his promise to grant them larger powers of jurisdiction with respect to title investigations. But no such legislation was to be either proposed or passed, and the Crown's continuing procrastination in implementing the 1883 Act only helped to further dampen the already dwindling enthusiasm for the Committees.

By 1887 the Bay of Islands Committee had apparently at last been able to commence title investigations. It had achieved some notable successes, for example by encouraging claimants who refused to submit their cases to the Native Land Court to bring them before the Committee, but had also found itself frustrated by a number of factors. Tawhai informed Ballance in March of that year that his Committee was 'now engaged in dealing with lands owned by individuals here at Kaikohe, which are in a very difficult state, and over which the said individuals nearly came to an open quarrel'.[70] Notwithstanding this the disputants had been persuaded to apply to the Committee to inquire into the disputed lands, and for the past month, Tawhai reported, 'seven very complicated land cases have been dealt with and both parties have been satisfied with the decisions of the Committee'. The people were, he added, 'very favourably impressed' with the working of the Committee, 'for they say that the Native Committee give their decision in accordance to the Native custom'. Tawhai reported, however, that during the course, of their investigations:

> a half-caste arrived from Hokianga, his object was to declare that my Committee had no authority to deal with cases respecting Native lands; the said half-caste made this declaration so as to prevent these disputed lands from being submitted for investigation by the Native Committee, he even went further to say, that those Native lands that have not yet been dealt with should be left for investigation of the Native Land Court, to which the owners of these blocks replied that they did not wish the Native Land Court to deal with them but the Native Committee. All the Kaikohe people therefore with all the hapus of Ngapuhi and Te Rarawa are submitting their lands for investigation by the Native Committee.

This challenge to the jurisdiction of the Committee prompted its members to actually examine the powers granted them under the Act, and despite much of the Maori translation of this proving 'so mixed up that no clear and intelligible meaning could be attached to it', Tawhai added that:

> In consequence...of the statement...that the Committee had no authority to deal with land matters, the Committee met again...to look through the clauses of the Act, and it was found that what he said was quite correct...[A]ll troubles in connection with Native lands are...referred to the Native Land Court, and all power of dealing with them is taken away from the Native Committee.

Tawhai therefore requested on behalf of its members that 'the Government would grant the Native Committee the necessary authority and power' to perform its duties, and that a surveyor be appointed to work under the direction of the Committee. Once surveys had been completed and the title had been investigated a report and accompanying plan should be forwarded to the Chief Judge of the Land Court, Tawhai suggested, following which 'certificate should be issued to those in whose favour the Committee had given its decision'. There were, moreover, strong financial grounds for supporting such a procedure. Tawhai pointed out that the Committee had sat for twenty days, settling seven very complicated land claims at no cost to the colony, having collected (unbeknown to its members perhaps, without legal authority) a sum sufficient to meet its expenses, whereas had the Native Land Court sat for a similar period, the costs to the Crown resulting from the salaries of the Judge, clerks, interpreters, Assessors, and so on, would have been considerable. 'For these reasons', Tawhai shrewdly informed Ballance, 'the Committee now request that powers be given them so as to strengthen them to carry on such an inexpensive course to the colony'.

Tawhai was informed in response that although the Native Minister was pleased to hear that the Bay of Islands Committee was working satisfactorily, he was to 'see that the Committee...does not exceed the powers the law has conferred upon it'; the Committee could only assist the Court, he was told, when both claimants and counter-claimants concurred with its findings and asked the Court to ratify them.[71] Lewis had put it more bluntly, recommending to Ballance that he remind the Committee 'not...to usurp the functions of the Native Land Court'.[72]

Undeterred, Tawhai wrote again a week later that he was now 'with a sorrowful heart' exhorting his Committee to settle land disputes amongst the Ngapuhi, and that the people supported this, despite the:

> very little encouragement given them by the clause dealing with land disputes in the Act of 1883. This weakness in that clause discouraged them but still they did all in their power to settle these troubles, so that the result has been that nine cases have been completed.[73]

Another thing which grieved him, Tawhai informed the Minister, was the:

> declaration of both Natives and Europeans that the Native Committee have no authority to deal with lands, and telling the Natives that they are wasting their money because the sum which the Committee impose upon all cases and counter-claimants, so as to support the Committee is 10/– and for administering the oath 1/–.

These fees, although entirely voluntary, do not seem to have deterred potential claimants, and Tawhai reported that they had another fourteen 'very complicated land questions to be dealt with' during their current sitting, and a further 36 applications awaiting a hearing. He had, however, deferred fixing a date for the hearing of the latter until informed by the Native Minister whether or not he approved of the actions of the Committee. Tawhai reminded the Minister that:

> These people are very obstinate in submitting their lands for investigation by the Native Land Court, it was only through this being a Native Committee, and as their decision is given in accordance with the Maori customs, that they now agree to submit their lands (to the Committee). This course has also prevented outsiders putting in claims as the Committee generally knows the position of the lands submitted and the people interested therein.

In a separate letter forwarded to the Minister a few days later, Tawhai again urged that he be told whether the government approved of the Committee's actions, and informed Ballance that Crown officials had been discouraging claimants from taking cases to the Committee for investigation:

> I am now engaged in endeavouring to suppress the troubles of this most troublesome place, Kaikohe, owing to advices being given by the Government officials and J.P.s to the Natives so as to prevent them from bringing their grievances and troubles to the Native Committee, as they greatly ridicule the capacity of the Native Committee to deal with them.
>
> I consider that this is like saying 'Do not take your grievances and

troubles to the Native Committee, lest they be dealt with and settled, but have it settled amongst yourselves by fighting "the thing" out as you were wont to do in days gone by'.[74]

Of course, the alternative explanation one might give for this advice was that Crown officials were instead anxious that the parties involved should fight out their battles in the Native Land Court. In any event, Tawhai was once again politely reminded that the Committee should be careful not to assume powers it did not have: 'The law...only authorises it to deal with cases submitted by agreement of all parties interested', he was told.

As Williams notes, unofficial committees 'could have done as much without any legal recognition at all'.[75] In these circumstances, it was hardly surprising that the Treaty of Waitangi Committee had been revived by 1889. After all, it was free of government control or supervision, could define its boundaries as it chose, received just as much funding from the Crown (nil), and stood just as much chance of having its decisions ratified by the Native Land Court. Tawhai's spirited leadership of the Bay of Islands Committee had proven insufficient to overcome the insurmountable obstacles placed in its way, and henceforth the Ngapuhi leader devoted his attentions to the Treaty of Waitangi movement he had stood aloof from in the early 1880s, when convinced that the solution to Maori grievances lay in legislative reforms such as the Native Committees Act.[76]

Perhaps one of the most surprising facts to emerge from Tawhai's correspondence with the government was that, although he had been a member of Parliament when the 1883 Act was passed, it was not till 1887, when Crown officials and others pointed it out, that he had become aware of the severely limited jurisdiction granted the Committees by law (which prompted him to also petition Parliament on the subject).[77] Ballance's 1885 travels through the North Island had shown that many were already alive to this, but some, it seems, continued to pin their hopes on the Committees in the belief or expectation that they might eventually be made effective instruments of self-government.

Even Tawhiao's supporters in the King Country, who boycotted the 1884 elections for the Kawhia and Waikato Committees, had by late in 1885 established their own unofficial King committees, prompted possibly by concern that the government had chosen to conduct its negotiations for the opening up of the district to the Native Land Court and railway construction through the official Committees. The Kawhia Committee under John Ormbsy had played a key role in talks with the Crown, and Wilkinson, the Government Native Agent at Alexandra, was able to report in May 1886 that at crucial and lengthy meetings held late in 1885:

> a number of matters were dealt with that tended towards the opening-up of the King country for settlement. A scale of prices was fixed for different classes of timber, a considerable quantity of which was then and is now being used by railway and other contractors. Arrangements were also made for granting by the Committee of temporary occupation-leases to contractors and storekeepers who wished to live in their district. These and other matters were settled by the Committee at that time; but the most important of all the subjects dealt with and disposed of by them was the agreeing to throw open the whole of the King country for gold-prospecting under certain conditions.[78]

Although no gold was to be discovered in the district, the Committee was able, through quiet diplomacy with Wilkinson and the government, to reach agreement for twelve experienced prospectors ('sober and respectable withal') to test out the country, thereby avoiding a general stampede from the Thames fields. Moreover, the Committee had even persuaded a King supporter who had threatened to burn down houses built on disputed land to submit his claims to it, after he had refused to refer the matter to the Native Land Court.

In the light of these successes, Wilkinson reported that in November 1885:

> the Natives at Whatiwhatihoe started what they called a 'King Committee' in opposition to the Kawhia Native Committee, which

consists of members most of whom have nothing in common with the King party, and who were duly elected in accordance with 'The Native Committees Act, 1883'; the King Committee being a Committee nominated (not elected) by and from amongst the supporters of the King party. Of course they had no other standing than that which the mana or power of Tawhiao – now but a shadow of what it once was – could give them. That, however, did not cause them to have any the less idea of their own importance, and they did not hesitate at issuing summonses to Natives to appear before them who belonged to 'the other side', and who would have nothing to do with them because they were not elected from amongst the people, and were not working in accordance with the law...This policy of the King party in setting up Committees was not only carried out at Whatiwhatihoe, but also at Kawhia, Aotea, Thames, Ohinemuri, Piako, and other places where Tawhiao had any supporters; and they have caused in some cases considerable trouble, especially at Aotea – where for a time they stopped the repairing of the road across the harbour – and also at Ohinemuri, where the Ngatihako Tribe only a few weeks ago stopped the survey of the Paeroa-Te Aroha Railway line.

These obstructions were, Wilkinson believed, part of a deliberate strategy:

> the policy that these Committees seem to have been instructed to carry out in every district in which I have come across them has been to stop, if possible, all Government works that are being carried out on Native land that has not yet passed the Native Land Court; and whenever they think that they can safely do so without running the risk of being punished for their action they do it, they looking upon it as a duty they owe to Tawhiao and the *tikanga* or King movement to stop everything that is being done on Native land unless it has first been sanctioned by Tawhiao himself.[79]

Yet if this stood in marked contrast to the Kawhia Committee's more diplomatic approach of seeking to negotiate the controlled entry of institutions of state and European settlement to the district, by 1886 the King committees were themselves looking to merge with Ormsby's and achieve official recognition under the

1883 Act. The Kawhia Committee, dominated by Ngati Maniapoto, appear to have interpreted this move, probably correctly, more in the light of a hostile takeover, than a friendly merger, and stated their opposition in no uncertain terms.[80] Apparently anxious not to upset its new-found Rohe Potae friends, the government declined to recognise the King committees.[81] An opportunity for rapprochement with the King movement had been sacrificed in favour of cementing ties with Ngati Maniapoto, who were, after all, the recognised customary owners of a vast tract of land which the Crown was anxious to see opened up to European settlement.

Despite the differences in strategy between Ngati Maniapoto and the King movement neither was anxious for the Native Land Court to adjudicate on their lands, as Ballance had been told in no uncertain terms in 1885. But when the Court did commence hearings on the Rohe Potae block in 1886, it was the pragmatic and resourceful leadership of Ormsby and the Kawhia Committee which helped to ensure that some of the worst excesses of Native Land Court sittings elsewhere were avoided. As Sorrenson says, 'there was none of the debauchery which was a feature of earlier Court sittings held in European towns'.[82] Tribal claims to the block were discussed by the Committee and later defined by the Court, which subsequently subdivided it on a hapu basis.[83] The Kawhia Committee appears to have played an important role in this process of determining hapu interests, and it was not until 1890, when G.T. Wilkinson commenced purchasing individual interests in the adjudicated lands, that Maniapoto tribal control over their lands through the mechanism of the Committee began to be seriously undermined.[84]

The Kawhia Committee achieved some short-term successes largely because of the geopolitical importance attached to the 'opening up' of the King Country at the time. But in other districts where such considerations did not apply there was to be little to show for the Committees' efforts, whatever the initial enthusiasm. In the Hawke's Bay district, for example, elections were held early in 1884 following Maori agitation, even though the area 'was not intended to be brought under the immediate operation of the Native Committees Act'.[85] Nearly 1200 votes were recorded, and Henare Matua, the former Repudiation movement leader, was subsequently chosen as Chairman.[86] Just over a year later, however, George Preece, the Napier Resident Magistrate, described the Act as 'a dead letter as far as this district is concerned'.[87] In 1887 this situation had not changed, Preece reporting that 'with the exception of one or two small land disputes they have had no duties'.[88] Requests for a separate Committee for the populous Wairoa district had been declined on the grounds that as there was 'no present urgency...the matter might be allowed to remain in abeyance',[89] and by 1891 the Hawke's Bay Committee was 'just "fooling round" with small and trivial cases, and, in fact, doing nothing in particular'.[90]

Other requests for Committees were also 'allowed to remain in abeyance', sometimes for surprising, if revealing, reasons.[91] The Tuhoe and Ngati Awa tribes had been included in the huge Opotiki Committee district, along with Whakatohea, Ngai Tai and Whanau-a-Apanui, but by 1886 were agitating to have their own separate Committees.[92] Ballance informed Ngati Awa that their 600-strong tribe was not large enough to justify a separate Committee, and that they would have to expand their boundaries to include more than 1000 people before he would consider the request.[93] By 1887 Ngati Awa had complied with this condition, and had even elected their own Committee in anticipation of the government's approval.[94] They had expanded their boundaries by incorporating Tuhoe within their proposed district, however, and apart from the indignant response this predictably provoked from the latter tribe, Bush, the Opotiki Resident Magistrate, reported a more fundamental reason for declining Ngati Awa's request:

> These natives seem most anxious for this Committee, but as more than likely a majority of its members when elected will be Te Kooti-ites, it is a question as to whether their request should be complied with. It would scarcely do to have a nominal Committee under the Native Committees Act, which while elected under that Act, were under Te Kooti's orders, and conformed to his wishes. It is stated by

> some persons, that all that is required is to have the sanction of the Government for their Committee, having obtained that, they propose working it on Te Kooti principles, under the circumstances I cannot see how their request can be complied with.⁹⁵

Ballance accordingly declined to establish a separate Committee district for Ngati Awa. By the following year, though, Tuhoe had also set up their own committee, possibly as a successor (or complement) to Te Whitu Tekau,⁹⁶ and were seeking official status for it. Rakuraku Rehua wrote to the Native Minister from Te Waimana in September 1888:

> This is to inform you of the election of a Committee for Tuhoe for the purpose of dealing with their local affairs within their own boundaries, as all strife, perverse dealings, and acts of violence have ceased, and all have mutually settled down under the law. They have passed resolutions touching their lands that all surveys are to be considered and dealt with by the Committee only, not by any one or two individuals or more, and that the question of Europeans wishing to prospect for gold and the granting of permission to do so is to be dealt with solely by the Committee, not by any one, two, or more individuals.
>
> The idea in this respect is to prevent difficulty and trouble arising within the boundaries of their territories.⁹⁷

The request to sanction the appointment of an official Committee for the Urewera district was ignored. Six months later Bush wrote that:

> You must bear in mind that the Urewera are all Kooti-ites. Rakuraku is one of his greatest supporters, and that consequently any Committee formed would probably be conducted on Te Kooti principles, which are to keep the country locked up. He does not approve of lands being surveyed, or passed through the Court, as he is evidently of opinion that these two things help the natives to part with their lands. If there would be any chance of the Urewera acting sensibly, and allowing gold prospecting, and such like within their territory, then certainly I think it would be a great advantage to constitute their country into a separate Committee district, but of

this I am doubtful. The Urewera have always had a tribal Committee termed the "Seventy". This Committee has always opposed the making of roads, surveys, and prospecting. The question is would another Committee be more amenable to reason. I am doubtful.[98]

With Tuhoe being so 'unreasonable' as to oppose the Native Land Court and surveys, there was little prospect of the tribe being granted their own Committee. Clearly, to the extent that the Committees were intended to do anything useful this was to be in the direction of facilitating the work of the Court. Yet most Maori had always looked upon their Committees, official or otherwise, as alternatives to the Native Land Court rather than as impotent appendages to it. Ironically, Tuhoe's 'unreasonableness' eventually compelled the Crown to grant them large powers of self-government over the Urewera district in return for limited concessions. Elsewhere, though, the failure of the Native Committees Act to meet Maori aspirations did little to stem the growing tide of opposition to the work of the Land Court, nor to quench the Maori appetite for representative and powerful committees as agencies of tribal control.[99]

# 8. Autonomy Denied: Continuing Maori Efforts

Maori efforts to gain real powers for representative tribal committees continued throughout the 1880s and 1890s. They were underlain by an increasing tendency towards intertribal cooperation, and even received occasional support from influential Pakeha. In 1884 Wi Pere, who had that year been elected MHR for Eastern Maori, endeavoured unsuccessfully to pass a Native Lands Act Amendment Bill intended to substantially increase Maori involvement in determining titles to land and in deciding collectively the fate of these once legal ownership had been determined.[1] Under this bill each Native Committee would have selected five persons to act as Assessors in the Native Land Court, at least three of whom would decide all questions of title in conjunction with the presiding Judge, with the concurrence of a majority of the Assessors required before any decision could be reached.[2] The owners of the block would have then elected their own committee empowered to decide on all dealings with respect to it, subject to ratification by at least three-quarters of the owners.

W.L. Rees, who along with Pere had set up the failed New Zealand Native Land Settlement Company in an effort to overcome the problems associated with individualised title,[3] also supported the idea of tribal control of land through the mechanism of the committee. In a lengthy memorandum on native land laws, which was laid on the table of the House in 1884, Rees wrote that

> the history of legislation for and administration of Native lands has been a scandal to the colony. The principal cause conducing to the ridiculous and perplexing number and contradictory character of the Native Land Acts is found in the efforts always made by their

> framers to deal with Maori tribes owning land as if they were Englishmen, owning in severalty under a title of freehold. It ought to be remembered that Maoris hold land not in severalty, but in common. The land is the heritage of the tribe or hapu. ...
>
> A very gross act of cruelty and bad faith as well as folly was perpetrated by us when we compelled the Natives to hold their lands as individuals. The Treaty of Waitangi assured them of 'all their rights in their lands'. The chief right of all was the right of tribal ownership – but a tribe of five hundred persons is totally different from five hundred distinct and opposing claimants. It is the tribe which owns the land, and it is the tribe which, in justice, ought to have sole power to use it or to deal with it.[4]

Rees believed that the one plan 'entirely consistent with Maori ideas' was for 'tribal dealings through the instrumentality of committees chosen by the owners of the different blocks of land, around all which dealings such restrictions and safeguards shall be placed as will satisfy justice and prudence'.

Ballance, the Native Minister, was ready enough to pay lip service to the idea of granting enlarged powers to the Native Committees set up under the 1883 Act, but as the course of the Native Lands Alienation Restriction Act of 1884 showed, was not yet willing to act on this. Although the Act was intended primarily to reimpose Crown pre-emption over an area of some four million acres in the vicinity of the North Island main trunk railway, Te Wahanui had informed both chambers of Parliament that the main concern of Ngati Maniapoto was that the Native Land Court should be excluded from the district, with the Native Committee empowered to rule on all land transactions.[5] Ballance, as was seen, promised to increase the powers of the Committees but was not prepared to admit that the Court should not continue to function as the primary institution for determining native title. John Bryce, Ballance's predecessor in office, not surprisingly also supported this view, considering that while they might act as 'assistants to the Court', it would be 'entirely hopeless to expect that any Maori Committee could progress in the settlement of title if left to themselves'.[6]

Wi Pere believed otherwise, and endeavoured unsuccessfully during the bill's committal stages to insert amendments giving Native Committees power to determine title and administer the lands.[7] When the bill was referred to the Legislative Council a few days later, several members were outspoken in their condemnation of speculative dealings with individual owners. J.C. Richmond launched a strong attack on the Native Land Court, which he described as:

> that Frankenstein power created by the State...which, blinded by its own fanaticism and vanity, proceeded remorselessly through thick and thin; and which insisted on finding what never existed – a Native land law – and insisted upon manufacturing it if it did not find it.[8]

The Council adopted Pere's proposed amendments giving power to the Committees, but when the amended bill was referred back to the House for approval the Premier, Robert Stout, outlined a number of reasons why the Council's amendments should not be approved, including that:

> there is no reason to suppose that Native Committees have yet attained the position which would justify the Legislature in placing them as arbiters between the owners of land and the representatives of the Crown.[9]

Sir George Grey considered Stout's objections 'baseless' and believed the Committees would be 'absolutely able' to conduct land dealings with the Crown. Te Puke Te Ao, the member for Western Maori, asserted that:

> the Native Committee is most fitted to decide who are the owners of the land, because the Europeans have not the knowledge of Maori customs which the Native Committees have. All that Europeans know about is the money...I do not think the Government should stand in the way of Committees administering the land. This House has already given authority to Native Committees in the year 1883. This House passed the Native Committees Act in 1883. Now, I have heard the Premier state that he will not consent to give that power to the Native Committees.

Why, then, was the power given to them last year, and why should it be taken from them now?[10]

Ihaka Hakuene, who had replaced Tawhai as the Northern Maori representative, was slightly more cautious, suggesting that the Committees manage the lands in conjunction with the government to prevent abuses by either party.[11] But it was Wi Pere who delivered the most ardent speech in defence of the Council's amendments, asserting that though the other chamber had 'evinced some consideration for them', 'this House is going to murder the Natives', and declaring his willingness to talk for as long as it would take to get the government to accept that the Native Committees should administer the lands. Pere's attempted filibuster inevitably provoked nothing more than the wrath of Stout, who made the familiar allegation that the 'obstructive course' the Maori members were taking had been instigated by designing Europeans. When the House's objections were referred back to the Legislative Council, P.A. Buckley, the Colonial Secretary, stated that:

> As to the amendments regarding Native Committees, I confess that at the time it was made its importance did not strike me. But I find that these Native Committees have not worked up to the present. No one knows anything about their working – no one knows what their position may be – no one, in fact, knows anything about them.[12]

Waterhouse, J.C. Richmond and Pollen all spoke in favour of the amendments, largely out of concern that Ngati Maniapoto would withdraw their support for the railway unless they were granted a voice in the management of their own lands. Wi Tako Ngatata also supported retaining the amendments, informing the Council that Te Wahanui had requested him to do so. But a motion that the amendments be insisted on was lost by eighteen votes to twelve.[13] A potentially promising opportunity for at least two of the Committees (Kawhia and Whanganui) to gain effective control over their own lands had been declined in favour of continuing the Native Land Court's hegemony over Maori.

The split which had developed between Ngati Maniapoto and the King party as the government sought to open up the King Country threatened to undermine Tawhiao's position as the effective ruler of a sizeable territory in the centre of the North Island. In 1883 he had abandoned his former policy of isolation and travelled around the North Island, and in 1884 he decided to follow the example set by Ngapuhi by travelling to England to lay his grievances before the Queen.[14] Like Taiwhanga's before it, Tawhiao's petition contained a lengthy recital of many of the familiar Maori grievances, including the Waitara purchase and subsequent war and confiscation, the treatment of Te Whiti, and the Maori people's exclusion from any real share of power over the administration of their lands or other affairs. The petition stated that:

> The Native Land Court, instituted...by the Government,...was adopted...in order to destroy the rights of the Maoris over their own land, rights secured to them by the Queen in the Treaty of Waitangi.
>
> A fresh rule was thus established, by which the Court had full powers, its authority was entirely in European hands, and the Maoris were denied all authority. It was established that ten persons were to be allowed claims over any section of ground, the majority were to rest satisfied with no land to live on, and the lands were ultimately alienated by purchase. Another rule was set up by the Court, that if the claimants failed to present themselves to the Court the land should be handed over to others, and thus the lands were sold, including the lands, the homesteads, and the plantations, and the real owners of the land were left destitute. When the Maori race asked that they might be allowed to deal with their own lands by means of their own committees, the Government declined. In cases where Europeans purchased land from Maoris who received money for lands not theirs, the purchase thus made was established to the purchasers. Assessors were, indeed, appointed for the Courts, but they had no power to say anything with regard to the lands dealt with by the Court.[15]

After referring to their under-representation in Parliament, Tawhiao requested that the Queen grant her Maori subjects their own separate government, empowered to pass laws with respect to their own lands and other local affairs, with a Maori commissioner appointed to mediate between the races on matters such as the leasing and selling of lands. The greater portion of the taxes paid by Maori should be handed over to their own government, and a commission should be appointed by the Queen to inquire into all confiscations and other wrongful taking of land. Beyond this, Tawhiao asked that:

> the European Judges in the Native Land Court be superseded, and that your Maori race be then permitted to direct their own affairs in that Court; that they may be empowered to appoint their own Judges over their own lands, lest they be all lost by the present doings of the Court; that they may be able to deal with these lands in accordance with their own customs, apportioning to each tribe their share, and, having made all ready for leasing or selling, to submit all rulings to the Commissioner appointed by you, that he may look into the whole affair, and see that no injurious effects come upon the Maori, and then he is to submit all to your Governor for confirmation.

Tawhiao was no more successful than Taiwhanga had been in gaining an audience with the Queen, but did get to present the petition to the new Secretary of State, Lord Derby, who once again referred the matter back to the New Zealand government for comment.[16] The official reply from Stout nearly nine months later was predictably hostile. The Premier suggested – misleadingly – that it would 'least embarrass' the Imperial government to refer only to matters since 1865, implying that the colonial administration bore no responsibility for native affairs prior to that year. Since that time, Stout asserted, there had been 'no infraction of the Treaty of Waitangi'. Section 71 of the New Zealand Constitution Act had been cited in support of Maori administering their own affairs, but he maintained that this provision had been intended to be used 'for a short time and under the then special circumstances of the colony'. Stout added that:

> So far as allowing the laws, customs, and usages of the Natives in all their relations to and dealings with each other to be maintained, Ministers would point out that this has been the policy of all the Native Land Acts. The Courts that have to deal with Native land...decide according to Native customs or usage...[17]

Perhaps someone should have told the Court's Judges this. Further comments by the Premier were just as far-fetched:

> What...the petitioners desire is really the setting up of a Parliament in certain parts of the North Island which would not be under the control of the General Assembly of New Zealand. Seeing that in the Legislative Council and the House of Representatives the Natives are represented by able chiefs, and that they have practically no local affairs to look after that cannot be done by their Committees – local bodies recognized by the Government – Ministers do not deem it necessary to point out the unreasonableness and absurdity of such a request.

The reality was that there were practically no local affairs that *could* be handled by the Committees, since they had been denied jurisdiction to do anything except arbitrate in petty disputes and inform the Native Land Court of their opinions on cases before them. Moreover, with the exception of minor private legislation such as the Taiaroa Land Act of 1883, there had been little to show for Maori representation in Parliament, with a long string of bills almost all of which sought to gain a greater say for Maori over their own affairs having been voted down by the Pakeha members.[18]

Tawhiao's reply to news of the petition's rejection is worthy of lengthy quotation. The Maori King informed the Governor that:

> with reference to the statement that since 1865, England ceased to interfere in the management of affairs in New Zealand, and left them to be managed by the Government of New Zealand, it may be so! But the Maori people are not aware of the reasons that led their pakeha friends to apply to have the sole management of affairs in New Zealand, and the assent thereto of the Queen's Government was given without considering the Maori people or making any

enquiries of them. Because the right of governing and the occupation of this island by Europeans dates from the Treaty of Waitangi, and it was left to the Chiefs, the Hapus of the Native people, and Her Majesty to carry out the provisions of the Treaty of Waitangi which became a covenant on the descendants.

And further with reference to the statement made by your Ministers that 'there has been no infraction of the Treaty of Waitangi' we would ask 'What portion of the Treaty of Waitangi, what Hapus or what Chiefs placed the authority over the Native Lands under the Native Land Court or gave the Europeans the sole power to deal with Maori lands in that Court; or what Hapus or Native Chiefs have had the direction of Native Lands according to Maori usage in that Court, as stated in the paragraph respecting the Native Land Court in that petition'.

And further with reference to the statement respecting the presence of Native Members in the Legislature, the status of those Members was pointed out in the petition – taking the basis of population one Native Member is returned for more than 20,000 persons, whereas one European Member is returned for every 5,000. When indeed have the applications of those Members for increased representation been acceded to by that Parliament? When indeed have the applications of those Members to have the grievances of the Native people redressed been acceded to by that Parliament? When indeed have the applications of those Members asking that the Natives should have the power of administering their own lands been acceded to by that Parliament?[19]

Tawhiao asked that a copy of this letter be forwarded to the Imperial government. Ballance, however, considered its 'tone' such that a simple acknowledgement would suffice, whilst Governor Jervois opined that 'the Natives generally have been exceptionally well treated in New Zealand & have nothing to complain about'.[20]

There remained no shortage of complaints, however, and following news of the failure of Tawhiao's petition about a thousand supporters of the King from throughout the central North Island met at Poutu, near Lake Taupo, where a number of resolutions were passed. According to Scannell, the Taupo Resident Magistrate:

> all were unanimous in agreeing that all the tribes were to unite as one people; to acknowledge Tawhiao as king of all the Natives in New Zealand, acknowledging the Queen's authority, but not that of the Colonial Government; to withdraw the adjudication of their lands from the Native Land Court; to allow no surveys, sales, or leases of lands; to allow no spirits to be sold or stores for the sale of European goods to be kept within the boundaries of what they call the King country..; to abstain from voting for Native members of the House of Representatives; [and] that Native Committees should be appointed under Tawhiao's authority throughout the Island to manage their local affairs.[21]

As was seen previously, by November 1885 King committees had been set up in the Rohe Potae and Hauraki districts, but were unsuccessful in their efforts to gain official recognition. In May of the following year Tawhiao forwarded to the government a proposed bill providing for the establishment of a Maori Council under the direction of the King, with all existing Native Committees placed under the administrative authority of the Council and empowered to 'deal with their difficulties, land claims, disputes, and other troubles concerning themselves'. The Treaty of Waitangi, section 71 of the 1852 Constitution Act, and Governor Gore Browne's 1860 reaffirmation of the Crown's commitment to honour the terms of the Treaty were all cited in support of the right of Maori to administer their own lands and other affairs and of the abolition of the Native Land Court and 'the many other things that create evil'.[22] Ballance, though, was again dismissive. The Native Land Court, he claimed, was supported by 'almost all the tribes', the Maori Councils envisaged by section 71 of the Constitution Act were intended to be of a 'temporary nature only' and to finally introduce them, 34 years later, would 'be acting directly contrary to the spirit of the Constitution Act itself'.[23]

While Tawhiao's proposal for the establishment of a Maori Council under his own personal supervision was acceptable to his supporters, it was less so to the tribes outside the King movement.[24] Kotahitanga still had some way to go, despite intermittent efforts during the 1880s at cooperation between the Kingitanga and tribes which had always remained aloof from it. Meanwhile, Ballance was able to cite the Native Lands Administration Act passed into law in August 1886 as evidence of his government's willingness to listen to Maori demands. But although the extensive consultation with Maori which preceded the passing of Ballance's Act was a novel and refreshing change, as was the recognition of tribal ownership of lands which it contained, the Native Lands Administration Act ultimately proved a dead letter because of the Minister's failure to listen to Maori concerns about the proposed legislation. Numerous requests that the Committees established under the 1883 Act be empowered to investigate titles were ignored by Ballance, despite his constant assurances to the contrary. The 1886 Act made no provision for greater powers to be granted to the District Committees, but instead provided for the owners of a block, once determined by the Native Land Court, to elect their own Committee empowered to decide on the terms of any sale or lease, which would be undertaken by a government-appointed District Commissioner. Scarred by their experiences under the ten-owner rule, many Maori feared placing their lands in the hands of a Committee over which the remaining owners had no control, and were even less enamoured with the notion of a Pakeha official undertaking to dispose of their lands.[25] James Carroll, for example, giving evidence to the Native Affairs Committee on an earlier version of the bill in 1885, stated that the Hawke's Bay and East Coast tribes he represented were concerned that the proposed legislation 'places too much power in the hands of the Government', and that by it 'they would be robbed in a great measure of their independence...in connection with their lands':

> there seemed to be a want in the Bill of some provision so that the owners might control the Committee. The Bill states that the Committee shall issue instructions to the Commissioner,

whereupon the Commissioner shall proceed to carry out these instructions. There is nothing in the Bill to show that these directions shall come from the owners of the block. They think it is possible that a Committee of seven might act on their own account, independent altogether of the wishes of the owners.[26]

Wi Pere's 1884 bill had stipulated that the block committees should first obtain the consent of three-quarters of the land's owners before proceeding with any proposed dealings. Under Ballance's legislation, however, the committees were not required to gain the consent of the owners before dealing with the land, and the only safeguard included was provision for the interests of dissentients to be partitioned out (and for the Committee to be dissolved upon application of two-thirds of the owners). Wahanui had also told the Native Affairs Committee that he wished the block committees set up in such a way that 'their only power is to carry out the wishes of the owners of the land', and again reiterated Ngati Maniapoto's opposition to the Native Land Court and their desire that land titles be investigated and determined by the existing Native Committees.[27]

Similar representations were made to the Native Minister at a widely-attended meeting convened at Waipatu, near Hastings, early in 1886. Ballance was informed that those represented at the meeting were in favour of committees being elected to administer Maori lands provided these acted in accordance with the wishes of the owners, and that they desired that 'Native Committees may be substituted for the Native Land Court'.[28] Wi Pere told the Minister that 'the Act of 1883 was deficient. There was no real power given to the Committees'.[29] Ballance, in reply, told the meeting that he was in favour of granting the Native Committees power to investigate titles, with a right of appeal to the Native Land Court, and that he hoped to introduce some measure along those lines. As further evidence of his willingness to strengthen the Committees, Ballance cited the fact that he had introduced salaries for their Chairmen and authorised them to frank mail, had instructed Land Court Registrars that copies of all applications for surveys should be forwarded to the Committees, and had proclaimed new Committee districts such as Tauranga.[30] Apparently satisfied with this explanation, and with Ballance's assurance that the government would ensure that the new block committees were directly accountable to the owners, the meeting ended with a general endorsement of the Minister's policies.

The Act eventually passed by Ballance barely reflected the extensive consultation that had preceded its passage through Parliament. While some of the Maori representatives were inclined to support it on the basis that it was at least an improvement on what had preceded it, the reception from the broader Maori community was almost universally hostile. Parliament was soon inundated with petitions calling for the repeal of the Act, and Hoani Taipua, the member for Western Maori, no doubt looking to boost his standing with the voters in election year, tried in 1887 to pass legislation repealing its provisions with respect to his electorate.[31] The Commissioners appointed under the Act were also flooded with letters from Maori around the country objecting to the mana over their lands being placed in the hands of the government,[32] and in 1888 reported that only one small block had been brought under its provisions.[33] As the Native Land Laws Commission of 1891 commented:

> The Native Land Administration Act of 1886 was inoperative owing to two reasons, the first of these being that the total control of their lands was taken away from the Maoris and placed in the hands of persons not in any way responsible to them; the second, that the Act was made optional and not imperative. The Natives objected to being totally deprived of all authority and management of their ancestral lands, and therefore they refused to bring those lands under the Administration Act.[34]

With many settlers and speculators also opposed to the prohibition on direct private purchase contained in the Act, the election of a government dominated by advocates of 'free trade' in Maori land late in 1887 spelled doom for Ballance's short-lived experiment with block committees, and under the Native Land Act 1888 individual owners were once again permitted to dispose

*Autonomy Denied*

of their interests however they saw fit.

While the Atkinson ministry claimed that in repealing the Native Lands Administration Act, thereby allowing Maori to dispose of their lands as they chose, they were meeting Maori aspirations, few tribal leaders viewed matters this way.[35] In April and May 1888 a series of large intertribal gatherings were held at Waiomatatini, Omaanu, Waitangi, and Putiki. At the last meeting a draft bill encapsulating the dominant Maori viewpoint on land legislation was drawn up for forwarding to Parliament. Central to the bill's provisions were clauses stating that:

> The Maori Committees, as appointed under 'The Native Committees Act, 1883', shall be empowered to act as the Native Land Court, and to have the same jurisdiction as the said Court.

> 'The Native Committees Act, 1883', shall be so amended that the said Committees shall be released from the control of the Government, and that the Chairman shall have the power, with his Committee, to deal with cases according to Native custom when any future Native Land Court Acts are being passed. The Committee to decide such matters as they may see clear.[36]

At this meeting a representative committee of chiefs, including Paora Tuhaere, Major Kemp and more than a dozen others, was elected to promote Maori interests in Wellington.[37] In August 1888 Tuhaere and two other chiefs, Wiremu Pomare of Whangarei and Akuhata Hori Tupaea of Tauranga, were permitted to address the Legislative Council on the subject of the Native Land Bills then before the Assembly. Tuhaere told the Council that they had been delegated by their people to express their opposition to the proposed measures and to request that further consideration of the bills be held over until after a meeting at Waitangi the following March. He also stated that Maori desired that:

> the Native Committees should have power to adjudicate on the title to Native lands and that the only work remaining for the Government to do should be to give effect to their decisions. Let me and my Native people have charge of our own lands for ourselves.[38]

Tuhaere's comments were echoed by the other two speakers but ignored by Parliament, which proceeded to pass the legislation regardless, and a further appeal to the Governor to ask the Queen to disallow the 1888 Native Lands Act met with no more success.[39] Hirini Taiwhanga, who had been elected MHR for Northern Maori in 1887, had tried to stonewall the passage of the legislation, and when he failed introduced his own bill providing for the appointment of a committee of eight Maori, including the four parliamentary representatives, to seek such relief for Maori whose rights and privileges under the Treaty of Waitangi had been abrogated as they deemed appropriate.[40] Predictably, this made little progress in the Assembly.

The election of a Liberal government intent on 'closer settlement' at the end of 1890 heralded a radical shift away from the 'free trade' approach of the previous administration, but hardly in the direction favoured by Maori. In the south, where little Maori land remained, such a policy may have been based on 'busting up' the estates of large European runholders, but in the North Island it was firmly premised on extensive Crown acquisitions of Maori territory. As Tom Brooking says, almost every aspect of Liberal Maori land policy in the 1890s 'was coercive and punitive'.[41] This occurred, moreover, despite the fact that one of the first acts of the new government was to appoint a commission of inquiry into native land laws, headed by W.L. Rees, long an advocate of Maori committees, with James Carroll, the part-European Ngati Kahungunu MHR for Eastern Maori, and Thomas Mackay, a former West Coast Commissioner, as the other members. Mackay dissented from many parts of the Commission's report, but died before completing his own. Mackay's unfinished report advocated that land titles should be investigated by tribal committees, convened under the supervision of district commissioners, each 'composed of one leading chief of each hapu or sub-tribe claiming to be owners', with decisions arrived at forwarded to the Native Land Court for confirmation and the existing committee or a new one deciding on the subsequent administration of the lands.[42] Indeed, that Maori committees should play a much greater role in the determination of titles and subsequent administration of land was possibly the only point on which all three Commissioners were in agreement, with Carroll dissenting from the Chairman's key recommendation that Crown pre-emption be reimposed, a position he reversed soon enough when appointed to the Executive Council in 1892.[43]

In their main report, Rees and Carroll condemned the evil effects of the Native Land Court system and the breakdown in tribal society which it had promoted. 'For a quarter century', they wrote:

> the Native-land law and the Native Land Courts have drifted from bad to worse. The old public and tribal method of purchase was finally discarded for private and individual dealings. Secrecy, which is ever a badge of fraud, was observed. All the power of the natural leaders of the Maori people was undermined. A slave or a child was in reality placed on an equality with the noblest rangatira (chief) or the boldest warrior of the tribe. An easy entrance into the title of every block could be found for some paltry bribe. The charmed circle once broken, the European gradually pushed the Maori out and took possession. Sometimes the means used were fair, sometimes they were not.
>
> The alienation of Native land under this law took its very worst form and its most disastrous tendency. It was obtained from a helpless people. The crowds of owners in a memorial of ownership were like a flock of sheep without a shepherd, a watch-dog, or a leader. Mostly ignorant barbarians, they became suddenly possessed of a title to land which was a marketable commodity. The right to occupy and cultivate possessed by their fathers became in their hands an estate which could be sold. The strength which lies in union was taken from them. The authority of their natural rulers was destroyed. They were surrounded by temptations.[44]

The intricacies of completing a transaction under the 1873 Native Lands Act had been such as to create 'a state of confusion and anarchy' that even lawyers were forced to admit they could not fully unravel. And the only redeeming piece of native land legislation, the Native Lands Administration Act of 1886, had proven inoperative because Maori objected to being totally deprived of all authority and management over their lands, whilst the Native Committees Act of 1883 was little more than 'a hollow shell' which mocked Maori with a mere semblance of authority.

The only solution to these problems, the Commissioners believed, was to return to tribal or corporate dealings in land. Summarising the considerable body of evidence presented to them, Rees and Carroll noted that:

> The unanimity of the Natives was not merely negative, and condemnatory of the past and present – it was also displayed in their wishes for the future. Everywhere they gave substantially the same evidence as to the desire of the tribes regarding the future management of their land. Titles they believe can be found and determined, boundaries can be settled, and lists of owners prepared, by the Maoris themselves, leaving only a few disputed cases to be determined by the Court.[45]

Although averse to selling the freehold to their lands, most Maori were, the report added, willing – indeed anxious – to lease part of their estates, and believed that a committee chosen from the owners could arrange this in conjunction with a government officer. Rees and Carroll proposed that the Native Land Court be retained 'to decide cases of dispute as a last resort', but remodelled through the appointment of district Judges. The Commissioners believed, however, that 'Maori Committees and runangas will be able generally to decide both as to boundaries and ownership, and the Court will only be called on to decide in extreme cases, and upon the evidence already given before the runanga'. Block committees acting under the supervision of a district commissioner would then decide on the disposal of the land, dealing exclusively with a Native Land Board, half of whose members would be appointed by the tribal committees.[46]

There was, not surprisingly, considerable support for the notion of committees determining titles and administering the lands amongst the many Maori communities visited by the Commission. The proposals put forward by Rees and Carroll were in many respects simply a reiteration of what Maori themselves had long been requesting, and many spoke of their frustration at the limited powers granted the Native Committees elected under the 1883 Act. At Cambridge, Hitiri Te Paerata informed the Commissioners that 'The Ngatituwharetoa have been praying the Government for a long time to give them a Committee, but without success'. What they wanted, he stated, was 'a separate and independent Committee, not one mixed up with another tribe' and 'clothed with the same power as that which the Land Court possesses'.[47] At Kawakawa, Wiremu Pomare told the Commission that Ngapuhi's own committees had laid down the boundary lines between different hapu and settled other disputes to the satisfaction of all parties, but the government would 'not listen to the decisions we have come to'.[48] And at Waipawa many Ngati Kahungunu speakers complained of the 'feeble' nature of the official Native Committees, Renata Pukututu stating that:

> At present the District Committee of Hawke's Bay are just 'fooling round' with small and trivial cases, and, in fact, doing nothing in particular. Their time is altogether taken up with the investigation of petty cases. We hope that the Government will clothe the Native Committees with proper and sufficient power.[49]

Further support for the granting of real and effective powers to the Committees came at a series of meetings held throughout the North Island in 1891, from which a delegation of 30 chiefs was selected to travel to Wellington to lay their concerns before the government. In a letter to the Maori parliamentary representatives, the delegation stated that:

> The principal points on which the natives were unanimous at these meetings are as follows, namely:
>
> (a) That the power to manage their own lands be returned to the Maori people.
>
> (b) That the Maori district committees be empowered to adjudicate upon native lands, and lands which have not been adjudicated upon by the Native Land Court, and also with subdivisions and successions, having similar powers to the Native Land Court.

(c) That the co-owners of any block of land should have power to appoint a committee to manage their lands.

(d) That a committee be appointed to decide any land disputes in which natives and Europeans or the Government are involved, and also to consider all oppressive laws, and all purchases, leases, and judgements, and all other grievances since the Treaty of Waitangi.

(e) That any sale of individual interests, whether to Government or other persons, be void and of no effect unless and until the land has been individualised.[50]

Unless these principles were agreed to, the Maori parliamentarians were informed, they should withdraw and take no further part in the proceedings of the House.

Yet despite the fact that a royal commission of inquiry had endorsed essentially the same principles, and had advanced detailed proposals for committees to investigate titles and administer lands once awarded, there remained little willingness on the part of the government to accept them. A Validation Court was established, a Native Land Purchase Board created, and Crown pre-emption effectively reimposed, but the proposals concerning committees were completely ignored as the Liberal government instead embarked on an aggressive land purchase policy.[51] In 1892 Carroll introduced an amendment to the Native Committees Act of 1883 providing for these Committees to have powers to investigate titles, and for the election of block committees to administer the lands, as had been recommended by the Native Land Laws Commission of which he was a member.[52] This bill failed to even gain a second reading. In a separate debate Eparaima Kapa, the member for Northern Maori, asked pointedly: 'What is there unreasonable in the demand we have made for many years that power should be given to our Native committees to investigate titles to our lands'.[53] And in the same debate Hoani Taipua of Western Maori stated that he had:

> often pointed out in this House that there is a simple method by

which the Court could be relieved of a great deal of its work, and things made much easier for all parties – that is, to set up Native committees, and give them sufficient power to fix tribal boundaries and deal with their lands, and then to apply to the Native Land Court to have all their proceedings confirmed. I have brought that question before the House at various times for several years, but it appears to find no favour in the eyes of the Ministry of the day...All the proceedings connected with the Native Land Court are ruinously expensive...The total sum which the Natives have to pay in the way of charges for investigating the title to their land sometimes amounts to as much as the land is worth. This costly method is the only method which the Natives have of investigating the title to their land. It is on account of all these difficulties that I am so persistent in urging that the experiment should be made of submitting the management of the Native land to Native committees, to see if they could not carry on the investigation in a better manner.[54]

Maori outside Parliament were equally persistent in their calls to be granted greater rights of self-government. In 1891 Te Arawa petitioned the Queen for the formation of 'a representative council, to be elected by your Maori subjects, as a mountain of rest from which all measures affecting the Maori people can be clearly reviewed, and all matters also affecting the Natives can be dealt with'.[55] In January 1892 representatives of tribes from throughout the country gathered at Parikino, on the Whanganui River, where they reached agreement to boycott the Native Land Court and refrain from further sales, and formed a committee of 80 to draft alternative legislation.[56] Boycotts of the Native Land Court were a frequent phenomenon in the 1890s; but despite the initial enthusiasm with which these were taken up by Maori around the country, they were hardly a sustainable form of protest, given the rich rewards available to individuals or hapu who ignored them, in the form of the lands of the boycotters. By the 1890s, even the formerly staunch 'loyalist' Major Kemp was wearily advising that it was 'no use as of old putting our words on paper and sending that to the government...as we would be replied to by deceit, and by words intended to make us believe one thing, when the contrary is meant'.[57] Instead, many Maori sought to gain acceptance for an assembly of their own, to oversee block committees with genuine powers to administer Maori lands.

In April 1892, more than a thousand Maori from throughout the country gathered at Waitangi and agreed to form a kotahitanga, or union of the tribes, to debate alternative policies and present a united front to the government on Maori grievances. Arrangements were made for the election of a Maori Parliament, to be convened at Waipatu in June 1892, and one of the fundamental tenets which the movement committed itself to at the Waitangi meeting was the abolition of the Native Land Court and its replacement by Maori committees.[58] At the second sitting of the Maori Parliament, also at Waipatu, in April and May 1893, a Federated Maori Assembly Empowering Bill crystallising many of the movement's demands was drafted for forwarding to the General Assembly along with a lengthy petition outlining Maori grievances with respect to their lands. The Maori people had, the petition stated, ever since the signing of the Treaty of Waitangi 'always desired to live in amity with the white people that come to settle in these Islands, as we have always had a desire to learn from them the way to acquire wealth and to live in peace'. But when Parliament was set up in 1854 'the Maori people could not understand it, and many apprehended evil', considering that 'the new Government would, by its work, deprive the Natives of their lands', in consequence of which a Maori King had been set up. War had resulted, the petitioners noting that many Maori had fought alongside the Queen's soldiers against their own relatives, and that had they not done so, 'the authority or sovereignty of and over New Zealand would have ceased long ago, and the white people would have abandoned these islands there and then'. Following the wars, the Native Land Court had been set up, the administration of which was 'becoming more and more confusing and unsatisfactory'. 'It injures, but never benefits, the people', the petition tersely stated. The practice of the Court was 'a complete innovation' to the

Maori people, who were debarred from dealing with their lands tribally and left 'like sheep without a shepherd, being driven hither and thither'. Maori were 'perfectly capable of taking care of themselves and their properties, if they were allowed to do so', but were denied the opportunity by Parliament, which continued to make unjust laws and treated Maori wishes as 'the murmuring of the wind'. What they desired, the petition stated, was:

> (1) That the right to manage our own property be given back to us; so that peace and happiness may reign throughout these islands.
>
> (2) That the power to govern the Natives be delegated to the Federated Maori Assembly of New Zealand.
>
> (3) That the said Assembly consist of an Upper and a Lower House. The Upper to consist of the chiefs by birth.
>
> (4) And the Lower House shall consist of Natives who shall be elected by the different tribes to represent them in the Assembly.
>
> (5) The said Federated Assembly to have power to appoint District Committees comprised of Maoris, who shall investigate titles to Native lands, and subdivide the same, according to the rules of equity and good conscience.[59]

The preamble to the accompanying draft bill again cited the Treaty of Waitangi and section 71 of the Constitution Act in support of Maori claims to self-government, along with a supporting petition signed by over 21,900 people (nearly half the entire Maori population). Most of the ten clauses in the draft bill concerned the appointment of district Maori committees, which were to operate under the direct control of the Federated Maori Assembly, though with the ultimate sanction of the Governor still required before any judgements could be confirmed. There was no place for the Native Land Court in the Maori Parliament's plans. Clause 10 of the draft bill provided simply for its abolition.

There was little prospect of a government which in private could boast about breaking the annual record for Maori land purchase[60], even contemplating for a moment the abolition of the one institution that made this state land grab possible, let alone providing Maori with the means to retain some tribal cohesion and ownership of their lands. Indeed, by 1894 even James Carroll, newly promoted to the Cabinet and no longer dependent on Maori votes for his political future, was describing the idea of Maori committees investigating land titles as an 'absurdity'.[61]

Carroll's comments came in a debate over the Maori Parliament's latest bill, which had been introduced into the House by Hone Heke, a leading figure in the Kotahitanga movement, who had been elected MHR for Northern Maori in 1893 at the age of just 24. Heke's Native Rights Bill provided simply for a constitution to be granted to all persons of the Maori race, 'providing for the enactment of laws by a Parliament elected by such persons', such laws to 'relate to and exclusively deal with the personal rights and with the lands and all other property of the aboriginal native inhabitants of New Zealand'.[62] Supported outside the House by a Maori committee led by Te Heuheu, Heke introduced the bill for its second reading by quoting in full from a number of documents which he believed supported Maori claims to some form of self-government, including the 1835 Declaration of Independence, the Treaty of Waitangi, section 71 of the Constitution Act, and King Tawhiao's 1886 bill providing for the establishment of a Maori Council. Every Act passed by Parliament since 1854 had been 'disastrous' to the Maori race, according to Heke, and all Maori now desired was a 'separate tribunal' to enable them to make their own laws.[63]

Carroll, in reply, stated that it would be a 'kindness' to free Maori from the 'delusion' that Parliament would ever grant them a separate constitution, and added that:

> They had been told that the Native Land Court was a source of great dissatisfaction to the Native people; but did the honourable gentleman propose in his Bill what should take its place? He had not told the House what the Native mind was as to the investigation of titles to their lands, and he presumed he meant that the work of the Native Land Court should hereafter be carried on by Native committees. If that were so, that experiment had been tried already.

> There was an Act passed in 1883 forming Native committees, but in actual experience that Act was found to be totally unworkable, and particularly to the Natives themselves, who had not the slightest idea of conceiving any method or laying down any principle for investigating their titles; they had no practical system by which they could reduce the ownership of land to anything like a simple form. They met and discussed their land affairs, disputed amongst themselves, – and they were very prone to dispute amongst themselves, – and, finally, they broke up on the verge of hostilities. He said this from personal experience. And the idea that Native committees were capable of doing the work of the Native Land Court in the investigation of titles to Native land was an absurdity.

Given that Carroll had co-authored (or at least penned his signature to) a report which described the Native Committees Act of 1883 as a 'hollow shell' which 'mocked and still mocks the Natives with a semblance of authority', and in 1892 had introduced a bill providing for the Committees established under this Act to be given real powers with respect to title investigations, his U-turn on this question when promoted from the backbenches to the Cabinet was about as convincing as his change of mind on the question of pre-emption. The Committees had not been given any responsibility for resolving questions of title, and it was therefore hardly surprising that some meetings had degenerated into petty squabbles. They were free to argue amongst themselves but had no obligation to decide anything – hardly an environment encouraging compromise and sensible agreement.

While some members expressed support for allowing Committees to administer Maori lands, the generally contemptuous attitude of most Pakeha politicians to any notion of Maori control over their own affairs was graphically conveyed as members filed out of the debating chamber until a quorum was no longer present, shelving consideration of the bill.[64] In 1896, after two further efforts to have it voted on, Heke's proposed legislation was finally defeated.

Wi Pere, who had resumed possession of the Eastern Maori seat from Carroll, keenly supported Heke's Native Rights Bill but had no more success in persuading Parliament to pass more moderate bills also aimed at giving Maori committees control over Maori-owned lands. In 1894 Pere introduced a Native Lands Administration Bill which again provided for the 1883 Native Committees to investigate titles to papatupu lands, with elected block committees empowered to farm, lease or sell these with the consent of the owners. In an effort to have the authority of the Maori Parliament recognised, any amendment to this measure was to require the consent of the Kotahitanga.[65] Possibly an even greater affront to the sensibilities of the Pakeha members, however, was provided by bills introduced by Pere in 1896 and 1897. Reversing what was perceived by most settlers to be the natural order of things, these provided for Maori to be appointed Judges of the Native Land Court, with Pakeha as their Assessors.[66]

These measures stood little chance of success, but in one district, at least, circumstances were conspiring to ensure that the government would eventually be compelled to grant limited self-government in return for some acknowledgement of the Queen's authority. The last Maori community in the country to retain a high degree of autonomy over its own affairs was to become the first to gain some measure of legal recognition of its right to administer its own lands, even if this was ultimately to prove little more than a 'benevolent deception'.[67]

## 9. 'To Keep Off the White Man and His Works': Te Urewera Committees and the Experiment of 1896[1]

The remote Urewera district, the home of Tuhoe and other related iwi, was the last region in the country to remain effectively outside the writ of British law and almost entirely unavailable for European settlement in the nineteenth century. Prior to the New Zealand Wars of the 1860s the Urewera tribes were described as having an 'intense suspicion and distrust of the Pakeha', with whom they had had negligible contact. C. Hunter Brown, who was probably the first Crown official to travel through the district, reported with respect to the Urewera people's attitude to Grey's runanga scheme that:

> Even when they could no longer refuse the praise of 'pai' and 'tika' ('good' and 'fair') to the Governor's new system, they still dreaded something behind, still feared a trap, and could, generally speaking, only be brought to such modified consent as 'Bring your new "ture" and let us see it closely', illustrated by handling a stick; 'if we approve, well and good; if not, we drop it', and other expressions to that effect.[2]

The Waikato War rendered Grey's new institutions a dead letter in the Urewera district. British sovereignty remained little more than a legal fiction, and the first contact many Maori from the region had with representatives of the Crown was probably in battle.[3]

Nearly a decade of bitter fighting and destruction did little to alleviate this suspicion. As Sian Daly says, Tuhoe's attitude in the period following the wars was clearly spelt out by a post erected on the confiscation line at Ruatoki which read 'hai arai i te pakeha me ana mahi – to keep off the white man and his works'.[4]

It was in the context of continuing 'suspicion and distrust' of the 'white man and his works' and the comparatively unsuitable

217

nature of much of the Urewera district for European settlement that in June 1872, Tuhoe and their allies held a meeting at Ruatahuna to set up a council of 70 (subsequently known as Te Whitu Tekau) to guard their lands, and define the boundaries of the territory within which the leasing or selling of lands would not be permitted. This was probably a revival of a similar council which appears to have been in existence prior to the wars.[5] McLean, the Native Minister, was informed of the resolutions of this meeting. His response is unknown, but in November 1871 the goverment's agent at Napier, J.D. Ormond, had written to several Urewera chiefs promising them that, if Te Kooti was given up for trial, Ngati Porou troops would be withdrawn from their territory and 'the management of your people will be left as we arranged to yourselves'.[6] Te Kooti was not captured but Tuhoe nevertheless gained the distinct impression that the Crown had endorsed – even entered into a compact to protect – an Urewera 'rohe potae', to be administered by Te Whitu Tekau.[7] On the day of the meeting, Te Whenuanui, Paerau and several other chiefs wrote to McLean to tell him of their decisions. After noting the boundaries of the area affected (which extended from the Bay of Plenty confiscation line south to Waikaremoana), the chiefs informed McLean that they were resolved on the 'uniting of the tribe – that their words should be one and that they should have one canoe, Matatua'. They had, they added, decided on the 'apportionment of chiefs among Tuhoe'. There would be seventy responsible for carrying out 'the work of this bird of peace and quietness' within their boundaries, where they had proscribed 'roads, leasing and selling of land'.[8]

H.W. Brabant, the Opotiki Resident Magistrate, reportedly told Tamaikowha that the plan of appointing 70 chiefs was a bad one, 'as they might have seventy different opinions'.[9] And although one deputation at the meeting appear to have opposed its resolutions, the proposals for a tribal veto against surveys and applications to the Native Land Court seem to have gained broad support. When, shortly after this meeting, one chief, Makarini Te Wharehuia, signed an agreement with the government agent Samuel Locke which effectively ratified the transfer of 'rebel' interests in lands to the south of Waikaremoana to a small number of predominantly 'loyalist' Ngati Kahungunu chiefs, he was rebuked by others for having 'parted with Waikaremoana'.[10] Probably, though, their primary concern was that the 'rohe potae' had been breached, as Pakeha farmers shortly thereafter took up leases on these lands in defiance of Te Whitu Tekau's ban on such transactions. When a neighbouring tribe was discovered to be leasing land at Galatea in 1873, for example, Te Whitu Tekau threatened to kill any cattle and sheep placed on this land, which had been included in the 'rohe potae'.[11]

Yet despite some incursions on the fringes of their territory, Tuhoe's rohe, under the protection of Te Whitu Tekau, remained largely inviolate, and Brabant reported after a visit to Ruatahuna in 1874 that Tuhoe appeared 'almost unanimous in their wish to keep roads, Magistrates, and other Government measures' out.[12] Brabant believed Te Whitu Tekau to be 'but little [different] from the runanga of any other Native tribe', adding somewhat cryptically that 'The distinction that the *Whitu Tekau* was supposed to exclude the chiefs is really inoperative'. The question of whether to accept or reject and seek the return of confiscated lands was one that had divided the Urewera tribes and Brabant reported that:

> The 'Seventy' had matured a scheme, which they hoped would come to a head at their *hui*, to get all the tribes to join them in a sort of land league, to forbid the sale and leasing of lands, roads, &c.; but they appear to have nearly abandoned it as impracticable, as not only the tribes outside refuse to join them, but they cannot even agree about it among themselves.[13]

Brabant's suggestion that Tuhoe were divided on the issue of land dealings is not borne out by the evidence, however, which seems to indicate that Tuhoe proper was strongly opposed to any form of alienation of their lands, with only neighbouring tribes on the northern fringes of their territory, who had been negotiating leases with government agents, standing aloof. Evidence that a tribal veto was in operation came from Hira Tauaki, a leading figure in Te Whitu Tekau, who informed Brabant that:

> the Urewera had had many things from the Government: they had received food and clothing after their surrender; they had also taken rations when they visited Napier, Opotiki, and other places; and worst of all, Kereru had taken money from Government. That they begged the Government to accept these *tahas* (calabashes) as payment for the rations and for the money which had been given to Kereru. That they feared the Government intended at some future time to exact land in payment. That the *tahas* were a small thing, but the Urewera were not rich; and that although individuals took rations from Government, the tribe wished the system to be stopped, as they thought that ultimately they would be called upon to pay for them in land.[14]

Kereru Te Pukenui, a paramount chief of Tuhoe, had obviously earned serious censure from Te Whitu Tekau and the rest of the tribe, and possibly was even denied membership of the Council of Seventy as a result, which might explain the reference to the exclusion of chiefs.[15] During the course of the meeting, Tauaki had stated firmly:

> What I say to the chiefs of Tuhoe is this, *'tiakina tou arero'* (guard your tongues). The chiefs (Kereru) have had their say. We (the 'Seventy') have one thing to say to you, Mr. Brabant.[16]

Clearly, though, whether or not Tuhoe's paramount chiefs had been excluded from Te Whitu Tekau they were just as much subject to its efforts to maintain a tribal veto over all dealings with outsiders as were those of lesser rank. Notwithstanding disputes as to the best strategy to pursue with respect to the confiscated blocks, Tuhoe remained a tribe with a high degree of cohesion, and it was this cohesion combined with the fact that government energies were initially focused on opening up more desirable lands in other regions, that allowed them to retain considerable autonomy over their own affairs, and to exclude the Native Land Court for so long.

Te Whitu Tekau barely features again in official correspondence concerning the Urewera district. Yet evidence that it survived for a considerable period thereafter comes from both Tuhoe oral traditions and from Bush's 1889 report, cited earlier, which noted that 'The Urewera have always had a tribal Committee termed the "Seventy". This Committee has always opposed the making of roads, surveys, and prospecting'.[17] Presumably Bush's use of the present tense was not accidental, and his use of the term 'always' certainly suggests that it survived longer than the mere three years for which there is official record of its existence. And the supposition that Te Whitu Tekau suffered a swift demise is even less convincing in the light of the relative lack of pressure facing Tuhoe in comparison with less cohesive tribal units in districts subject to regular Native Land Court hearings.

Nevertheless, by the 1880s Tuhoe were beginning to come under the spotlight. Prior to this decade the factors already mentioned, combined with an expectation on the part of the government that Land Court and purchase activity on the fringes of the district would lead eventually to its opening up, seem to have encouraged a lassez-faire approach to the region, with Tuhoe for the most part being left to their own devices.[18] But with speculation as to the existence of gold and other valuable minerals in the district mounting from the mid-1880s, and the government's success in the opening up of the King Country (which left the Urewera as the only district in the country still substantially outside the bounds of British sovereignty and almost entirely unavailable for European settlement), a more active approach was adopted. Surreptitious surveys and prospecting became an increasing problem for Tuhoe, even if those who undertook these activities did so at some risk. In the Waimana Valley, for example, one chief had erected a notice warning that any European who passed beyond it 'will make relish for my food'.[19]

It was undoubtedly with a view to dealing with the pressures resulting from wild rumours of the riches to be found in their district that Tuhoe sought official status for a committee elected in 1888 to deal with all surveys and 'the question of Europeans wishing to prospect for gold and the granting of permission to do so'. Edwin Mitchelson, the Native Minister, was informed that the sole object of this step was 'to prevent bloodshed in connection with our lands and prevent other people or hapus dealing with them and thereby produce trouble'.[20] Whether this committee was intended as a successor to Te Whitu Tekau, or as a sort of Cabinet-style executive to the more unwieldy Council of Seventy, is unclear. In any event, as was seen in an earlier section, Tuhoe's application was ignored by the Minister, largely on the basis of Bush's report that any official committee constituted for the Urewera district would more than likely continue to oppose roads, surveys, prospecting and the Native Land Court.[21]

In April 1889 Samuel Locke visited Te Urewera at the request of the Native Minister to 'make such arrangements as would lead to the opening-up of that part of this Island for prospecting for gold and other minerals, and for utilising the forests, &c., which are said to contain a large quantity of totara'. According to Locke's account, after being greeted 'in the most cordial manner', he was asked to explain the purpose of his visit. Locke told those assembled at Ruatoki that he had been asked by the government to help overcome the difficulties recently posed by Europeans exploring for gold, timber and other valuable objects in their part of the country, and that his idea was that 'a proper understanding between the Government and themselves' might be reached if Tuhoe were to appoint a number of chiefs empowered to receive letters from the Crown authorising such explorations in their part of the country. The response he received hardly indicated any great shift in Tuhoe attitudes:

> I was met by the reply that they were a very secluded people, not accustomed to Europeans' ways, and that they were very much annoyed by the manner in which the surveyors around them had been carrying on for some time past without their knowledge or consent. As they put the point: They might be quietly cultivating at their kaingas, and suddenly receive a notice to attend a Native Land Court for the adjudication of lands within their boundaries, the surveys of which they had never heard, and such conduct would probably lead to some one being knocked on the head. As to the gold, they knew nothing and cared nothing about; but they would not have people, without their consent and knowledge, wandering about their country.[22]

After several days of discussion, Locke persuaded Tuhoe to write to the Native Minister, outlining the boundaries of their 'rohe potae' and agreeing to select a number of chiefs to consider proposals to explore it.[23] Locke (somewhat optimistically) concluded that 'with ordinary care and caution, the whole country can be explored for minerals, timber, and other objects', adding that most of this 'mountainous, forest covered region...such as the Waikaremoana Lake and other parts' was 'very romantic, but quite unfit for the purpose of agriculture'.

However optimistic Locke may have been, he remained astute enough to warn the government against 'surreptitious interference', which would only tend to undermine Tuhoe confidence in the Crown's intentions. Despite this, in the early 1890s efforts were made to force through surveys and Land Court sittings on the Urewera perimeter, with only minority support from the Tuhoe tribe. In 1892 surveyors attempting to enter the Urewera were forcibly turned back.[24] The following year Alfred Cadman, the Native Minister, 'ruthlessly forced a survey', again with only minority support, which led to the arrest of some of the Tuhoe who had confiscated the surveyors' instruments.[25] Serious violence was threatened until Te Kooti (who had attended the opening of the meeting house built in his honour at Ruatahuna, Te Whai-a-te-motu, in 1891, when it was 'unanimously agreed that no gold prospectors, surveyors, or Europeans were to be allowed inside the Urewera boundary') persuaded the protesters to allow the survey to continue and to work within the law.[26]

As Cadman had instructed the government officials on the ground to threaten that 'persistent opposition to the Law' by Tuhoe could lead to the extension of the confiscation line 'further into their Country',[27] Te Kooti's plea for moderation was probably accepted as the wisest course of action in the circumstances. For although the government's forcible surveys of the Urewera were condemned by the Kotahitanga, which feared that 'mischief will be done, and perhaps blood will be shed because those Maoris are not accustomed to European ways',[28] attention had now been turned on the Urewera as the last district in the country still outside the bounds of Pakeha law.

In a situation which was clearly unsatisfactory for both Tuhoe and the government, the former appear now to have sought some sort of legislative sanction for their 'rohe potae', in accordance with the recognition which they understood McLean to have given this in the early 1870s, whilst the Crown was anxious to establish some sort of foothold in the district which would at the very least allow it to ensure that the Urewera was at last brought within the realm of the law.

At a large gathering of the Tuhoe tribe held in early 1894 which lasted more than a month, these issues were debated at length and a number of resolutions were passed. According to Numia Kereru:

> One matter that was determined was the territorial boundary of what land was to be surveyed under command of the Government, and internal surveys within these boundaries would not be consented to at the present time, and that searching for gold would not be agreed to by them, and that the sale of their land would not be acquiesced in by them, and the laying-off of roads through their land would not be agreed to, and that the leasing of their lands was also to be prohibited, that committees should be established, and that the duty of these committees was to deal with troubles that might arise in reference to their lands.[29]

Numia outlined the decisions reached at this gathering at a meeting held with the Premier, R.J. Seddon, and James Carroll at Ruatoki just a few weeks later. Seddon and Carroll were midway through an extensive tour of North Island Maori communities, the primary object of which was to explain the reimposition of Crown pre-emption. The Urewera district remained a special case, however, and the attention devoted to it on this tour gives some indication of the importance attached to it at this time. Yet if Seddon believed that a personal touch would help to overcome Tuhoe wariness and suspicion of government motives, the surviving accounts of his meetings at Ruatoki and elsewhere suggest he was not entirely successful. Kereru Te Pukenui, for example, welcomed Seddon and Carroll as men who had 'come to benefit me or to injure me – even though it may be to strike the land or the people', adding that he had heard rumours – which he was inclined to believe – that they were 'evilly disposed' towards Tuhoe and had come to destroy them.[30] Those who had attended the recent meeting had 'wished to retain within their own hands the administration of the affairs relating to their lands' Numia Kereru stated, since:

> Lands that get under the control of the Government are simply squandered away; those who have possessed land become landless, they are those who are supported by the Government.[31]

Tuhoe had seen what had happened to other tribes around the country, he added, and did not wish for a 'temporary prosperity'. Surveys combined with the operations of the Native Land Court led to the alienation of land, and for this reason Tuhoe wanted their own committees to administer their affairs.

Seddon, in reply, suggested that Tuhoe were too divided to control their land themselves, adding that if one particular faction 'got the ear of the committee', those not represented on it might resort to violence in order to get their way.[32] The Premier added that Tuhoe opposition to surveys was 'almost suicidal', since it would be impossible for the government to maintain them in possession of their lands unless it knew exactly where these were, (ignoring the fact that there was little dispute as to the tribe's ownership of most of Te Urewera, and that Tuhoe had consented to the surveying of the external boundaries of their district). He wished to see a clean slate, and if Tuhoe would wipe off the conclusions arrived at during its earlier meeting he would ensure that the right people got the land, and that surveys were undertaken by the government at the least possible cost. Otherwise, he and Carroll warned, the government could by law compel them to accept surveys and the determination of titles by the Native Land Court – the only 'committee' which could confirm Tuhoe ownership of the Urewera district, according to Carroll.[33]

Yet while Ngati Manawa at Galatea and Ngati Whare at Te Whaiti both indicated their desire to remain outside the Tuhoe 'rohe potae', at Ruatahuna Seddon and Carroll were again informed of the tribe's desire to administer its own affairs. Te Whare Kotua, for example, stated that:

> We want our territorial boundary defined. We want the Government to let a committee of Tuhoe be established to carry out our affairs. We would not then need the Government to carry out our affairs within this boundary...We do not want other people to prosecute the survey, and cut up our land while we are trying to arrange with the Government. We want a proper understanding to be arrived at. We want our boundary confirmed, and our titles to the land indorsed, without a survey if possible. We want the Government to give legal effect to the establishment of a committee, who will manage our affairs in connection with our land.[34]

Te Pukeiotu told Seddon and Carroll of the precedents for this course of action, referring to the agreement which Tuhoe always understood to have been reached with McLean at the time of their surrender to the Crown:

> the two great chiefs of this country, Paerau and Te Whenuanui, in the days that are past and in the days of the voice of Sir Donald McLean, arranged that this territory should be kept inviolate, and that they should reign supreme in this part, and that was given effect to by Sir Donald McLean...These chiefs arranged that all Government matters should be excluded from this boundary – namely, roads, leases, wrongful sales, mortgages, and everything that is vile. There was then a protectorate over this place, to protect these people against the advances of the Europeans.[35]

Seddon claimed to be visiting Tuhoe with the same friendly intentions as McLean, but at the same time warned them that there could be but one law and one government in the country, to which the people of Te Urewera should either submit or suffer the consequences. He told the Ruatahuna gathering that:

> you cannot have protection unless you acknowledge the sovereignty of the Queen, who governs all...If you want to have a committee amongst yourselves to meet and discuss matters so as to condense and bring down to a focus what is in your interest, it is wise you

should do so...But, if you want a committee that is to pass laws to have effect in the land of Tuhoe and to act antagonistically to the Government, I may tell you at once it is impossible, and the sooner you get that out of your minds the better it will be for all of you. That has been the cause of all your trouble.[36]

Tuhoe speakers stated that they simply wanted 'a committee for our own district to settle matters amongst ourselves, not between ourselves and other people – a committee to protect and control our own affairs', and suggested that the government could give effect to its decisions, before finally acquiescing under Seddon's adamant reiteration that there could be but one government to a committee 'to advise the government in matters on behalf of the people'.

Yet while Seddon and his accompanying entourage of officials and reporters seem to have regarded this first visit by a Premier to the Urewera district as having successfully overcome the 'difficulties' standing in the way of further surveying and prospecting in the region, subsequent events indicate that Tuhoe certainly did not see it in the same way. Gerhard Mueller, the Auckland Commissioner of Crown Lands, appears to have joined Seddon's party for the Urewera section of their journey largely in order to make a reconnaissance of the country, and was later reported in the *Auckland Star* to consider a large part of the land admirably suited for settlement and as believing there to be 'no doubt it will prove gold-bearing'. Commenting on political matters, Mueller opined that:

> there will be no further trouble with the Ureweras. The past is past, and they will trust the Government and the Europeans to deal fairly and justly by them in future. They recognise that the balance of power has passed from the Native people to the Europeans, and that it is futile to oppose the extension of settlement.[37]

Proof that Tuhoe had not abandoned their opposition to the 'extension of settlement' came in April 1895 when two government survey parties attempting to undertake a triangulation survey in the northern Urewera were turned back by Tuhoe and had their instruments seized. Seddon, perhaps miffed that his much lauded 'settlement' of the Urewera problem had been exposed as nothing of the kind, despatched a detachment of the Permanent Artillery to the scene to enable the continuation of the survey. James Cowan, who accompanied this expedition, later described the scene on its arrival at Ruatoki on 21 April:

> We found all the leading men of the Urewera, from Ruatoki to Waikare-moana, assembled there, to the number of about two hundred, seated in half-moon formation on the *marae*. It was an ominous reception. No call of welcome; not a word from the sullen mountain-men squatting there glowering at us. When at last they did speak their speeches were decidedly hostile. They wanted no surveyors in their country; they did not see any necessity for mapping it; they feared some of their land might be taken to pay for the survey. We found, afterwards, that many of the younger men were ready and eager to fight; and practically every man had a gun and ammunition, although they did not parade their arms before us.[38]

Clearly the Premier's visit the previous year had resolved little. Attempting to save face, Seddon blamed Wi Pere and Hone Heke for inciting trouble.[39] Yet as Daly suggests, the most surprising aspect of this whole affair was the apparent lack of consultation with Tuhoe prior to the commencement of the survey, notwithstanding the tribe's repeated opposition. Only someone with Seddon's considerable ego could have departed from Te Urewera in 1894 under the impression that surreptitious surveys would now be tolerated by the tribe.[40] Intervention by Carroll saved Seddon's misjudgement from resulting in bloodshed and the survey was permitted to proceed, presumably pending later negotiations for a more permanent settlement of the problem.

In September 1895 a Tuhoe delegation visited Wellington at Seddon's invitation in an effort to reach an agreement with the government on the future administration of Te Urewera. Tuhoe were now willing to have their land titles adjudicated upon, though not by the Native Land Court, and continued to insist that they be allowed to elect their own committees to take charge of their affairs. Beyond this, they sought schools, sanitary instruction and agricultural improvements, and for the whole of the Urewera district to be set aside as an inalienable reserve for their benefit.[41]

Learning perhaps from his earlier misjudgement that Tuhoe was not a tribe to be taken lightly, Seddon was now prepared to compromise on some points provided Tuhoe recognised and accepted the rule of law. On 25 September he outlined the government's response to Tuhoe's requests in a letter addressed to the tribe's representatives in Wellington. On the question of surveys and land title adjudication, the Premier remarked:

> you ask that the *rohe-potae* of the Tuhoe land...be permanently determined; and, in order to do this, that a Commissioner be appointed to define the boundary known as the *rohe-potae*. I do not see why this cannot be done...The boundaries of these lands can be determined by the trig. stations that have been erected. You ask also that a Commissioner be appointed to inquire into the title of the persons owning land within the said *rohe-potae*, and to determine the boundaries of land belonging to hapus and persons who consider that the land is theirs, his decision to be down in writing; the Commissioner also to make a sketch-plan of the country, to be approved by the Surveyor-General, the boundaries of the land belonging to the hapus being determined by landmarks where possible to do so; if not to be surveyed with the concurrence of the owners of the land. In coming to such a decision, the Commissioner must pay due consideration to Native manners and customs, and, where it is possible to do so, he must follow the boundaries of the several hapus, each block to be dealt with in a clear and proper manner.[42]

Seddon's agreement to effectively exclude the Native Land Court from Te Urewera and to only undertake surveys with the concurrence of the owners were major concessions, given that the government had the legal power to have titles investigated by the Court, and to authorise surveys, without consulting those concerned. Indeed, Seddon even consented to the election of local committees, out of which a general committee was to be selected:

> When the Commissioner has concluded his investigation into the title of the several blocks, then the Maoris who are in a block of land belonging to a hapu may elect a Local Committee, the members of which must not exceed seven in number. This Committee to be an administrative one, to act for the owners of the land for the period for which they were elected. The number of these Local Committees should be determined by the number of the hapus and the owners of the blocks of land.
>
> You ask further that a General Committee be appointed to deal with the tribal lands generally, and that the decisions and proceedings of the said Committee be binding on the Local Committees and hapus; its proceedings to be conducted in accordance with Maori manners and customs. I think that such a Committee should be appointed, and, in order to give effect to this, I agree that each Local Committee or hapu should elect one of their number to be a member of the General Committee, all the decisions of the General Committee to be communicated to the Local Committees for their guidance.

In return for granting these requests, Seddon noted that he was:

> very much pleased to learn from you that you have opened your land to tourists, who will now have an opportunity of seeing the wonders of your country, and the extent of your forests, with its lakes and its rivers. It is a cause of gratification to the Governor, and to me also, to hear that you acknowledge that the Queen's mana is over all, and that you will honour and obey her laws.

This was the crux of the matter as far as Seddon was concerned: Tuhoe had acknowledged the mana of the Queen, and having done so could now safely be granted limited self-government over their lands, in the absence of any willingness on their part to alienate them.

Shortly after the Tuhoe delegation's visit to Wellington an Urewera District Native Reserve Bill was introduced in the House, and after being referred to the Native Affairs Committee, which made some amendments to it, was finally passed into law on 12 October 1896. Described in its long title as 'An Act to make provision as to the Ownership and Local Government of the Native Lands in the Urewera District', the Act largely accorded with Seddon's outline of his arrangement with Tuhoe of the previous September. An area of approximately 656,000 acres, extending as far south as Waikaremoana, was declared to be a native reserve, within which the Native Land Court Act of 1894 would not apply. Instead, the Governor could appoint seven persons to be Commissioners, of whom two were to be Europeans 'and the remainder Natives of the Tuhoe Tribe'. These Commissioners were to divide the district into blocks, and 'with due regard to Native customs and usages' investigate the ownership of each, 'adopting as far as possible hapu boundaries' in order to 'arrive at a just and equitable decision in each case'. All expenses associated with implementing the Act were to be borne by the Crown, including the cost of preparing the sketch-plans upon which the ownership of each block could be determined. Each order of the Commissioners (which was to include the relative shares of those families and individuals declared owners) was to be published in the *Kahiti*, after which aggrieved persons had twelve months to appeal to the Minister of Native Affairs, who could 'direct such expert inquiry and report' as he saw fit, and who had the final decision in any appeal.

After being confirmed by the Governor or the Minister, each order was to operate as a certificate of ownership which would record the names of the members of the Local Committee and the General Committee, along with any change of ownership in the block, or any dealings in respect of it. Provisional Local Committees of between five and seven members were to be appointed by the Commissioners, and once permanent Committees had been elected for every block, a General Committee of one representative from each Local Committee was to be established. Whereas the powers of the Local Committees were to be confined to 'the internal affairs of the block', the General Committee was 'to deal with all questions affecting the reserve as a whole, or affecting any portion thereof in relation to other persons than the owners', and was to retain the sole right to 'alienate any portion of the district to Her

Majesty, either absolutely or for any lesser estate, or by way of cession for mining purposes'. The Governor could, however, lay out roads and landing-places without the General Committee's permission, and could also acquire up to 400 acres for accommodation houses and camping grounds under the provisions of the Public Works Act 1894.

In introducing the Bill for its second reading in the House on 24 September 1896, Carroll informed members that the land affected by it was 'not fit...for settlement in any shape whatever'. Despite this, it was 'full of natural beauties' and would have a strong attraction for tourists, as well as being a 'convenient' place for its owners to live. Because of the unsuitability of the district for settlement and the lack of European interests involved, Carroll believed it would be 'gracious and considerate on our part...if we conceded to them the modified form of local government' outlined in the bill. First, however, it was 'absolutely necessary...to clothe the country with a legal title', and Carroll interestingly justified the establishment of a Maori-dominated commission for this purpose on the grounds that it would be a far superior means of determining native title in the absence of European interests:

> This sort of tribunal was considered necessary rather than calling in the assistance of the Native Land Court, because there are no European interests involved, and the investigation of the title of that land must proceed according to Maori law, usage, and custom, – and if any one can understand Maori law, usage, and custom in reference to land-tenure it must be held, and it must be maintained, that it is the Maoris themselves, and especially the owners of the country.[43]

Carroll added that the government saw 'no harm' in the establishment of committees to administer the Tuhoe tribe's affairs. Parliament had not often conceded to Maori what they desired, he added, noting that:

> They have been clamouring for years by way of petition, or through their representatives, for certain concessions to be made to them in the government of their lands. We never saw fit to make it before

because European interests were so mixed up with Native interests affecting various blocks of land and various tracts of country in this colony that we deemed it to be imprudent to make those allowances when they were asked for.

Again, however, the fact that no European interests were involved made it safe to concede these rights of limited self-government, and the result, Carroll predicted, would be the eventual 'advancement of these Natives up to a state of civilisation equal to that of their pakeha brethren', whereby the government would be enabled to 'impose upon them all the responsibilities and liabilities which all other subjects of Her Majesty are subjected to at the present time'.

Seddon also pointed to the 'exceptional circumstances in connection with the Tuhoe' as justification for granting limited self-government. 'If matters had continued as they were', he stated:

> it was practically a reserve, but not a reserve supported by legislation; it was a stronghold of the people who were determined that Europeans should not be in their midst – that our Courts and our present course in respect to Native lands procedure should not obtain in their part of the colony. That was the position. It was practically so, for years, under the old Maori custom. I say it would be much better to have a reserve such as this is made now, with the sanction and approval of our Parliament, with the mana of the Queen admitted freely and without the slightest reservation, than to have, as we had only a few years ago, a representative of Her Majesty the Queen going to the borders of the Urewera Country and then turning back, deeming it not to be advisable to proceed further.[44]

Seddon also referred several times to the promise, which he had 'no hesitation whatever in saying was made by Sir Donald McLean', that Tuhoe lands should be reserved from alienation. Respective governments had ignored this promise for years, he believed, leading to serious trouble at times with respect to the Urewera. Now the government had an opportunity to redeem McLean's promise in a manner which would ensure that no further trouble would arise and the authority of the law would be recognised.

The Leader of the Opposition, Captain Russell, did not view the bill quite so kindly, describing it as 'a complete and revolutionary change in the Native legislation of the Government', which proposed a Maori governing body 'with a novel and peculiar system of land-regulation over a very large area of the country'.[45] Yet although the bill gave the appearance of granting Tuhoe control over their own affairs, Russell believed it would do nothing of the sort:

> The Tuhoe people have no doubt been very much pleased, but deluded by the Government; they think they are going to have the control of their lands; they believe they have scored a point. I can assure them they have done no such thing. This is our old friend 'the thin end of the wedge' once again; when once the Government have got power under this Bill, and the land is subdivided, the autocratic Native Minister [Seddon] will do what he chooses, and the instant the Tuhoe people have brought their land under the operations of this Act they will find before long that all they have wished to avoid has come upon them, and that settlement will follow on subdivision.

Russell believed this outcome would be right and proper, and considered that the only feature to recommend the bill was that 'the Government have been able to effect by a side-wind what they could not do directly'.[46] The suitability of the district for settlement was an 'open question', and Russell pointed to its potentially valuable forests and the possibility of gold being discovered. No reason had been offered for the bill other than the fact that the Tuhoe people wished to manage their own affairs. Yet Russell believed that once the lands had been subdivided the Commissioners would be done away with and the land brought under the administration of the Native Land Court.

Hone Heke also considered the bill a 'sham', believing the 'real Act' would be entirely governed by regulations made by the Governor-in-Council, which could give the Native Land Court jurisdiction over the district. Although he fully supported giving Tuhoe the right to administer their properties as they saw fit, the bill was, in his view, 'nothing else than one of those measures introduced by the Government to entrap the Tuhoe Natives'.[47] Moreover, the bill contained provision for the alienation of Tuhoe lands, even though the Urewera people had requested that their territory should be absolutely inalienable.

Yet despite Heke's suspicion, the three other Maori members were positive in their response to the bill. Wi Pere shared Heke's concern regarding the Crown's proposed right of acquisition under it, but aside from this considered that it would probably serve as a model for other tribes also wishing to administer their own lands.[48] Ropata Te Ao, the member for Western Maori, thought the bill would 'be the means of saving the Tuhoe people', and stated that it was a 'waste of time' to discuss its provisions, since 'Maori tribes in other parts of the North Island, as well as the Tuhoe people' approved of it. If the Act was found to work well other tribes would probably ask for similar measures to be passed with respect to their own lands, and he wondered why these requests should not be granted. Opposition to the bill was, he suspected, based on the knowledge that it would allow Tuhoe to retain control of their lands.[49]

The prospect that other tribes would seek similar control over their own affairs had been one of the Opposition's further objections to the proposed legislation. Russell informed the House that:

> The effect is that already this promise of Maori self-government having been made to these people has become widely known, and the Natives throughout the colony are beginning to agitate to be allowed to deal with their own lands in exactly the same way as the Tuhoe people, and the end will be that disappointment must ensue, for local self-government by the Maori people cannot and will not be allowed to prevail, and what cannot be granted to all should not be permitted to a few.[50]

But although Seddon had been careful to emphasise the 'exceptional circumstances' of the Urewera district, he was not adverse to suggestions that a similar measure might be adopted more generally. Earlier, in debate on Heke's Native Rights Bill, the Premier had conceded that he believed 'they should find something for the Natives to do'.[51] Heke's bill went too far in the direction of promoting separate institutions for Maori, in Seddon's view, but if the Urewera legislation proved a success in that district he would be willing to consider granting similar powers with respect to their lands to Maori elsewhere.

The Urewera District Native Reserve Act of 1896 did indeed provide a basis for legislation passed in 1900 which extended similar measures to the rest of the country, though this can hardly have been justified by the success of the Urewera legislation, since titles to most of the district remained unsettled until at least 1907. Despite the intention to subdivide the Urewera district on the basis of hapu boundaries, the Commissioners, under the chairmanship of a Pakeha official, discovered soon after their initial round of hearings in 1899 that:

> practically there are no such things as defined hapu boundaries such as were acknowledged by the people as belonging to any given hapu to the exclusion of others. As a matter of fact, nearly the whole area is subject to overlapping claims, sometimes three or four claims one on top of the other with discordant boundaries; and the hapus are so mixed by intermarriage that it is difficult to say to what hapu any particular individual of the tribe belongs.[52]

This was always going to be a problem for any tribunal charged with the task of deciding on definite boundary lines where none had previously existed. The complex and overlapping nature of hapu rights in the Urewera district was also to have a major effect on the make-up of the Commission itself. In 1900 an amendment was passed to the Urewera District Native Reserve Act disqualifying Commissioners with a personal interest in any block from voting on its ownership. According to Carroll, by this time Native Minister, this safeguard had become necessary because 'wherever the Commissioners sat it was found that two or three, or in some cases the whole, of the [Maori] Commissioners were personally interested'.[53] Yet though there was provision for the European Commissioners to temporarily appoint Tuhoe individuals to sit on cases in which they themselves were not personally interested, this power does not appear to have been used to any significant extent. In fact, many of the orders of the Urewera Commission were made by a Pakeha majority, undermining the original intent of the 1896 Act that the people of Te Urewera should, with some guidance and assistance from the two European Commissioners, essentially determine their own land titles themselves.[54] Instead, the Commission became, to all intents and purposes, a slightly less expensive and more amenable version of the Native Land Court, operating under a Pakeha tikanga rather than a Maori one.

Perhaps because of the Commission's domination by its two Pakeha members (who had suggested the 1900 amendment and were given discretion as to whether to implement it), its operations were conducted more along the adversarial 'winner-takes-all' lines of a Land Court hearing than with the more pragmatic and conciliatory approach which might have prevailed had Tuhoe been left to settle ownership themselves. Nearly three years after commencing investigations, the Commission's Chairman, W.J. Butler, in reporting on the conclusion of its hearings, informed the Native Minister that:

> The time occupied in the ascertainment of title to the blocks which came before the Commission was much longer than was anticipated. Tuhoe were new to the work, and would not make the smallest concession, the result being that the ownership of each block was fought out to the bitter end, notwithstanding the efforts made by the European members of the Commission to induce them to settle the ownership of, at any rate, the smaller blocks among themselves.[55]

With more than 200 appeals being lodged against the decisions of the Commission, this was far from the end of the matter. The second Urewera Commission, which heard these appeals in 1906-7, had no Tuhoe representation, with Paratene Ngata of Ngati Porou the only Maori appointed to this three-man panel of 'experts'.

As with the Native Land Court in other regions, this lengthy process of litigation also appears to have had drastic consequences for Maori health in the Urewera district, with Tuhoe one of the few tribes in the country to record a drop in numbers in the 1901 census. M.P.K. Sorrenson's figures indicate that the population fell by nearly a quarter in just five years, and this at a time when total Maori numbers were beginning to recover after nearly three decades of Land Court and purchase activity in many parts of the North Island.[56] This, combined with the already impoverished and precarious state in which many Tuhoe lived, made the Crown's de facto disavowal and eventual repeal of the 1896 Act a great deal easier to achieve. In 1909 the Native Land Court's jurisdiction was extended to the Urewera district, and in the rush to acquire lands in the area a provisional General Committee of dubious legal standing was finally convened in the same year, only to be subverted and eventually ignored by the Crown when it became clear that it was not going to sanction widespread Crown purchasing in the district. By 1910 the Crown had begun purchasing individual interests in blocks in the Urewera, later using retrospective validating legislation to overcome the fact that the 1896 Act had specified that all land alienations were to be negotiated through the General Committee. By 1915 this policy had been extended to virtually all of the 656,000-acre 'reserve'.

In 1896 Seddon had grandly maintained that the government was finally honouring a 25-year-old promise by a former Native Minister, Donald McLean, to keep the Urewera a permanently inalienable protectorate for the benefit of its Maori owners. A quarter-century later, in 1921, when the Urewera District Native Reserve Act of 1896 was finally repealed and a consolidation scheme introduced, nearly three-quarters of the district had passed into Crown ownership as a result of the policy of large-scale acquisitions of individual interests. If the 1896 Act might initially have been viewed as a bold and novel attempt to recognise tribal authority over Maori lands, by the 1920s it had taken on something of the appearance of Russell's 'thin end of the wedge'. With the benefit of hindsight, Heke was right to be sceptical that the government would ever grant Maori genuine authority over their own lands, even if this was not apparent at the time that the 1900 Maori Lands Administration Act, an even more short-lived 'experiment' in recognising tribal authority, was passed.[57]

# 10. Tentative and Temporary Steps: The 1900 Legislation[1]

According to the Stout–Ngata Commission of 1907–8, while Maori in the 1890s were divided on many points, there were two issues upon which they were practically unanimous:

(i). That the Crown cease the purchase of Native lands;

(ii). That the adjudication, management, and administration of the remnant of their lands be vested in controlling Councils, Boards, or Committees composed of representative Maoris.[2]

Early in 1898 Seddon visited many Maori communities throughout the North Island, and was told that Maori wished the purchase of all lands remaining in their ownership to be stopped, and control over them vested in committees. Some Maori suggested that the now defunct District Native Committees created under the 1883 Act might be revived and used to ensure Maori retained control over their fast-dwindling estates.[3] Similar sentiments had also been expressed in a petition drafted by the Kotahitanga and forwarded to Queen Victoria on the occasion of her Diamond Jubilee. More than 60 million acres of Maori land had passed into the hands of private persons or the Crown since the commencement of British colonisation, and they now asked to be enabled to retain and utilise the remaining five million or so acres themselves, with any portions they could not profitably use being put up for lease 'for the purposes of settlement and the development of the colony'.[4] Their 'wish, desire, and request' to hold onto the remnant of their tribal lands could, however, 'only be given effect to by passing...legislation prohibiting forever the sale of our surviving lands to the Crown and private persons'.

As Williams comments, if this request for paternal legislation might have seemed, on the face of it, a surprising reversal of the usual Maori demand for full control and management over their own lands, in reality it was not. Maori did not view autonomy and government protection as contradictory.[5] They sought autonomy over their own lands because this would provide them with the means to retain possession of them, but at the same time were wise enough to appreciate that no amount of nominal autonomy would be sufficient to withstand coercive legislation and institutions which facilitated alienation. They wanted control over their own lands in an environment which did not, block–by–block, systematically undermine this control.

During the 1898 parliamentary session, Seddon introduced a bill which, citing this petition in its preamble, purported to meet many of the grievances long expressed by Maori.[6] Under this bill the Native Land Court would be abolished and land purchases prohibited, with Native Land Boards assuming the powers of the Court and responsibility for leasing surplus lands. Yet while most Maori welcomed the proposed abolition of the Land Court, just as in 1886 few welcomed the prospect of placing their lands in the hands of what were intended to be European-controlled boards.[7] As Williams writes: 'Far from being agents of local or tribal control, the boards looked to the Maoris very much like government bodies which would act in the interests of the Pakehas'.[8]

Whether to support the proposed measure and press for changes that would give Maori greater control under the new system, or to reject it and continue to seek legal recognition for the Maori Parliament, was the key issue debated at the 1898 meeting of the Kotahitanga, which ended in acrimony. The 'home rule' party, bolstered for the first time by the attendance of 30 delegates from the King, walked out of the meeting rather than even consider Seddon's measure. Distrustful of the settler-dominated Assembly, this faction continued to seek a legal forum in which to decide their own affairs, and embodied this demand in Henare Kaihau's Maori Council Constitution Bill. Introduced into Parliament in both 1897 and 1898, this bill provided for a

Council partly elected and partly nominated by the King to assume full power over Maori matters, with the Native Land Court replaced by committees operating under the supervision of the Council.⁹

Recognising the futility of attempting to gain authority for a Maori Parliament through the General Assembly, the more moderate faction of the Kotahitanga nonetheless remained committed to the abolition of the Land Court and the investigation of titles by Maori committees. These changes, and a Maori majority on the proposed boards, were the key amendments to Seddon's bill resolved on at the Kotahitanga meeting, with the influence of the Young Maori Party evident in further suggestions that the committees should also take on responsibility for sanitary conditions in Maori villages and other social issues.¹⁰

Seddon's bill was amended slightly and again brought forward in the 1899 session, but made little headway while Maori continued to debate the merits of its contents. Meanwhile, as an interim measure, legislation was passed preventing the Crown from entering into any fresh negotiations for the purchase of Maori land.¹¹ Since the resumption of Crown pre-emption in 1892, some 2.7 million acres of Maori land had been purchased by the Crown at a total cost of about £775,500.¹² The Crown's aggressive land purchase policy had been so successful that there was no longer a pressing need to acquire more lands for settlement. Indeed, there was a strong case for easing up on this front. As Seddon told Parliament in 1899, if land sales were not prohibited 'a large landless body of Natives' might emerge to become 'a burden on the State'.¹³

Most Maori certainly preferred to lease rather than sell any land they could not use, and while the 1899 session of the Kotahitanga at Waitangi was marred by the absence of the more moderate southern and eastern leaders, at its fully attended 1900 meeting, held at Rotorua, the youthful Apirana Ngata successfully converted the proponents of 'home rule' to further consideration of the government's proposed legislation.¹⁴ Led by Ngata and Heke, the Kotahitanga drafted a new bill, based on the amendments made to Seddon's proposed legislation of 1898 by the moderate faction. Again, no lands were to be sold, and the Native Land Court was to be abolished and replaced by local committees operating under the supervision of six District Land Boards.[15]

These suggestions, along with the proposals of Ngata and the Young Maori Party for health reform, were incorporated into two pieces of legislation passed by the General Assembly in 1900.[16] Under the Maori Councils Act, elected Maori Councils based on tribal boundaries were to be empowered to pass regulations 'for the promotion of the health and welfare and moral well-being of the Maori inhabitants of the district', with Village Committees enforcing by-laws on sanitary and other matters. The Maori Lands Administration Act provided for the establishment of six Maori Land Councils, but differed in some important ways from the proposals of the Kotahitanga. In spite of Maori objections, the Land Councils were to have a Pakeha majority; and contrary to earlier proposals, the Native Land Court was to remain, although Maori claiming to be the owners of any particular block of papatupu land were to be empowered to form a Papatupu Block Committee, which could investigate title to the land and, subject to confirmation by the Council and provided there was no appeal against their decision to the Court, have this ratified as if it were an order of the Court. Moreover, the Act was made permissive rather than compulsory. Papakainga lands were to be absolutely inalienable, and lands owned by more than two Maori could only be leased with the consent of the Council, with alienation of the freehold permitted only with the consent of the Governor in Council.

The preamble to the Maori Lands Administration Act outlined the raison d'être for this revolutionary change in Maori land legislation:

> Whereas the chiefs and other leading Maoris of New Zealand, by petition to Her Majesty and to the Parliament of New Zealand, urged that the residue (about five million acres) of the Maori land now remaining in possession of the Maori owners should be

> for their use and benefit in such wise as to protect them from the risk of being left landless: And whereas it is expedient, in the interests both of the Maoris and Europeans of the colony, that provision should be made for the better settlement and utilisation of large areas of Maori land at present lying unoccupied and unproductive, and for the encouragement and protection of the Maoris in efforts of industry and self-help: And whereas it is necessary also to make provision for the prevention, by the better administration of Maori lands, of useless and expensive dissensions and litigation...

Carroll's legislation was intended to provide a reasonable compromise between the needs of European settlers and those of Maori, and in many respects embodied what tribal leaders had long been urging.[17] Yet after more than three decades of 'useless and expensive dissensions and litigation', the Act was in more ways than one a case of 'too little, too late'. In some districts, for example, the Native Land Court had proven such an effective tool for extinguishing native title that practically no papatupu lands remained, rendering the provision allowing Maori to investigate titles themselves largely redundant.[18] And despite Opposition cries of 'native landlordism', the voluntary nature of the legislation, combined with the domination of the Maori Land Councils by Pakeha officials, made many Maori reluctant to vest their lands in them. As the Stout–Ngata Commission was to comment, while large areas of land were vested in the Councils in some areas, in many others the Act proved inoperative for much the same reasons as had Ballance's Native Land Administration Act of 1886. Maori 'objected to being deprived of all authority and management of their ancestral lands', and, wary of continual changes in Maori land legislation, 'suspected that the new policy was only another attempt to sweep into the maw of the State large areas of their rapidly dwindling ancestral lands'.[19]

The Maori Lands Administration Act was premised on the assumption that Maori would voluntarily place their lands in the hands of Maori Land Councils for disposal by way of lease, thereby averting settler pressure to acquire the freehold. This underestimated the extent both of Maori distrust of government intentions after decades of legal chicanery directed against them, and of Pakeha opposition to having Maori landlords. In 1904, more than 6000 Maori signed petitions demanding that Land Councils be composed solely of Maori members.[20] And with the Pakeha press and the Opposition also criticising the failure of the government's so-called 'taihoa' policies, the Liberal administration was forced to admit by 1905 that its reliance on the voluntary vesting of lands in the Councils created under the 1900 Act had failed.

Already, in 1904, Parliament had passed legislation providing for the compulsory vesting of land in the Councils for non-payment of rates, with the Minister of Native Affairs empowered by the same Act to apply to the Native Land Court to have title to any land ascertained if he considered that the owners were delaying making such an application in order to avoid this liability.[21] The Maori Land Settlement Act of 1905 extended this principle even further by allowing the Minister to initiate Land Court investigations of title at his discretion, and at the same time replaced the partially elected Maori Land Councils with wholly nominated Maori Land Boards with a Pakeha majority. Moreover, this Act also provided for the compulsory vesting of land in the new Boards in the Tai Tokerau and Tairawhiti districts, with provision also made for the Crown to spend up to £200,000 per annum on the purchase of Maori land. As Williams put it, these changes 'meant a substantial loss of Maori control over Maori land'.[22] Any pretence that the Councils or Boards were intended to provide a means of self-government for Maori was essentially abandoned, with the government instead succumbing to intense settler and Opposition pressure and reverting to coercive legislation to compel Maori to make land available for European settlement. And although the Stout–Ngata Commission of 1907-8 partly went against this trend by providing Maori with an opportunity to put forward their views as to what should be done with their remaining land, it was the Pakeha-dominated Land Boards, not the Maori owners, which were to control and decide the fate of Maori lands for most of the twentieth century. Nor were the bodies created under the Maori

Councils Act of 1900 allowed to develop into more effective institutions of local self-government for Maori. Starved of funds, and tending to exceed their limited powers, the Councils rapidly lost support once the carefully circumscribed authority delegated to them became apparent to Maori.[23]

In fact, one of the few success stories of the short-lived 1900 legislation was the Papatupu Block Committees. These were so successful in gaining Maori confidence that the President of the Tai Tokerau Maori Land Council was driven to complain that he was being overwhelmed by reports of completed title investigations and did not have time to scrutinise them all.[24] By 1905, whereas only some 7000 acres had been voluntarily vested in the Councils for leasing, more than 30,000 Maori had obtained titles to an area of about 347,000 acres under the legislation.[25] Commenting on the work of these Committees, Stout and Ngata noted in 1908 that although they had been 'given to understand that this method of investigation had ignobly failed', its results were nothing short of 'astonishing', and had saved a great deal of time and money.[26] Despite this, by 1909 these Committees had been abolished, and the Native Land Court had again been declared to have 'exclusive jurisdiction to investigate the title to customary land, and to determine the relative interests of the owners thereof'.[27] Maori had again been marginalised in the process of determining title to their own lands.

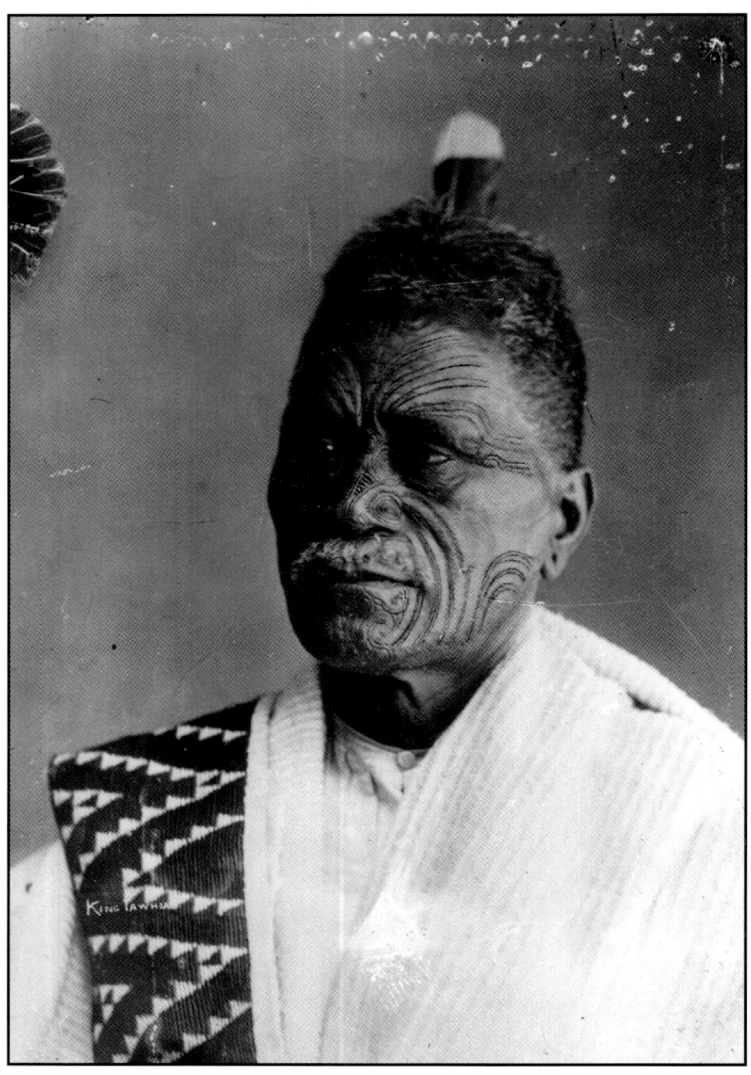

*Tawhiao Matutaera Potatau Te Wherowhero (King Tawhiao)*
ALEXANDER TURNBULL LIBRARY F- 50875-1/2 -

*Hone Mohi Tawhai*
ALEXANDER TURNBULL LIBRARY F- 96631-1/2 -

*Tutakangahau (left), and Numia Kereru*
ALEXANDER TURNBULL LIBRARY, F- 4156-1/2 -

*Te Wahanui*
ALEXANDER TURNBULL LIBRARY F- 91903-1/2 -

*Wi Pere*
ALEXANDER TURNBULL LIBRARY F- 34936-1/2 -

*Hone Heke*
ALEXANDER TURNBULL LIBRARY F- 188-35MM-A

*Hirini Taiwhanga*
ALEXANDER TURNBULL LIBRARY, F-146999-1/2 -

# 11. Conclusion

Although the specific focus of this publication has been on Maori committees, both official and unofficial, in the nineteenth century, a much broader and more fundamental issue has inevitably arisen throughout it. Maori consistently sought to establish committees and to have these recognised by the Crown not because they were simply looking to mimic Pakeha structures, but because they sought a place for themselves in the new colonial order that would not involve being entirely subsumed by it. Committees of various kinds were close enough to traditional tribal runanga (and, indeed, in some cases virtually indistinguishable from them) to allow Maori to feel that they had found a flexible and adaptive means by which they might engage with the colonial order on terms of mutual benefit. For Maori, this meant preserving tribal authority and control – rangatiratanga – and retaining sufficient autonomy to administer their lands and other affairs in a considered and collective manner, as both the Treaty of Waitangi and the New Zealand Constitution Act of 1852 had apparently promised them. Insofar as Pakeha were concerned, however, the key to Maori 'civilisation' and advancement in the nineteenth century lay in the destruction of tribal structures and the individualisation of titles to Maori land. Maori would, it was hoped, eventually become amalgamated into the mainstream of colonial society, taking their place as brown-skinned versions of their European colonisers.

From the perspective of late twentieth-century New Zealand it is easy to ascribe cynical and sinister motives to those Crown officials and settlers who worked towards the destruction of tribal institutions in the nineteenth century. Clearly they were only too alive to the fact that by undermining the collective cohesion of

Maori society they were also helping to facilitate the alienation of Maori lands on terms beneficial to Pakeha, and this knowledge undoubtedly played a big part in the process of Maori disempowerment which the Crown encouraged from the mid-1850s. Yet on the other hand, most cultures throughout history have tended to be guilty of ethnocentrism, and one should not condemn nineteenth-century Pakeha purely because they sought to impose their own institutions and ideas on Maori. Most of those who argued against allowing Maori committees to investigate titles to land were undoubtedly sincere in stating that the Native Land Court could undertake this process more effectively, even whilst appreciating that it would also help to expedite the alienation of Maori lands.

Whatever the actual motivations, however, it is clear that in the early years of British rule in New Zealand, the Crown was hardly in a position to enforce its will on Maori, and because of that Maori institutions and involvement in the system of government were of necessity tolerated. Yet while the Constitution Act of 1852 had envisaged the establishment of districts within which Maori customs and authority might be recognised, its practical effect was to transfer power to the settlers, leaving Maori increasingly excluded from any real say in the administration of the colony. This, combined with increasingly dubious Crown land purchase tactics, often involving surreptitious sales transacted with compliant individuals without consultation with the rest of the tribe, prompted many Maori communities to develop more formal tribal and supra-tribal structures aimed at retaining some measure of collective cohesion in the face of efforts to undermine this. The proto-nationalist Kingitanga was one outcome of these developments, and the revival of tribal runanga another.

It was the emergence of a pan-tribal political movement, opposed to land sales and intent on preserving Maori autonomy, which was most feared by Crown officials and settlers; and with local runanga being revived spontaneously, the government increasingly moved towards a strategy of co-opting these into the system and using them to counter the perceived threat of the

King movement. Indirect rule, not genuine self-government for Maori, was the goal, underlain by the desire to investigate and individualise land titles, thereby facilitating alienation for the purposes of settlement. William Fox, the Premier, put this succinctly in 1862 in defending the involvement of runanga in the investigation of titles by stating that the government had 'no choice but to use it, it exists as a fact...and, if we do not use it for good purposes, it will assuredly be used against us for bad'. Tribal authority was recognised reluctantly, and only until such time as the government might be in a position to subvert it. Unable to enforce its will, the state instead sought to rule through the runanga, while at the same time encouraging them to make land available for settlement by determining and individualising titles.

Grey's 'new institutions' scheme was ultimately undermined by the ulterior motives which had underlain it. And once it became clear that runanga were not prepared to simply throw open Maori lands for full-scale settlement, the scheme also became discredited in the eyes of many settlers. In 1861 the Judges of the Supreme Court had informed Governor Gore Browne that a formal court of law was not an appropriate place for determining titles to Maori land, instead advocating that Maori should themselves be entrusted with this task, perhaps with the assistance of the local Resident Magistrate. The 1862 Native Lands Act, which formed an integral part of the 'new institutions' scheme, had also envisaged that a local panel of chiefs would decide on titles under the supervision of the local government agent but proved largely inoperative owing to the Waikato War, after promising beginnings in the north.

By 1865, however, settler attitudes had hardened, and F.D. Fenton, appointed first Chief Judge of a newly-constituted Native Land Court, set about creating a highly formal institution, based on the Supreme Court, which provided for minimal Maori involvement in the process of determining titles to their own lands. The Court as created under the 1865 Native Lands Act was one which applied a rigid and distorted view of customary Maori land tenure, with an adversarial and highly expensive 'winner-takes-all' system of land title adjudication fomenting dissension between rival claimants and encouraging spurious claims and false evidence. Tribal authority was grievously undermined by the fact that any individual could initiate an investigation, compelling other owners to also participate or risk losing their land altogether, and alienation was facilitated both by the high costs involved in obtaining title and by the fact that each individual was free to dispose of his or her interests once determined without reference to the rest of the tribe. This process, fundamentally at odds with customary Maori land tenure and the collective decision-making process which lay at the heart of tribal autonomy, was introduced without consultation with Maori, who were not represented in Parliament at the time that the Court was established.

By the early 1870s the operations of the Court, combined with those of land sharks and speculators, in parts of the country such as Hawke's Bay, had become a colonial scandal, and when Maori got an opportunity to express their views on the Court to a commission appointed in 1871, few were flattering in their comments. Paora Tuhaere of Ngati Whatua and Te Wheoro of Waikato, for example, both suggested that the Court should be done away with, and Maori allowed to determine titles themselves through runanga or committees selected by the claimants. Similar suggestions were made by other Maori, and many complained about the costs associated with the Court and the fact that the legislation under which it operated had never been translated into Maori.

Yet despite support from influential figures such as Sir William Martin and Edward Shortland for greater Maori involvement in the process of determining titles to their own lands, little was done in this direction. In 1872 the Native Minister, Donald McLean, introduced a Native Councils Bill, which provided for the election of local councils in any district in which Maori were in the majority and retained their lands, councils which were to be headed by 'presidents' under the supervision of the local Resident Magistrates. As well as being empowered to pass by-laws on a wide range of matters of local concern, the proposed councils would also investigate and decide on land disputes, with their decisions to be ratified by the Native Land Court if agreement could be reached between the parties. Even these very limited proposed rights for Maori were enough, however, to spark fears that the bill would destroy the authority of the Native Land Court and lead to the councils assuming a much wider range of powers. In the face of this opposition, McLean was forced to withdraw the bill in 1873, notwithstanding the considerable support it had gained from Maori communities around the country, and some alleged that the government had never seriously intended to pass the bill, but had merely used it to buy support for McLean's new Native Land Act.

Despite the failure of McLean's bill, Maori agitation for the legal right to determine land titles themselves if anything intensified during the remainder of the 1870s, and in the absence of legally-constituted committees, numerous unofficial bodies were continually established and revived as a means of maintaining some degree of tribal control and cohesion in the face of overwhelming pressures towards fragmentation. But so long as the Native Land Court remained in existence the authority of these committees was tenuous. Disgruntled individuals or hapu could ignore committee decisions and instead try their luck in the Land Court. In Wairarapa, where a very active committees movement had emerged in the 1870s, for example, E.S. Maunsell reported that local Maori were inclined to withhold their lands from the operations of the Native Land Act 'except in cases of claims to succeed deceased grantees, and of disputed titles forced into Court by one party having animosity towards the other, and of mercenary motives, when sullenness and indisposition to allow the hearing to proceed on the objecting side result'. And while out-of-court settlements between contending claimants were often ratified by Land Court Judges, more formal Maori structures for investigating titles tended to be viewed with a mixture of jealously and contempt, as also occurred in Wairarapa, where on at least one occasion the presiding Judge informed the claimants that the Court in no way recognised Maori committees or their findings and would therefore disregard the agreement arranged by one such committee with respect to a disputed block.

Unofficial committees seem to have fared best in districts that the Native Land Court had yet to fully reach, such as the King Country, Te Urewera, Upper Whanganui, Taupo and Rotorua. Yet even in the absence of the Court, efforts to maintain some degree of tribal control and cohesion were continually in danger of being undermined by both Crown and private land purchase agents, who frequently plied individuals with groundbait in the form of advance payments when they could not induce tribal gatherings to agree to sell their lands and to submit their claims to the Court for investigation. In the Rotorua district, for example, committees were set up in the early 1870s largely in order to combat the activities of Crown land purchase agents. But even Tuhourangi's Putaiki, perhaps the most active and successful of these committees, could do little to prevent Crown and private parties from advancing sums to other sections of Te Arawa in respect of lands to which they laid claim.

The Komiti Nui o Rotorua, which claimed a wider jurisdiction, also faced similar problems, its members apparently targeted by Crown agents for cash advances in the hope of undermining its authority. Despite this, the Komiti Nui remained in a powerful if increasingly tenuous position, and when Fenton arrived in the district in November 1880 to seek an arrangement with Te Arawa for the formation of a township, he soon discovered that he could achieve little without the support of the Komiti. The agreement reached by Fenton that 99-year leases for a township site would be publicly auctioned by the Crown on behalf of the land's owners once these had been determined by the Native Land Court was signed by several members of the Komiti; correspondence between its Chairman and the Chief Judge strongly suggested that this agreement was conditional on the Court sitting merely to confirm the Komiti's prior award with respect to the land. Despite this, however, H.W. Brabant's prediction that the Fenton agreement would prove to be 'the thin end of the wedge which will eventually open their lands to European settlement' was ultimately proved correct.

*Conclusion*

When the Court opened at Ohinemutu in January 1881, 'The Rotorua Committee tried to have their standing recognised, but the Court could not do so'. When the township block was awarded almost in its entirety to Ngati Whakaue, other claimants wrote to Fenton to complain that this ignored the decision reached by the Komiti. Ngati Whakaue then attempted to include the names of others on their list of owners, but were warned by Fenton that 'The Komiti should not return to things that have once been settled' – thus ignoring the fact that it was the Native Land Court which had returned to matters already settled by the Komiti. Ngati Whakaue subsequently sought to repudiate the agreement, but found it was already too late, as groups rushed to have their lands investigated and put through the Court in order to protect their interests, setting off two decades of almost continuous Native Land Court sittings at Rotorua which would see less than one per cent of the district remaining as papatupu lands early in the new century. By late in 1881 the Komiti Nui, riven by internal divisions resulting from the Native Land Court's introduction to the Rotorua region, had along with the Putaki been reduced from the status of an effective local government to that of an impotent bit player, notwithstanding later partially successful efforts to revive it.

While Te Arawa's committees were for most of the 1870s seeking to defend tribal autonomy, in districts where the Court had already penetrated many tribes were trying to reassert this autonomy. The Hawke's Bay-based Repudiation movement, led by Henare Matua and backed up by its newspaper *Te Wananga*, played an important proselytising role in encouraging the formation of committees in districts such as Taupo and Upper Whanganui, at the same time urging tribes to petition Parliament on the subject. In fact, by the late 1870s committees appear to have become the rule rather than exception in most Maori communities, and with Paora Tuhaere's Orakei Parliament and Ngapuhi's Treaty of Waitangi movement also demanding the right to investigate titles to their lands themselves, through their own elected committees, it was becoming increasingly difficult for the government to issue its standard retort that the Native

Land Court was the 'committee' appointed by law.

In 1880 Hone Mohi Tawhai, the member of Parliament for Northern Maori, drafted a bill providing for committees 'to have authority to enquire into disputes arising in the district in connection with the surveying of land, applications for the investigation of title to lands, and the sale of lands upon the application of the persons interested in the land under dispute'. John Bryce, the Native Minister, undertook to have this bill printed and translated and 'properly drawn' out; by the time the member for Eastern Maori, Henare Tomoana, introduced it into the Assembly in 1881, any reference to surveys or sales had been omitted, although the committees were still empowered to investigate title disputes, with the Native Land Court obliged to 'take judicial notice' of their decisions in the event that both parties agreed to abide by this. In 1882 this bill got as far as a second reading, despite Bryce's belief that it would be 'most inadvisable to bind the Native Land Court to decisions reached by Maori committees', with several members suggesting that these might actually help to expedite the Court's work. Bowing to this pressure, Bryce in 1883 introduced a much-modified bill which would allow the committees to report their decisions merely 'for the information of the Court', and to arbitrate on petty disputes with the agreement of both disputants. Though some members argued that the committees should be given genuine powers in order to assist the Native Land Court in its work, most apparently concurred with the view of the Premier, Whitaker, that the measure was a 'harmless' one, innocent enough in itself, of which settlers need have no fear. In other words, it was a sop to Maori aspirations to administer their own lands: the Native Land Court would remain in the driving seat. Even Bryce admitted as much, within months of having successfully sponsored the bill through Parliament, when he informed the Governor confidentially that the notion that Maori committees could successfully determine titles was 'utterly impracticable'.

This attitude was reflected in the manner in which the Native Committees Act was implemented. As with McLean's proposed measure of 1872, Maori had begun electing committees and discussing boundaries in anticipation of the bill's passage. Unfortunately, while most of these committees were based on tribal boundaries, Bryce had already instructed his Native Under-Secretary that he did not wish the districts to be too numerous – six or seven...would be enough for the North Island'. As Williams says, initial Maori enthusiasm for the Act was not sustained, as many came to realise that, even without legal standing, their own committees were preferable. After all, the latter were free from government control or supervision, could define their own boundaries as they chose, received just as much funding from the Crown (nil), and stood just as much chance of having their decisions confirmed by the Native Land Court.

With old enemies often being lumped together into one huge district, most Maori took little interest in the proceedings of the Committees, allowing Bryce to assert hypocritically he would have to reconsider whether the legislation was of any real value. For those who did become involved, this involvement mostly took the form of 'squabbling between tribal groups for control of the committee elections and requests for more committees representative of smaller units'.[1]  Energetic and enthusiastic figures such as Hone Mohi Tawhai, the Chairman of the Bay of Islands Committee, strove hard to make them a success but were ultimately frustrated by their lack of any power, whilst other committees, of which the Hauraki Committee was typical, wrote to the Native Under-Secretary asking 'to be informed of the nature of their duties, seeing that they have now met three times and have had nothing to do'.

Tawhai found it difficult to persuade northern Maori that there was any point in taking their claims before the Committee, given that the Native Land Court was free to ignore any decision which it reached, a situation apparently exacerbated by Crown officials who poured ridicule on the Committee's lack of any real authority. And according to W.L. Rees, who considered the 1883 Act little more than 'an impotent and cruel farce', the Native Land Court, 'jealous of this new tribunal, and looking with disfavour upon the possible loss of any of its own power or prestige, treated the finding and the reports of the committees with contempt; they were immediately relegated to the waste paper basket'.

While John Ballance, Bryce's successor as Native Minister, proved slightly more sympathetic to the Committees, even granting them a short-lived allowance for expenses (albeit no more between twelve Committees, with up to 144 members, than what one Native Land Court Judge received annually by way of salary), on the key promise of granting them greater jurisdiction with respect to investigating titles there was to be no action. Ballance's Native Lands Administration Act of 1886, which provided for block committees elected by the owners to administer the lands once title had been determined by the Court, was one of the few pieces of legislation to recognise the right of tribal or communal dealings with respect to Maori lands. Even so, the Act proved inoperative because of Maori objections to the large powers conceded to a government-appointed Pakeha official under the legislation.

Maori continued to petition, lobby, and introduce bills calling for the right to investigate the titles to and manage their own lands themselves, through committees of their own choosing, often without reference to the Native Committees Act, which even Pakeha politicians were describing as a 'dead letter' as early as 1884. These appeals for the most part fell on deaf ears, however, notwithstanding the support they received from the Native Land Laws Commission of 1891, which condemned individual dealings in Maori lands and described the 1883 Act as a 'hollow shell' which 'mocked and still mocks the Natives with a semblance of authority'. In 1892 a Kotahitanga, or union of the tribes, was formed, with one of its fundamental tenets being the abolition of the Native Land Court and its replacement by Maori committees. Yet despite a petition signed by nearly half the Maori population in support of this demand, and occasionally successful boycotts of the Court, this aspiration received little support from the Liberal government, which was more intent on the large-scale acquisition of Maori land to enable 'closer settlement' by Pakeha, using coercive legislation designed to compel Maori to submit their claims for investigation before the Court.

There was, however, one district which remained a special case. The Urewera region was the last part of New Zealand still effectively outside the writ of British law and almost entirely unavailable for European settlement. At the conclusion of hostilities in their district, in June 1872, Tuhoe and other iwi of the Urewera held a meeting at which a council of 70 (Te Whitu Tekau) was established to define their rohe and defend it against 'roads, leasing and selling of land'. When H.W. Brabant, the Opotiki Resident Magistrate, visited Ruatahuna in 1874, he found that Te Whitu Tekau had appointed a secretary, had their own flag (described as 'showing the bust of a black man on a red ground') and had 'matured a scheme...to get all the tribes to join them in a sort of land league, to forbid the sale and leasing of lands, roads, &c'. Despite Brabant's exaggerated assertion that Tuhoe could not even agree on this amongst themselves, the fact that the Urewera district was not immediately coveted for the purposes of European settlement meant that they were able to maintain a high degree of tribal cohesion and autonomy.

Tuhoe had gained the impression that Donald McLean, Native Minister in the early 1870s, had sanctioned the creation of their protectorate, yet in the late 1880s found their requests for an official Committee under the 1883 Act denied on the grounds that any such Committee would more than likely continue to 'keep the country locked up'. With speculation as to the existence of gold in the district and the successful 'opening up' of the King Country, attention had begun to focus on Te Urewera. Although the Liberal administration initially sought to 'open up' the latter region by undertaking surreptitious surveys with only minority support from the tribe, with armed conflict dangerously close, by 1895 Seddon was forced to concede Tuhoe's demand that legally-constituted committees manage the tribe's affairs. In order to gain a foothold in the region, the Crown had been compelled to accept the first piece of legislation which gave Maori any serious say in the investigation of titles to and subsequent administration of their lands – even if the underlying principles of the Urewera District Native Reserve Act of 1896 were to be cynically ignored in the early decades of the twentieth century, when the opportunity arose to purchase individual interests from an impoverished Tuhoe people.

By the late 1890s the Crown's aggressive land purchase policy had been so successful that it was in a position to ease up slightly, and in 1900 legislation was passed providing for the establishment of district Maori Land Councils which were to be responsible for leasing Maori lands to Europeans, thereby averting settler pressure for the acquisition of the freehold. Yet with the Councils having Pakeha majorities, many Maori were understandably wary of vesting their lands in them, and by 1905 the government, also facing pressure from Europeans critical of so-called 'native landlordism', returned to coercive measures, renewing large-scale purchasing of individual interests and providing for the compulsory vesting of Maori lands in the Councils. By 1909 the Papatupu Block Committees provided for under the Maori Lands Administration Act of 1900 had also been swept away, even though they had reportedly achieved 'astonishing' results, disproving any notion that Maori were incapable of determining land titles themselves. The Native Land Court, temporarily marginalised, returned to centre stage as the Crown once again unilaterally assumed the right to decide for itself the best means of determining the ownership of customary Maori lands. The Crown's much-vaunted policies purportedly aimed at amalgamation continued into the twentieth century, concomitant with Maori attempts to find a place for themselves which was not completely subordinate to that of the Pakeha. To return to the Waitangi Tribunal's *Taranaki Report*:

> Through war, protest, and petition, the single thread that most illuminates the historical fabric of Maori and Pakeha contact has been the Maori determination to maintain Maori autonomy and the Government's desire to destroy it. The irony is that the need for mutual recognition had been seen at the very foundation of the State, when the Treaty of Waitangi was signed.[2]

# Endnotes

## Chapter 1
1. Waitangi Tribunal, *The Taranaki Report: Kaupapa Tuatahi*, Wellington: GP Publications, 1996, p.5.
2. Ibid.

## Chapter 2
1. Ibid., p.199.
2. A. Ward, *A Show of Justice: Racial 'Amalgamation' in Nineteenth Century New Zealand*, Auckland: Auckland University Press/Oxford University Press, 1973, p.96.
3. Cooper to McLean, 29 November 1856, *Appendices to the Journals of the House of Representatives (AJHR)*, 1862, C–1, p.323.
4. Cooper to McLean, 9 May 1859, ibid., p.342.
5. Cooper to McLean, 12 March 1860, ibid., p.350. On the Hawke's Bay runanga movement see S.M. Cole, 'The Repudiation Movement: A Study of the Maori Land Protest Movement in Hawkes Bay in the 1870s', MA History thesis, Massey University, 1977, pp.9–19; on Poverty Bay, see K.M. Sanderson, '"These Neglected Tribes": A Study of the East Coast Maoris and their Missionary, William Willliams, 1834–1870', MA History thesis, University of Auckland, 1980; and W.H. Oliver and J.M. Thomson, *Challenge and Response: A Study of the Development of the Gisborne East Coast Region*, Gisborne: East Coast Development Research Association, 1971.
6. Ward, *Show of Justice*, p.97.
7. Ibid., p.98.
8. Cited in R.S. Hill, *Policing the Colonial Frontier: The Theory and Practice of Coercive Social and Racial Control in New Zealand, 1767–1867*, pt 2, Wellington: Government Printer, 1986, p.805.
9. A. Ward, 'Law and Law-enforcement on the New Zealand Frontier, 1840–1893', *New Zealand Journal of History*, vol 5, no 2, October 1971, p.138.

10  Ibid. See *AJHR*, 1860, E–1C, for Fenton's reports from Waikato.
11  Ward, *Show of Justice*, p.107; B.J. Dalton, *War and Politics in New Zealand 1855–1870*, Sydney: Sydney University Press, 1967, p79.
12  Ward, *Show of Justice*, p.108; AJHR, 1860, E–6B, pp.3–5.
13  Minutes of Kohimarama Conference, 18 July 1860, *AJHR*, 1860, E–9, p.10; see also C. Orange, 'The Covenant of Kohimarama: A Ratification of the Treaty of Waitangi', *New Zealand Journal of History*, vol 14, no 1, April 1980.
14  Minutes of Kohimarama Conference, 18 July 1860, *AJHR*, 1860, E–9, p.11; Ward, *Show of Justice*, p.117.
15  Cited in Dalton, *War and Politics*, p.145.
16  Governor to Chief Justice and Judges of the Supreme Court, 6 May 1861, *AJHR*, 1861, E–3, p.13.
17  Chief Justice and Judges of the Supreme Court to Governor, 9 May 1861, ibid.
18  Gore Browne memorandum, 25 May 1861, *AJHR*, 1861, E–3A, p.3.
19  *New Zealand Parliamentary Debates (NZPD)*, 1861–63, 25 August 1862, p.610.
20  Grey memorandum, October 1861, *AJHR*, 1862, E–2, p.11.
21  Ibid., p.12.
22  Fox, minute by Ministers, 31 October 1861, ibid., p.15.
23  Grey minute, n.d., ibid., p.16.
24  Fox, minute by Ministers, 31 October 1861, ibid., p.15.
25  Ward, Show of Justice, p.125.
26  Ibid., p.150.
27  *NZPD*, 1861–63, 22 July 1862, p.422.
28  Ward, *Show of Justice*, p.152.
29  *NZPD*, 1861–63, 25 August 1862, p.610.
30  Cited in S. Cross and B. Bargh, 'The Whanganui District' (Rangahaua Whanui Working Paper: First Release), Waitangi Tribunal, April 1996, p.28.
31  Ward, *Show of Justice*, p.152.
32  *Daily Southern Cross*, 30 June 1864.
33  J. Rogan to Native Secretary, 9 June 1864, Rogan letterbook, BADW A588 530, National Archives – Auckland.
34  Ward, *Show of Justice*, p.180.
35  Ibid.; W.L Renwick, 'Fenton, Francis Dart', in *The Dictionary of New Zealand Biography (DNZB), Volume One, 1769–1869*, Wellington: Allen & Unwin/ Department of Internal Affairs, 1990, p.122.

36 Ward, *Show of Justice*, p.180.
37 Ward, 'Law and Law-enforcement', p.140–1.
38 Ward, *Show of Justice*, p.213.
39 See, for example, H.A. Ballara, 'The Origins of Ngati Kahungunu', PhD History thesis, Victoria University of Wellington, 1991.
40 Waitangi Tribunal, *Taranaki Report*, p.281; for an example of the latter see B.D. Gilling, 'By Whose Custom? The Operation of the Native Land Court in the Chatham Islands', *Victoria University of Wellington Law Review*, vol 23, no 3, October 1993.
41 Ward, *Show of Justice*, p.186.
42 Report of the Native Land Laws Commission ('Rees–Carroll Report'), *AJHR*, 1891, Session II, G–1, p.xi.
43 Ibid., minutes of evidence, p.145.
44 *NZPD*, 29 August 1870, vol 9, p.361.
45 Waitangi Tribunal, *Report of the Waitangi Tribunal on the Orakei Claim (Wai–9)*, Wellington: Waitangi Tribunal, 1987, p.123
46 Ward, *Show of Justice*, p.186.
47 Cited in A. Ward et al., 'Historical Report on the Ngati Kahungunu Rohe', Crown–Congress Joint Working Party, 1993, p.75.
48 Rees–Carroll Report, *AJHR*, 1891, Session II, G–1, p.vii.
49 Cited in Ward, *Show of Justice*, p.217.
50 M.P.K. Sorrenson, 'The Purchase of Maori Lands, 1865–1892', MA History thesis, Auckland University College, 1955, p.129; Rees–Carroll Report, *AJHR*, 1891, Session II, G–1, p.x.
51 W.L. Rees memorandum, n.d., *AJHR*, 1884, Session II, G–2, p.4.
52 Ward, *Show of Justice*, p.256.
53 Ward et al., 'Ngati Kahungunu' p.69.
54 M.P.K. Sorrenson, 'Land Purchase Methods and their Effect on Maori Population, 1865–1901', *Journal of the Polynesian Society*, vol 65, no 3, 1956, p.186.
55 Minutes of evidence, *AJHR*, 1891, Session II, G–1, p.9.
56 Sorrenson, 'Land Purchase Methods', pp.192–6; I. Pool, *Te Iwi Maori: A New Zealand Population Past, Present and Projected*, Auckland: Auckland University Press, 1991, pp.88–103.
57 *NZPD*, 5 August 1885, vol 52, p.515.
58 F.D. Fenton, *Important Judgements Delivered in the Compensation Court and Native Land Court 1866–1879*, Auckland: Native Land Court, 1879, p.19.
59 Ward, *Show of Justice*, p.187.
60 Waitangi Tribunal, *Taranaki Report*, pp.285–6
61 Premier to Administrator, 12 December 1882, *AJHR*, 1883, A–6, p.5.

## Chapter 3

1. *AJHR*, 1883, J–1, p.1.
2. Cooper to J.C. Richmond, Native Minister, 14 August 1867, *AJHR*, 1867, A–15.
3. Fenton to Richmond, 11 July 1867, *AJHR*, 1867, A–10, p.4.
4. Ward, *Show of Justice*, p.216.
5. See Ward *et al.*, CCJWP 'Ngati Kahungunu', pp.105–8.
6. Haultain to McLean, 18 July 1871, *AJHR*, 1871, A–2A, pp.3–4. Haultain remarked that 'scarcely a Native...examined...expressed a desire to see the Court abolished or materially altered in its constitution'.
7. Joint evidence of Te Wheoro and Tuhaere, 18 February 1871, ibid., pp.25–6.
8. G. Scott, 'Te Wheoro, Wiremu Te Morehu Maipapa'; S. Oliver, 'Tuhaere, Paora', *DNZB*, vol 1, pp.524, 552.
9. Joint evidence of Te Wheoro and Tuhaere, 18 February 1871, *AJHR*, 1871, A–2A, p.26.
10. Ibid.
11. Wi Te Wheoro to Haultain, 23 May 1870 [1871?], ibid., p.28.
12. Ibid.
13. Ibid., p.29.
14. B.D. Gilling, 'Engine of Destruction? An Introduction to the History of the Maori Land Court', *Victoria University of Wellington Law Review*, vol 24 no 2, 1994, p.127.
15. Sorrenson, 'Purchase of Maori Lands', p.39.
16. Evidence of Hemi Tautari, n.d., *AJHR*, 1871, A–2A, pp.29–30.
17. Evidence of Wiremu Pomare, n.d., ibid., p.35.
18. Evidence of Henare Tomoana, 31 May 1871, ibid., p.37.
19. Karaitiana Takamoana to General Assembly, 29 July 1871, ibid., p.40.
20. Evidence of Wiremu Patene, n.d., ibid., p.36.
21. Evidence of Wiremu Hikairo, 20 April 1871, ibid., p.31.
22. Ibid., p.33.
23. Ibid., p.32.
24. Ibid., p.34.
25. Ibid., p.33.
26. Ward, *Show of Justice*, p.253.
27. General Report by Chairman, *AJHR*, 1873, G–7, p.9.
28. *AJHR*, 1891, Session II, G–1, p.x.
29. H.T. Clarke to Native Under-Secretary, 27 January 1871, *AJHR*, 1871, F–6A, p.7.

Notes to pages 50-56

30 D.A. Armstrong. 'Ngati Makino and the Crown: 1880–1960', 1995, p.46.
31 Clarke to Native Under-Secretary, 14 February 1872, *AJHR*, 1872, F–3A, p.7.
32 Hamlin to Native Minister, 15 July 1872, *AJHR*, 1872, F–3, p.9.
33 Brabant to Native Minister, 24 June 1872, ibid., p.11.
34 Locke to Native Minister, 4 July 1872, *AJHR*, 1872, F–3A p.32.
35 Clarke to Native Minister, 27 December 1871, *AJHR*, 1872, F–4, p.4.
36 Te Whenuanui and others to the government, 9 June 1872, *AJHR*, 1872, F–3A, p.25. See chapter 9 for a more detailed discussion of the Urewera district.
37 *AJHR*, 1872, H–11, p.5.
38 *NZPD*, 11 October 1872, vol 13, p.587.
39 *Bills Rejected*, 1873; memorandum re Native Councils Bill, n.d. [1873], McLean Papers, MS–Papers–32–31, Alexander Turnbull Library.
40 *NZPD*, 22 October 1872, vol 13, p.895.
41 Ibid., p.897.
42 Ibid., p.896.
43 Ibid., p.897.
44 Ibid., p. 899.
45 Ibid., p. 898.
46 R.W. Woon to Native Under-Secretary, 10 May 1873, *AJHR*, 1873, G–1, p.17.
47 Brabant to Native Under-Secretary, 23 May 1873, ibid., p.10; Campbell to Native Under-Secretary, 17 May 1873, ibid., p.13.
48 Clarke to Native Under-Secretary, 9 June 1873, ibid., p.6.
49 Ibid., p.8. In an earlier report, Clarke had noted that Ngati Whakaue 'looked upon the measure as their own'. Ngati Uenukukopako and Ngati Rangiteaorere 'expressed themselves highly satisfied, and only regretted that it was not law now as they had several land disputes amongst themselves and with other hapus of the Arawa which they were anxious should be settled', while Ngati Pikiao gave the same expressions of support, suggesting only that the Council rather than the Governor should be given the power to select the president as its members would have a better knowledge of who would be capable of filling that office. Clarke to Native Under-Secretary, 23 December 1872, *AJHR*, 1873, G–1B, p.3–4.
50 Memorandum re Native Councils Bill, n.d. [1873], McLean Papers, MS–Papers–32–31, Alexander Turnbull Library.

271

51  Ibid.
52  Ward, *Show of Justice*, p.248.
53  *NZPD*, 25 July 1873, vol 14, p.108.
54  *NZPD*, 30 September 1873, vol 15, p.1514.
55  J.D. Ormond to McLean, 8 October 1873, McLean Papers, MS–Copy–Micro–0535–077 (folder 486), Alexander Turnbull Library.

## Chapter 4

1   *NZPD*, 30 September 1873, vol 15, p.1514
2   Ward *et al.*, 'Ngati Kahungunu', appendix 1, p.149; P. Goldsmith, 'Wairarapa' (Rangahaua Whanui Working Paper: First Release), Waitangi Tribunal, 1996, p.83.
3   Cited in C.L. Andrews, 'Aspects of Development: The Maori Situation, 1870–1890', MA Anthropology thesis, University of Auckland, 1968, p.97.
4   *Te Wananga*, 26 May 1877.
5   Ibid., 9 June 1877.
6   Ibid., 7 July 1877.
7   E.S. Maunsell to Native Minister, 23 April 1880, *AJHR*, 1880, G–4, p.12.
8   Ibid., 28 July 1877.
9   Whatakoari [?] and four others to Native Minister, 10 December 1879, N.O. 80/15, MA 23/13A, National Archives.
10  Maunsell to Native Under-Secretary, 23 May 1885, MA 23/13A, NA.
11  M.P.K. Sorrenson, 'The Politics of Land', in J.G.A. Pocock (ed.), *The Maori and New Zealand Politics*, Auckland: Blackwood & Janet Paul, 1965, p.40.
12  *Te Wananga*, 15 April 1876.
13  A. Ballara, 'Takamoana, Karaitiana', in *DNZB, vol 1*, p.419.
14  Ibid., p.420.
15  See V. O'Malley, 'Report for the Crown Forestry Rental Trust on the East Coast Confiscation Legislation and its Implementation', 1994, pp.149–55.
16  Cited in K. Sinclair, *Kinds of Peace: Maori People After the Wars 1870–1885*, Auckland: Auckland University Press, 1991, p.103.
17  'The Ngai Tahu Tribe' to the Speaker of the House of Representatives and colleagues, 21 October 1873, Le 1, 1874/121, NA.

18  A. Ballara and G Scott, 'Crown Purchases of Maori Land in Early Provincial Hawke's Bay', 1994, pp.172–3.
19  Translation of panui for meeting at Pakowhai, 1876, Sinclair, *Kinds of Peace*, p.107; a contemporary translation of the same notice can be found in *AJHR*, 1876, G–5, p.8.
20  *Te Wananga*, 15 April 1876.
21  In February 1878 T.W.R. Porter reported from Waiapu on plans for a 'large or general council...to be established throughout the east coast from Wairarapa to Tauranga[,] the district to be sub divided and a representative elected for each musterings of the council to be held half yearly'. Porter to R.J. Gill, AD 103/8 NA.
22  A. Ballara, 'Matua, Henare', in *DNZB vol 1*, p.285.
23  L. Cox, *Kotahitanga: The Search for Maori Political Unity*, Auckland: Oxford University Press, 1993, p.65.
24  A. Ward, 'Whanganui Ki Maniapoto' (Preliminary Historical Report Wai–48 and Related Claims), 1992, p.20.
25  Ibid., pp.20–2.
26  Cross and Bargh, 'Whanganui District', p.33.
27  Woon to Assistant Native Secretary, 21 February 1872 *AJHR*, 1872, F–3A, p.19.
28  Cross and Bargh, 'Whanganui District', p.36.
29  Woon to Native Under-Secretary, 10 May 1873, *AJHR*, 1873, G–1, p.17.
30  Woon to Native Under-Secretary, 16 June 1874, *AJHR*, 1874, G–2, p.14.
31  Cross and Bargh, 'Whanganui District', p.46.
32  Woon to Native Under-Secretary, 16 June 1874, *AJHR*, 1874, G–2, p.15.
33  Ibid.
34  Woon to Native Under-Secretary, 21 May 1875, *AJHR*, 1875, G–1, pp.11–12.
35  Ward, *Show of Justice*, p.242.
36  Woon to Native Under-Secretary, 22 May 1877, *AJHR*, 1877, G–1, p.16.
37  Ibid.
38  Woon to Native Under-Secretary, 28 May 1878, *AJHR*, 1878, G–1, p.13.
39  Woon to Native Under-Secretary, 24 May 1879, *AJHR*, 1879, Session I, G–1, p.9.
40  Woon to Native Under-Secretary, 28 May 1878, *AJHR*, 1878, G–1, p.13.

| | |
|---|---|
| 41 | Ward, 'Whanganui Ki Maniapoto', p.29; Cross and Bargh, 'Whanganui District', p.51; T. Dreaver, 'Te Rangihiwinui, Te Keepa', in *DNZB*, vol 1, pp.492–3. |
| 42 | Ward, 'Whanganui Ki Maniapoto', pp.29–30. |
| 43 | *AJHR*, 1883, J–1. |
| 44 | Sorrenson, 'Purchase of Maori Lands', p.118; Cross and Bargh, 'Whanganui District', p.121. |

## Chapter 5

| | |
|---|---|
| 1 | This section is largely based on V. O'Malley, 'The Crown and Te Arawa, c. 1840–1910: An Overview Report Commissioned by the Whakarewarewa Forest Trust', 1995, chs. 4 and 5. |
| 2 | *AJHR*, 1874, I–3, p.2. |
| 3 | Ibid. |
| 4 | Evidence of Wiremu Maihi Te Rangikaheke, 24 August 1874, Le 1, 1874/9, NA. |
| 5 | Davis and Mitchell to Native Under-Secretary, 24 April 1876, *AJHR*, 1876, G–5, p.2. |
| 6 | *AJHR*, 1874, I–3, pp.2–3 |
| 7 | Davis and Mitchell to Native Under-Secretary, 24 April 1876, *AJHR*, 1876, G–5, P.2. |
| 8 | Te Rangipuawhe to Native Minister, 17 August 1882, MA–MLP 1, 1882/342 pt1, NA. |
| 9 | Davis and Mitchell to J.D. Ormond, 23 August 1873, MA–MLP 1, 1873/159, NA. |
| 10 | *Bay of Plenty Times*, 20 August 1873. |
| 11 | Davis and Mitchell to Native Minister, 30 October 1874, MA–MLP 1, 1882/107, NA. |
| 12 | Under section 42 of the Immigration and Public Works Amendment Act 1871, Crown agents (unlike private parties),were permitted to negotiate land purchases prior to any award of the Native Land Court where the land in question was specifically required for gold–mining, special settlements, or railways. In practice, however, this clause was interpreted much more liberally as allowing the Crown to legally make advances on any lands. In the case of Te Arawa this clause was used in combination with powers granted it under the Native Land Acts of 1866 and 1873 to suspend the operations of the Native Land Court in any district in order to advance sums on a considerable area of land, thereby preventing private parties from completing any transactions if it appeared unlikely its own would be finalised. Moreover, the Government |

Native Land Purchases Act 1877 was even more explicit, allowing the Governor to exclude private purchasers from any lands under negotiation by the Crown. The Waitangi Tribunal has commented that 'the payment of tamana [advance money] was undoubtedly an established pressure tactic, an unfair practice designed to purchase land as quickly and cheaply as possible, and incompatible with the Crown's fiduciary duty under the Treaty. Tamana was a sprat to catch the mackerel'. Waitangi Tribunal, *The Te Roroa Report 1992*, Wellington: Brooker & Friend, 1992, p.60.

13  Davis and Mitchell to Ormond, 23 August 1873, MA–MLP 1, 1873/159, NA.
14  Davis and Mitchell to Native Under-Secretary, 24 April 1876, *AJHR*, 1876, G–5, p.3.
15  *New Zealand Gazette*, 21 August 1873, no.51, pp.475–6. In 1874 a further proclamation was issued, confirming the previous suspension under the provisions of the Native Lands Act 1873. *New Zealand Gazette*, 17 September 1874, no 50, p.632.
16  *Bay of Plenty Times*, 1 November 1873.
17  Notes of meeting with Tuhourangi, 19 December 1873, *AJHR*, 1874, G–1, p.16.
18  Te Keepa Te Rangipuawhe informed a Land Court hearing in 1882 that in 1866 Tuhourangi had conducted a series of meetings in order to define their boundaries. Maori Land Court Rotorua Minute Book 3, pp.196–7, Alexander Turnbull Library.
19  Notes of Meeting held with Tuhourangi, 19 December 1873, *AJHR*, 1874, G–1, p.17.
20  Hamlin to Native Under-Secretary, 19 June 1874, *AJHR*, 1874, G–2A, p.1.
21  *Te Wananga*, 24 October 1874.
22  Ibid., 26 January 1875.
23  Ibid., 26 February 1875.
24  Ibid., 30 September 1876.
25  Taekata Rawiri and others to Native Minister, 21 May 1874, MA–MLP 1, 1874/316, NA.
26  Hamlin to Native Under-Secretary, 19 June 1874, *AJHR*, 1874, G–2A, p.1.
27  Clarke to Native Minister, 29 June 1874, MA–MLP 1, 1874/316, NA.
28  Clarke to Mitchell and Davis, 7 August 1874, MA–MLP 1, 1874/316, NA.
29  Mitchell and Davis memorandum, 9 April 1875, MA–MLP 1, 1875/146, NA.

30  Hamlin to Native Under-Secretary, 28 May 1875, *AJHR*, 1875, G–1, p.15.
31  Davis and Mitchell to Native Under-Secretary, 10 July 1875, MA–MLP 1, 1875/320, NA.
32  Davis to Native Under-Secretary, 18 June 1876, *AJHR*, 1876, G–5, p.6.
33  Gilbert Mair, Journal, 12 February, 17–29 March 1876, MS–Papers–92–49, Alexander Turnbull Library.
34  Cited in Davis to Native Under-Secretary, 15 June 1876, *AJHR*, 1876, G–5, p.7.
35  Clarke memorandum, 25 May 1876, MA–MLP 1, 1885/17, NA.
36  *Bay of Plenty Times*, 26 July 1876; Clarke memorandum for A. Mackay, 22 November 1876, MA–MLP 1, 1885/17, NA; *New Zealand Gazette*, 22 February 1877, no 18, p.187.
37  *Bay of Plenty Times*, 11 April 1877.
38  Mitchell to Native Under-Secretary, 30 June 1877, *AJHR*, 1877, G–7, p.12.
39  *Bay of Plenty Times*, 6 October 1877.
40  Ibid., 19 December 1877 (citing *New Zealand Times*, 3 December 1877).
41  Mair to Editor, *New Zealand Times*, 16 December 1877, Gilbert Mair Papers, MS–Papers–92–2B, Alexander Turnbull Library.
42  Mair to Native Minister, 2 January 1878, ibid.
43  *Bay of Plenty Times*, 12 December 1877.
44  Ibid., 19 December 1877.
45  Ibid., 22 December 1877.
46  Ibid., 29 December 1877.
47  Ibid., 9 January 1878.
48  Ibid., 30 January 1878.
49  Ibid., 20 March 1878.
50  Ibid., 3 April 1878.
51  Ibid., 8 May 1878. Typically, other correspondents disputed this assertion.
52  Ibid., 4 May 1878.
53  Undated transcription from *Te Wananga*, Don Stafford Collection, Rotorua Public Library.
54  *Bay of Plenty Times*, 5 June, 12 June 1878; D.M. Stafford, *The Founding Years in Rotorua: A History of Events to 1900*, Rotorua: Ray Richards Publisher/Rotorua District Council, 1986, p.149.
55  *Bay of Plenty Times*, 10 October 1878.
56  Evidence of Aporo Tipi Tipi on petition no 349/1882, Native Affairs Committee, LE 1, 1882/6, NA.

57  *New Zealand Herald*, 11 December 1878; Stafford, *Founding Years*, pp.149–50.
58  New Zealand Herald, 11 December 1878.
59  M. Hikairo and others to Chief Judge Fenton, 12 August 1881, N.L.C. 81/4276, MA 13/79, NA.
60  *New Zealand Herald*, 13 January 1879.
61  *Bay of Plenty Times*, 24 December, 28 December 1878.
62  Ibid., 13 February 1879; *New Zealand Herald*, 5 February 1879.
63  Ibid., 4 April 1879.
64  H.W. Brabant to Native Under-Secretary, 31 May 1879, *AJHR*, 1879, Session I, G–1, p.18.
65  Dalton to Under-Secretary, Native Land Purchase Department, 12 April 1879 (telegram), MA–MLP 1, 1879/23, NA.
66  *Bay of Plenty Times*, 3 February 1881.
67  Mitchell to Under-Secretary, Native Land Purchase Department, 9 July 1879, MA–MLP 1, 1879/218, NA.
68  Mitchell to R.J. Gill, Under-Secretary, Native Land Purchase Department, n.d., MA 13/57, cited in D. Moore and S. Quinn, 'Alienation of Rotomahana Parekarangi Lands Within the Whakarewarewa State Forest', 1993, p.13.
69  *New Zealand Herald*, 9 April 1879.
70  Ibid., 7 June 1879.
71  Ibid., 20 September 1879.
72  Ibid., 17 September 1879. It was also reported that all liquor licences at Rotorua were likely to be cancelled by the Komiti Nui, which had also taken action against individuals who had sold timber to a settler.
73  *Bay of Plenty Times*, 21 August 1879.
74  Brabant to Native Under-Secretary, 15 May 1880, *AJHR*, 1880, G–4, p.7.
75  *Bay of Plenty Times*, 11 May 1880.
76  Ibid., 29 May 1880.
77  *New Zealand Herald*, 24 May 1880.
78  *Bay of Plenty Times*, 5 June, 5 August 1880.
79  R.J. Gill to Native Minister, 7 June 1880, MA–MLP 1, 1885/17, NA.
80  *Bay of Plenty Times*, 27 March 1880.
81  Ibid., 7 October 1880.
82  *NZPD*, 15 June 1880, vol 35, p.259.
83  Bryce to Fenton, 10 November 1880 (telegram), N.L.C. 80/5876, MA 13/79, NA.

84  Fenton to Bryce, 18 December 1880, N.L.C. 80/6110, MA 13/79, NA.
85  R. Haupapa and others to Fenton, 22 November 1880 (translation by Te Kuru-o-Te-Marama Waaka, September 1995), N.L.C. 80/5876, MA 13/79, NA.
86  Haupapa to Fenton, 23 November 1880 (translation by Te Kuru-o-Te-Marama Waaka, September 1995), N.L.C. 80/5876, MA 13/79, NA.
87  Haupapa to Fenton, 24 November 1880 (translation by Te Kuru-o-Te-Marama Waaka, September 1995), N.L.C. 80/5876, MA 13/79, NA.
88  Haupapa to Fenton, 17 December 1880, N.L.C. 80/6170, MA 13/79, NA.
89  Fenton to Bryce, 18 December 1880, N.L.C. 80/6110, MA 13/79, NA.
90  *Bay of Plenty Times*, 3 February 1881.
91  Ibid., 18 June 1881.
92  P. Te Pukuatua to Fenton, 24 June 1881 (telegram), N.L.C. 81/2980, MA 13/79, NA.
93  M. Hikairo and others to Fenton, 12 August 1881, N.L.C. 81/4276, MA 13/79, NA.
94  Mair to Fenton, 30 June 1881 (telegram), N.L.C. 81/3118, MA 13/79, NA.
95  Symonds to Fenton, 4 July 1881 (telegram), N.L.C. 81/3118, MA 13/79, NA.
96  Fenton to Symonds, 16 July 1881 (telegram), N.L.C. 81/3380, MA 13/79, NA.
97  Fenton to P. Te Pukuatua, 7 July 1881, (telegram), N.L.C. 81/3148, MA 13/79, NA.
98  Fenton to Symonds, 16 July 1881, (telegram), N.L.C. 81/3380, MA 13/79, NA.
99  Rolleston to Fenton, 4 July 1881 (telegram), N.L.C. 81/3120; Fenton to Rolleston, 16 July 1881 (telegram), N.L.C. 81/3448, MA 13/79, NA.
100 Symonds to Fenton, 8 July 1881 (telegram), N.L.C. 81/3606, MA 13/79, NA.
101 H. Te Pukuatua to Fenton, 8 August 1881, N.L.C. 81/4104, MA 13/79, NA.
102 *Bay of Plenty Times*, 6 September 1881.
103 Brabant to Native Under-Secretary, 31 May 1881, *AJHR*, 1881, G–8, p.11.

104 Brabant to Native Minister, 30 May 1882, *AJHR*, 1882, G–1, p.5.
105 R. Boast, 'The Hot Lakes: Maori Use and Management of Geothermal Areas from the Evidence of European Visitors', 1993, pp.105–6.
106 *AJHR*, 1908, G–1E, pp.1, 11.
107 Hall to Fenton, 3 March 1882 (telegram), N.L.C. 82/1244, MA 13/79, NA.
108 H.M. Morton, 'Notes of a Visit to the Lake District', c.1882–83 (transcription by R.P. Boast), NZ MSS 683, Auckland Public Library.
109 *New Zealand Herald*, 2 July 1883.
110 *Bay of Plenty Times*, 7 July 1883.
111 R.J. Gill, Under-Secretary, Native Land Purchase Department, to Brabant, 8 August 1881, MA 13/57, NA.
112 These included a Waitaha committee which was apparently active in the mid-1870s (who informed McLean in 1876 that they did 'not approve of the Native Lands Court') and a Ngati Pikiao committee, the secretary of which issued a notice in November 1879 describing the boundaries of the district within which the committee claimed the sole right 'to settle all disputes which may arise in respect to land and to prevent surveys and sale (of land)' other than those which it authorised. In 1880 the latter committee petitioned Parliament, requesting 'power to adjudicate upon their own blocks of land with the full powers of the Native Land Court, and further, that the Treaty of Waitangi be carried out'. Committee of Waitaha to McLean, 6 June 1876, *AJHR*, 1876, G–5, p.7; E.R. Rangihoro, Secretary, Ngati Pikiao Committee, 18 November 1879, N.O. 80/328, MA 23/13A, NA; *AJHR*, 1880, I–2, p.1; Armstrong, 'Ngati Makino', p.51.

## Chapter 6

1 *AJHR*, 1872, H–1, p.5; *AJHR*, 1876, I–4, p.6.
2 *NZPD*, 13 July 1882, vol. 42, p.305.
3 Ibid., p.306.
4 *Te Waka Maori o Niu Tirani*, 19 December 1876.
5 *Te Wananga*, 30 June 1877.
6 Ibid., 16 February 1878.
7 Ibid., 5 January 1878.
8 Ibid., 16 February 1878.
9 Ibid., 11 May 1878.
10 See *AJHR*, 1879, Session II, G–8.

11  J. McRae, 'Participation: Native Committees (1883) and Papatupu Block Committees (1900) in Tai Tokerau', MA Maori Studies thesis, University of Auckland, 1981, p.30.
12  Ibid., p.32
13  E. Baker, the Wairoa Resident Magistrate, noted in 1880 that 'each small kainga in this district has its *komiti*, and...most Native cases are tried by this tribunal'. Similar reports from other Crown officials around the country were common. Baker to Native Under-Secretary, 15 May 1880, *AJHR*, 1880, G–4, p.11.
14  Porter to Native Under-Secretary, 5 June 1878, *AJHR*, 1878, G–1, p.12.
15  G. Kelly to Native Under-Secretary, 11 June 1880, Mangonui Resident Magistrate's letterbook, BAFO A760/8, National Archives – Auckland.
16  Kelly to Raima Takanga and others, 9 June 1880, BAFO A760/8, National Archives – Auckland.
17  Kelly to Native Under-Secretary, 16 May 1881, *AJHR*, 1881, G–8, p.1.
18  Petition of Hepeta Maitai and 34 others, no. 239, Session II, 1879, MA 23/13A, NA.
19  Pineamine Tuhaka to Native Minister, 17 January 1881, MA 23/13A, NA.
20  J. Bryce minute, N.O. 80/15, 2 April 1880, MA 23/13A, NA.
21  Enclosure in Tawhai to Native Under-Secretary, 21 January 1881, N.O. 81/370, MA 23/13A, NA.
22  Tawhai to Native Minister, 6 October 1880, N.O. 80/3665, MA 23/13A, NA.
23  Bryce minute, 1 November 1880, N.O. 80/3665, MA 23/13A, NA.
24  Native Committees Empowering Bill, *Bills Rejected*, 1881.
25  P. Tuhaka to Native Minister, 17 January 1881, N.O. 81/367, MA 23/13A, NA.
26  W. Rolleston minute, 21 February 1881, N.O. 81/367, MA 23/13A, NA.
27  Fenton minute, n.d. [c. April 1881], N.O. 81/370, MA 23/13A, NA.
28  *Journals of the House of Representatives*, 19 July 1881, p.111.
29  *NZPD*, 15 September 1881, vol. 40, p.661.
30  Bryce minute, 12 January 1882, N.O. 82/106, MA 23/13A, NA.
31  Bryce minute, 11 May 1882, N.O. 82/106, MA 23/13A, NA.
32  *NZPD*, 13 July 1882, vol. 42, p.297.
33  Ibid., p.296.

34 Ibid., p.298.
35 Ibid., p.300.
36 Ibid., p.304.
37 Ibid., p.303.
38 *NZPD*, 3 August 1882, vol 43, pp.127–8.
39 Ibid., p.128.
40 Ibid., p.132.
41 Ibid., pp.128–9.
42 Ibid., p.134.
43 Ibid., p.129. Others outside Parliament were equally fearful of the bill's consequences. F.E. Maning, a retired Native Land Court Judge, for example, considered the bill 'a brutal invention' which would 'virtually take the Government of the country districts out of the hands of the European Government and hand them over to the tyranny of savages'. Cited in McRae, 'Participation', p.100.
44 *NZPD*, 3 August 1882, vol 43, p.137; *Journals of the House of Representatives*. 3 August 1882, pp.23–34.
45 *AJHR*, 1883, A–5, pp.2,3.
46 Ibid., p.4.
47 See, for example, F.E. Maning to Native Under-Secretary, n.d. [c. October 1882], MA 23/1, NA. Taiwhanga was described in this report (which was sent to New Zealand's Agent-General in London) as 'a scheming unprincipled native and notorious mischief maker'.
48 Premier to Administrator, 12 December 1882, *AJHR*, 1883, A–6, p.5.
49 'The Petition from the Tribes of New Zealand to England', MA 23/1, NA; C. Orange, *The Treaty of Waitangi*, Wellington: Allen & Unwin/Port Nicholson Press, 1987, p.210.
50 *New Zealand Herald*, 18 December 1883, MA 23/1, NA.
51 F.W. Chesson to Earl of Derby, 12 October 1883, MA 23/1, NA.
52 Bryce to Governor, 11 January 1884, MA 23/1, NA.
53 Bryce to Governor, 11 February 1884, G 49/20, NA.
54 E.S. Maunsell to Native Under-Secretary, 4 June 1883, *AJHR*, 1883, G–1A, p.12. This committee appears to have continued to function even after an official, but apparently ineffectual, District Native Committee was appointed under the 1883 Act. See A.G. Bagnall, *Wairarapa: An Historical Excursion*, Masterton: Hedley's Bookshop for the Masterton Trust Lands Trust, 1976, p.230.
55 *AJHR*, 1883, J–1, p.1.
56 Waitangi Tribunal, *The Pouakani Report 1993*, Wellington: Brooker & Friend, 1993, p.96.

57     *AJHR*, 1883, I–2, p.9.
58     The petition had been presented to the House on 26 June; the Native Committees Bill was given its first reading on 24 July. For the progress of the bill through the House see *Journals of the House of Representatives*, 1883, p.xli.
59     Tawhai and Taiaroa to Native Minister, 11 July 1883, MA 23/13A, NA.
60     The only part of the bill amended during its progress through the House was clause 14, dealing with the power of the committees with respect to title investigations which was amended by the House in Committee. The *Journals of the House of Representatives* give no indication of the nature of this amendment. See *Journals*, 24 August 1883, p.227.
61     *NZPD*, 22 August 1883, vol 46, pp.153–4.
62     *NZPD*, 29 August 1883, vol 46, pp.341–2.
63     Ibid., p.342.
64     Ibid. pp.342–3.
65     Ibid., p.345.
66     Ibid., p.341.
67     Ibid., p.342.
68     Section 14 of the Act stated that:
In any of the following cases–
(1.) Where it is desired to ascertain the names of the owners of any block of land being or to be passed through the Native Land Court; or
(2.) Where it is desired to ascertain the successors of any deceased Native owner; or
(3.) Where disputes have arisen as to the location of the boundary between lands claimed by Natives,
the Committee may make such inquiries as it shall think fit, and may report their decision thereon, certified in writing in the Maori language under the hand of the Chairman of the Committee, to the Chief Judge of the said Court for the information of the Court.

## Chapter 7

1     J.A. Williams, *Politics of the New Zealand Maori: Protest and Cooperation, 1891–1909*, Auckland: Oxford University Press, 1969, p.83.
2     McRae, 'Participation', p.103.
3     Orange, *Treaty of Waitangi*, p.201.
4     Andrews, 'Aspects of Development', p.98.

5 R.J. Martin, 'Aspects of Maori Affairs in the Liberal Period', MA History thesis, Victoria University College, 1956, p.186.
6 Ward, *Show of Justice*, p.290; Ward, 'Whanganui Ki Maniapoto', p.39.
7 Waitangi Tribunal, *Pouakani Report*, p.306.
8 *NZPD*, 8 November 1884, vol 50, p.489.
9 Rees–Carroll Report, AJHR, 1891, Session II, G–1, p.xvi.
10 W.L. Rees, *To the Honourable the Premier*, 15 March 1893 (published pamphlet), Alexander Turnbull Library.
11 For information concerning the establishment and operations of this committee see *Te Wananga*, 26 January, 9 February, 11 May 1878.
12 Hemopo Hikarahui to Native Minister, 8 November 1883, N.O. 83/3590, MA 23/13A, NA.
13 Bryce minute, 1 November 1883, N.O. 83/3322, MA 23/13A, NA.
14 Lewis minute, 1 January 1884, N.O. 83/3590, MA 23/13A, NA.
15 Te Rangikaheke to Native Minister, 23 October 1883, N.O. 83/3322, MA 23/13A.
16 Bryce minute, 27 September 1883, MA 23/13A, NA.
17 Lewis minute, 1 November 1883, N.O. 83/3322, MA 23/13A, NA.
18 Notes of Meeting with Tauranga Tribes, 21 February 1885, *AJHR*, 1885, G–1, p.62.
19 *AJHR*, 1884, Session II, I–2, p.19. Major Scannell, the Taupo Resident Magistrate, reported in 1885 that the Native Committees Act did not affect the Taupo people, the relevant Committee being 'too far away to be of any use'. Scanell to Native Under-Secretary, 14 April 1885, *AJHR*, 1885, G–2, p.13.
20 Hoera Te Mahirahi and the Committee to Native Minister, 10 December 1883 (and Bryce minute thereon), N.O. 84/145, MA 23/13A, NA.
21 Raika Whakarongotai to G. Wilkinson, 7 November 1883, MA 23/13A, NA.
22 W.H. Taipari to Wilkinson, 6 December 1883, MA 23/13A, NA.
23 Bryce minute on ibid., 13 December 1883.
24 McRae, 'Participation', pp.91–2.
25 *New Zealand Gazette*, 24 January 1884, no.8, pp.110–12. The districts proclaimed under the Act were: Bay of Islands, Kaipara, Waikato, Thames, Kawhia, Rotorua, Opotiki, East Cape, Hawke's Bay, Whanganui, Taranaki, and Wairarapa. Despite the sometimes misleading names, these districts encompassed the entire North Island.

26 Even so, South Island Maori occasionally forwarded requests to the Native Office for their own Committees to be established. One letter in 1888, for example, asked that a Native Committee 'be authorised to act as a Local Town Board to deal with funds accruing from taxes &c. on Kaiapoi Reserve'. MA 1888/102 (register entry), NA.
27 Ward, *Show of Justice*, p.290.
28 H.W. Bishop to Native Under-Secretary, 30 April 1885, *AJHR*, 1885, G–2, p.4.
29 Bishop to Native Under-Secretary, 12 May 1884, *AJHR*, 1884, Session II, G–1, p.3.
30 Brabant to Native Under-Secretary, 14 May 1884, ibid., p.14.
31 Bush to Native Under-Secretary, 8 May 1884, ibid., p.16.
32 Ward to Native Under-Secretary, 14 April 1884, ibid., p.20.
33 G.T. Wilkinson to Native Under-Secretary, 14 May 1884, ibid., p.11.
34 Ward, *Show of Justice*, p.290; 'Whanganui Ki Maniapoto', passim.
35 Parris to Native Minister, 23 April 1884, N.O. 84/1330, MA 23/13A, NA.
36 Bryce minute, 29 April 1884, N.O. 84/1330, MA 23/13A, NA.
37 Tauranga, for example, finally received its own Committee in 1886.
38 *NZPD*, 1 November, 6 November 1884, vol 50., pp.427, 555–6.
39 *NZPD*, 1 November 1884, vol 50, p.315.
40 Ibid., p.316.
41 *Thames Advertiser*, 28 May 1884, N.O. 84/1767, MA 23/13B, NA.
42 R. Whakarongotai [to Native Under-Secretary], 31 October 1884, N.O. 84/3270, MA 23/13B, NA.
43 Whakarongotai to Native Minister, 25 August 1885, N.O. 85/2938, MA 23/13B, NA.
44 The rules as published included provision for the Chairmen of the Committees to issue summonses but provided no means of compelling reluctant witnesses to attend and give evidence, or of punishing those who refused to do so, rendering this provision null and void. A similar situation applied to the scale of fees the Committees were permitted to charge applicants appearing before them. The Committees were advised that these could only be levied with the consent of the parties. For the rules under which the Committees were supposed to operate (none of which, it seems, were legally enforceable) see *New Zealand Gazette*, 3 June 1886, no.32, p.705.
45 Te Rangipuawhe to Native Minister, 6 March 1889, N.O. 89.638, MA 23/13B, NA.

46  Notes of Meeting with the Wanganui Tribes, 7 January 1885, *AJHR*, 1885, G–1, p.2.
47  Martin, 'Aspects of Maori Affairs', p.183.
48  Notes of Meeting with the Wanganui Tribes, 7 January 1885, *AJHR*, 1885, G–1, p.3.
49  Notes of Meeting at Kihikihi, 4 February 1885, ibid., p.15.
50  Ibid., p.17.
51  Native Under-Secretary to R. Parris, 13 February 1884; Bryce minute, 11 February 1884, N.O. 84/407, MA 23/13A, NA.
52  Martin, 'Aspects of Maori Affairs' p.184; Ward, *Show of Justice*, p.294; both Wiremu Kingi, the chairman of the Opotiki Committee, and Whakarongotai of the Thames Committee informed the Native Department in 1886 that they incurred considerable expense in supplying their respective Committees with food and other provisions when meetings were held at their homes. Kingi was informed that how the money was used was entirely up to him, but that no other funds would be provided to meet the Committee's expenses. But when Tawhai wrote the following year that he was 'greatly perplexed' as to what the sum was intended to cover, he was informed that 'the chairman should receive as his emoluments of office any portion of the £50 that is not appropriated for the expenses of the Committee, or the whole of it if the Committee do not object'. MA 23/13A–B, NA.
53  B.D. Gilling, 'The Nineteenth Century Native Land Court Judges: An Introductory Report' (Report Commissioned by the Waitangi Tribunal), 1994, p.30.
54  Notes of Meeting with Tawhiao, 6 February 1885, *AJHR*, 1885, G–1, p.27.
55  Notes of Meeting with the Thames Native Committee, 12 February 1885, ibid., pp.30–2.
56  Lewis minute, 11 October 1884, N.O. 84/2991, MA 23/13B, NA.
57  Minutes of Interview with Premier, Rotorua, 14 February 1889, N.O. 89/638, MA 23/13B, NA. This request also came down partly to the question of expenses. The Premier was informed that it was sometimes difficult for the full Committee to visit settlements where cases were to be investigated, as the residents were required to feed them, placing undue burden on their hosts.
58  Notes of Meeting at Rotorua, 16 February 1885, *AJHR*, 1885, G–1, p.43.
59  Notes of Meeting at Whakarewarewa, 19 February 1885, ibid., p.55.

60  Te Awekotuku and others to Native Minister, 10 July 1885, N.O. 85/2398, MA 23/13A, NA.
61  Lewis minute, 22 August 1885, ibid.
62  As was supposed to have occurred under the commission of five Tuhoe and two European officials which adjudicated on the titles to Urewera lands between 1899 and 1902 (See chapter 9).
63  Maunsell to Native Under-Secretary, 25 April 1886, *AJHR*, 1886, G–1, p.17.
64  J.H. Greenway to Native Under-Secretary, 16 April 1885, *AJHR*, 1885, G–2, p.5.
65  McRae, 'Participation', pp.75, 86, n.46.
66  Ibid., p.75.
67  Tawhai to Native Minister, 2 June 1885, MA 23/13A, NA.
68  Tawhai to Native Under-Secretary, 21 July 1885, N.O. 85/2709, MA 23/13A, NA.
69  Lewis minute, 29 August 1885, N.O. 85/2709, MA 23/13A, NA.
70  Tawhai to Native Minister, 17 March 1887, N.O. 87/891, MA 23/13B, NA.
71  Native Under-Secretary to Tawhai, n.d. (draft), N.O. 87/891, MA 23/13B, NA.
72  Lewis minute, 22 April 1887, N.O. 87/891, MA 23/13B, NA.
73  Tawhai to Native Minister, 24 March 1887, N.O. 87/982, MA 23/13B, NA.
74  Tawhai to Native Minister, 29 March 1887, N.O. 87/1032, MA 23/13B, NA.
75  Williams, *Politics of the New Zealand Maori*, p.83.
76  Orange, *Treaty of Waitangi*, p.224; R.J. Walker, 'Tawhai, Hone Mohi', in *The Dictionary of New Zealand Biography, Volume Two, 1870–1900*, Wellington: Bridget Williams Books/Department of Internal Affairs, 1993, p.508.
77  *AJHR*, 1887, I–2, p.3.
78  Wilkinson to Native Under-Secretary, 25 May 1886, *AJHR*, 1886, G–1, p.4.
79  Ibid., p.5.
80  J. Ormsby to Wilkinson, 30 June 1886, N.O. 86/1966, MA 23/13B, NA.
81  Lewis minute, 15 July 1886, N.O. 86/1966, MA 23/13B, NA.
82  Sorrenson, 'Purchase of Maori Lands', p.110.
83  Ward, 'Whanganui Ki Maniapoto', pp.79 ff.
84  Ward, *Show of Justice*, p.299.
85  Lewis minute, 5 March 1884, N.O. 84/653, MA 23/13B, NA.

| | |
|---|---|
| 86 | G. Preece to Native Under-Secretary, 26 April 1884, N.O. 84/1357, MA 23/13B, NA. |
| 87 | Preece to Native Under-Secretary, 8 June 1885, *AJHR*, 1885, G–2, p.17. |
| 88 | Preece to Native Under-Secretary, 5 March 1887, N.O. 87/734, MA 23/13B, NA. |
| 89 | Lewis minute, 1 July 1887, N.O. 87/1908, MA 23/13B, NA. |
| 90 | Minutes of Meetings with Natives and Others, *AJHR*, 1891, Session II, G–1, p.46. |
| 91 | Applications for existing committees to be recognised under the 1883 Act continued to be received. In 1888, for example, Waiheke Island Maori informed the Native Minister that they had their own committees 'which have not received the sanction of the Government – consequently they do not act with the required amount of spirit'. Rawiri Puhata and others to Native Minister, January 1888, N.O. 88/675, MA 23/13B, NA. |
| 92 | R.S. Bush to Native Under-Secretary, 3 May 1886, *AJHR*, 1886, G–1, pp.13–14. |
| 93 | Extracts from Notes of Native Meetings, Opotiki, 24 April 1886, MA 23/13B, NA. |
| 94 | Wepiha Apanui and others to Native Minister, 21 February 1887, MA 23/13B, NA. |
| 95 | Bush to Native Under-Secretary, 27 May 1887, MA 23/13B, NA. |
| 96 | See chapter 9. |
| 97 | Rakuraku Rehua and others to Native Minister, 30 September 1888, MA 23/13B, NA. |
| 98 | Bush to Native Under-Secretary, 4 April 1889, N.O. 89/821, MA 23/13B, NA. |
| 99 | The Native Committees Act 1883 was finally repealed in 1902, but had been a virtual dead letter for most of the preceding decade. Intermittent requests for Committees to be revived continued to be received throughout the 1890s. In 1896, for example, W.W. Te Paa and others, writing from Te Kopuru in the Kaipara district, requested that an official Committee be 'properly empowered to adjudicate with the tribes of our district'. One Justice Department official noted that this appeared to be a request for a Committee under the 1883 Act, and that 'These committees have for a number of years been left in abeyance – as it is a well known fact that they could not enforce their decisions'. J 1, 1897/223, NA. |

## Chapter 8

1. See Native Lands Act Amendment Bill, *Bills Rejected*, 1884.
2. In the marginalia to Pere's bill it is stated that the five persons to be appointed Assessors would be members of other District Committees. However, this is not specified in the text of the bill.
3. See A.D. Ward, 'The East Coast Maori Trust', MA History thesis, Victoria University College, 1958, pp.17–46.
4. Rees memorandum, n.d., *AJHR*, 1884, Session II, G–2, pp.1, 4.
5. *NZPD*, 1 November, 6 November 1884, vol 50., pp.427, 555–6.
6. *NZPD*, 1 November 1884, vol 50, p.322.
7. Ward, 'Whanganui Ki Maniapoto', p.48.
8. *NZPD*, 6 November 1884, vol 50, pp.435–6.
9. *NZPD*, 7 November 1884, vol 50, p.478.
10. Ibid., p.480.
11. Ibid., p.485.
12. *NZPD*, 8 November 1884, vol 50, p.486.
13. Ibid., p.489.
14. Orange, *Treaty of Waitangi*, p.211.
15. *AJHR*, 1885, A–2, pp.3–5.
16. Orange, *Treaty of Waitangi*, pp.212–13.
17. Stout to Governor, 12 March 1885, *AJHR*, 1885, A–1, p.32.
18. For a list of unsuccessful Bills presented to Parliament by the Maori members between 1868 and 1909, see *The Maori Land Legislation Manual/Te Puka Ako Hanganga Mo Nga Ture Whenua Maori*, Wellington: Crown Forestry Rental Trust, 1994–95, appendix D, pp.109–10.
19. Tawhiao to Governor, 21 September 1885, G 49/20, NA.
20. Jervois minute, 27 November 1885, G 49/20, NA.
21. D. Scannell to Native Under-Secretary, 23 September 1885, *AJHR*, 1886, G–3, p.1.
22. Tawhiao to Native Minister, 17 May 1886, *AJHR*, 1886, G–14, pp.2–3.
23. Ballance to Tawhiao, 8 June 1886, ibid., pp.4–5.
24. Orange, *Treaty of Waitangi*, p.219.
25. Ward, *Show of Justice*, pp.296–7.
26. Evidence of James Carroll, 14 August 1885, *AJHR*, 1885, I–2B, p.1.
27. Evidence of Wahanui, 19–20 August 1885, ibid., pp.4–14.
28. Notes of Meeting at Waipatu, January 1886, AJHR, 1886, G–2, pp.5–6, 10.
29. Ibid., p.17.
30. Ibid., p.11.

31 Native Land Administration Act 1886 Amendment Bill, *Bills Rejected*, 1887; NZPD, 11 May 1887, vol 57, pp.210–20.
32 See MA–MLA 51, NA.
33 Commissioner, Native Land Administration Act, to Native Under-Secretary, 21 May 1888, *Appendices to the Journals of the Legislative Council*, 1888, no 16, p.1.
34 Rees–Carroll Report, *AJHR*, 1891, Session II, G–1, p.xvi.
35 Ward, *Show of Justice*, p.298.
36 *AJHR*, 1888, G–7, p.1.
37 Orange, *Treaty of Waitangi*, pp.222–3.
38 *NZPD*, 21 August 1888, vol 63, p.209.
39 Orange, *Treaty of Waitangi*, p.223.
40 Maoris Relief Bill, *Bills Rejected*, 1888.
41 T. Brooking, '"Busting Up" the Greatest Estate of All: Liberal Maori Land Policy, 1891–1911', *New Zealand Journal of History*, vol 26, no 1, 1992, p.84.
42 Unfinished report by T. Mackay, *AJHR*, 1891, Session II, G–1A, pp.22–3.
43 On Carroll's early political career, see S. Sweetman, 'James Carroll 1887–96: "A Wholesome Blend"', M A History thesis, Massey University, 1973.
44 Rees–Carroll Report, *AJHR*, 1891, Session II, G–1, p.x.
45 Ibid., p.xix.
46 Ibid., pp.xxi–xv.
47 Ibid., 'Minutes of Meetings with Natives and Others', p.14.
48 Ibid., p.16.
49 Ibid., p.46.
50 Cited in W.L. Rees, *To the Honourable the Premier*.
51 Sections 122–130 of the Native Land Court Act of 1894 provided for the owners of any block to be incorporated by order of the Court with the consent of the majority, and empowered the Court to appoint a committee nominated by the owners to administer the block. However, the only specific power granted to the committees under this legislation was to authorise alienations, and with all proceeds from any transaction to be paid to the Public Trustee, these provisions do not appear to have gone anywhere near meeting Maori aspirations for full control over their own lands. According to the Stout–Ngata Commission, they were included in the Act in order to 'facilitate alienation and to overcome the difficulties of communal ownership'. *AJHR*, 1907, G–1C, p.4.
52 Native Committees Act 1883 Amendment Bill, *Bills Rejected*, 1892.

| | |
|---|---|
| 53 | *NZPD*, 29 September 1892, vol 78, p.517. A Native Empowering Bill promoted by Sir George Grey, which provided for the formation of Maori incorporations to administer and settle disputes with respect to Maori lands, fared no better than Carroll's bill. See Williams, *Politics of the New Zealand Maori*, p.86; *Journals of the House of Representatives*, 1892, p.L. |
| 54 | *NZPD*, 29 September 1892, vol 78, pp. 516–17. |
| 55 | *AJHR*, 1892, A–1, p.9. |
| 56 | Williams, *Politics of the New Zealand Maori*, pp.51–2. |
| 57 | Ibid., p.51. |
| 58 | Cox, *Kotahitanga*, p.67; Martin, 'Aspects of Maori Affairs', p.45. |
| 59 | *AJHR*, 1893, J–1, p.2. |
| 60 | Brooking, '"Busting Up" the Greatest Estate', p.82. |
| 61 | Carroll became the MHR for the general (European) seat of Waiapu in 1893, transferring from Eastern Maori. In addition to supporting the concept of committees helping to determine titles and administer lands as a member of the Native Land Laws Commission of 1891, and introducing a bill along these lines in 1892, he had also in 1893 successfully sponsored, along with Rees and Pere, a private member's bill, which provided for a large block of land north-east of Gisborne with more than 180 owners to be administered as an incorporation through a committee of management. See Mangatu No 1 Empowering Act (Private) 1893 and Ward, 'East Coast Maori Trust', pp.199–218. |
| 62 | Native Rights Bill, *Bills Rejected*, 1894. |
| 63 | *NZPD*, 10 September 1894, vol 85, pp.550–4. |
| 64 | Williams, *Politics of the New Zealand Maori*, p.56. |
| 65 | Native Lands Administration Bill, *Bills Rejected*, 1894. |
| 66 | Native Land Bill, *Bills Rejected*, 1896, 1897. |
| 67 | S. Webster, 'Urewera Lands 1895–1926: A Tentative Historical Survey of Tuhoe and Government Relations as Reflected in Official Records'. University of Auckland, 1985, p.3. |

## Chapter 9

| | |
|---|---|
| 1 | This section is partly adapted from V. O'Malley, 'The Crown's Acquisition of the Waikaremoana Block, 1921–25' (A Report for the Panekiri Tribal Trust Board), 1996, chapters 2–4. |
| 2 | C. Hunter Brown, Report of an Official Visit to the Urewera Tribes, June 1862, *AJHR*, 1862, E–9, Section IV, p.28. |
| 3 | V. O'Malley, 'The Crown and Ngati Ruapani: Confiscation and Land Purchase in the Wairoa–Waikaremoana Area, 1865–1875' |

(A Report for the Patunamu State Forest [Wai–144] Claim), 1994, p.9.
4   E. Best, *Tuhoe: The Children of the Mist*, Wellington: Reed, 1925, p.665, cited in S. Daly, 'The Background to the Urewera District Native Reserve Act 1896' (draft Rangahaua Whanui chapter), Waitangi Tribunal [1995], p.1.
5   H. H. Turton reporting on a visit to the district in 1861, noted that 'Their great council of 70 members actually sat during five long nights, in adjudicating a case which ended after all in a verdict of 8s'. H. H. Turton, report respecting the Maori Runanga, 20 November 1861, *AJHR*, 1862, E–5A, p.8.
6   [Ormond] to Whenuanui and Paerau, 20 November 1871 AGG–HB 4/8, NA. On the same date Ormond wrote to Erueti Tamaikowha at Waikaremoana that – 'it is to you the regulation of affairs within your boundaries will be entrusted'. There is also evidence that McLean had met Tuhoe chiefs during peace negotiations and discussed with them the boundaries of an Urewera 'protectorate'. One chief reportedly told the meeting that he had 'spoken before Mr McLean's face at Napier about that law setting forth the boundaries of the land'. Henare Kepa Te Ahuru and others to Native Minister, 9 June 1872, *AJHR*, 1872, F–3A, p.29. According to Daly (p.2), a Tuhoe delegation had travelled to Napier in 1870 and held discussions with McLean concerning the establishment of an Urewera 'rohe potae'.
7   When the Premier, R.J. Seddon, visited Ruatahuna in 1894 he was informed by Te Pukeiotu that McLean had 'given effect' to an arrangement made at this time that the lands of Tuhoe 'should be kept inviolate'. Seddon subsequently referred to McLean's promise in Parliament in support of the Urewera District Native Reserve Bill, which was, he argued, 'redeeming' this promise ignored by successive governments since the time of McLean. *AJHR*, 1895, G–1, p.74; *NZPD*, 24 September 1896, vol. 96, p.166.
8   Te Whenuanui and others to Government, 9 June 1872, *AJHR*, 1872, F–3A, p.29.
9   Brabant to Native Minister, 4 July 1872, ibid., p.28.
10  Hetaraka Whakaumua to J.D. Ormond, 15 September 1872, AGG–HB, NA, cited in Daly, 'Background to the Urewera District Native Reserve Act', p.5. See O'Malley, 'The Crown and Ngati Ruapani', pp.106–114.
11  Te Whareraupo to Brabant, 22 December 1873 *AJHR*, 1874, G–9, p.2.

| | |
|---|---|
| 12 | Report by Brabant, 1 April 1874, *AJHR*, 1874, G–1A, p.3. |
| 13 | Ibid. |
| 14 | Ibid., p.2. |
| 15 | Daly, 'Background to the Urewera Native Reserve Act', p.5. |
| 16 | Report by Brabant, 1 April 1874, *AJHR*, 1874, G–1A, p.5. |
| 17 | R.S. Bush to Native Under-Secretary, 4 April 1889, N.O. 89/821, MA 23/13B, NA. For a discussion of the oral histories associated with Te Whitu Tekau, and in particular Te Kooti's role in encouraging the union of Tuhoe, see J. Binney, *Redemption Songs: A Life of Te Kooti Arikirangi Te Turuki*, Auckland: Auckland University Press/Bridget Williams Books, 1995, pp.469ff. |
| 18 | Daly, 'Background to the Urewera District Native Reserve Act', p.9. |
| 19 | Cited in Binney, *Redemption Songs*, p.470. |
| 20 | Rakuraku Rehua and others to Native Minister, 30 September 1888, MA 23/13B, NA. |
| 21 | Mitchelson minute, 17 April 1889, N.O. 89/821, MA 23/13B, NA. |
| 22 | Locke to Native Minister, 27 April 1889, *AJHR*, 1889, G–6, p.1. |
| 23 | Kereru Te Pukenui to Native Minister, 17 April 1889, ibid., p.2. |
| 24 | Williams, *Politics of the New Zealand Maori*, p.92. |
| 25 | Ward, *Show of Justice*, p.304. |
| 26 | Ibid.; Binney, *Redemption Songs*, pp.472, 487–9. |
| 27 | Cited in Binney, *Redemption Songs*, p.487. |
| 28 | Cited in Williams, *Politics of the New Zealand Maori*, p.92. |
| 29 | *AJHR*, 1895, G–1, p.52. |
| 30 | Ibid., p.49. |
| 31 | Ibid., p.52. |
| 32 | Ibid., p.53. |
| 33 | Ibid., pp.54–6. |
| 34 | Ibid., p.76. |
| 35 | Ibid., p.74. |
| 36 | Ibid., p.78. |
| 37 | Ibid., p.94. |
| 38 | J. Cowan, *The New Zealand Wars: A History of the Maori Campaigns of the Pioneering Period*, Wellington: Government Printer, 1922 [1983 reprint], vol.2, p.497. |
| 39 | Williams, *Politics of the New Zealand Maori*, p.93. |
| 40 | Daly, 'Background to the Urewera District Native Reserve Act', p.32. |
| 41 | Williams, *Politics of the New Zealand Maori*, p.94. |
| 42 | See Second Schedule to Urewera District Native Reserve Act 1896, no.27, pp.69–71. |

43   *NZPD*, 24 September 1896, vol 96, p.158.
44   Ibid., p.167.
45   Ibid., p.159.
46   Ibid., p.160.
47   Ibid., p.163.
48   Ibid., pp.164–5.
49   Ibid., p.166.
50   Ibid., p.161.
51   *NZPD*, 24 June 1896, vol. 92, p.312.
52   *AJHR*, 1899, C–1, p.xi.
53   *NZPD*, 18 October 1900, vol 142, p.425.
54   See *AJHR*, 1903, G–6 for the orders of the first Urewera Commission.
55   W.J. Butler to Native Minister, 6 August 1902, *AJHR*, 1902, G–6.
56   Sorrenson, 'Land Purchase Methods', (1956), p.193.
57   For a more detailed discussion of Urewera land dealings in the early twentieth century see O'Malley, 'Waikaremoana Block'; E. Stokes *et al.*, *Te Urewera: Nga Iwi Te Whenua Te Ngahere/People, Land and Forests of Te Urewera*, Hamilton: University of Waikato, 1986; Webster, 'Urewera Lands'.

## Chapter 10

1   The Maori Lands Administration Act and the Maori Councils Act of 1900 are both, strictly speaking, outside the scope of this study, which includes a brief consideration of them solely for the purposes of continuity. For a fuller consideration of this legislation see: Williams, *Politics of the New Zealand Maori*; Martin, 'Aspects of Maori Affairs'; G.V. Butterworth, 'Maori Land Legislation: The Work of Carroll and Ngata', *New Zealand Law Journal*, August 1985; B.R. Gilmore, 'Maori Land Policy and Administration During the Liberal Period, 1900–1912', MA History thesis, University of Auckland, 1969. See also D.M. Loveridge. 'Maori Land Councils and Maori Land Boards: A Historical Overview, 1900 to 1952' (Rangahaua Whanui Series: First Release), Waitangi Tribunal, December 1996. This deals comprehensively with the subject but was unavailable at the time of writing.
2   *AJHR*, 1907, G–1C, p.5.
3   Martin, 'Aspects of Maori Affairs', pp.66–7.
4   *AJHR*, 1898, I–3A, p.113.
5   Williams, *Politics of the New Zealand Maori*, p.73.
6   See Native Lands Settlement and Administration Bill, *AJHR*, 1898, I–3A, pp.94ff.

7   See petitions for and against the bill in ibid., pp.1–4.
8   Williams, *Politics of the New Zealand Maori*, p.98.
9   Ibid., p.103; See Maori Council Constitution Bill, *Bills Rejected*, 1897, 1898.
10  Williams, *Politics of the New Zealand Maori*, p.101; for the Kotahitanga's proposed amendments to Seddon's bill, see *AJHR*, 1898, I–3A, pp.110–12.
11  Native Land Laws Amendment Act 1899, section 3.
12  *AJHR*, 1907, G–1C, p.5.
13  Cited in Martin, 'Aspects of Maori Affairs', p.70. Daly, 'Background to the Urewera District Native Reserve Act', (p.41) suggests that the passing of the Urewera District Native Reserve Act of 1896 might also be explained in terms of this slackening of pressure for the purchase of Maori land.
14  Williams, *Politics of the New Zealand Maori*, p.107.
15  Ibid., p.108.
16  Butterworth, 'Maori Land Legislation', p.244.
17  Williams, *Politics of the New Zealand Maori*, p.150.
18  Just over 6000 of the more than 600,000 acres in the broader Rotorua district, for example, remained papatupu by 1907. The remaining 99 per cent had all passed through the Court since 1881. *AJHR*, 1908, G–1E, p.11.
19  *AJHR*, 1907, G–1C, p.6.
20  Williams, *Politics of the New Zealand Maori*, p.120.
21  Native Land Rating Act, *New Zealand Statutes*, 1904, no 41.
22  Williams, *Politics of the New Zealand Maori*, p.128.
23  Ibid., p.116; for a detailed discussion of the Councils, see also Martin, 'Aspects of Maori Affairs', pp.82–110.
24  McRae, 'Participation', p.98.
25  Butterworth, 'Maori Land Legislation', p.244.
26  Cited in McRae, 'Participation', p.77.
27  Native Land Act, *New Zealand Statutes*, 1909, no 15, section 90.

## Chapter 11

1   Ward, *Show of Justice*, p.174.
2   Waitangi Tribunal, *Taranaki Report*, p.6

# Select Bibliography

## A. Primary Sources

### I. Unpublished Archives and Manuscripts

**Alexander Turnbull Library, Wellington**
McLean, Donald. Papers
Mair, Gilbert. Papers
Native Land Court. Rotorua Minute Books

**National Archives, Wellington**
G 49/20 (correspondence concerning Maori petitions).
Le 1, 1893/130 (petition of the Federated Assembly of Maori Tribes).
MA 13/79 (Rotorua township papers).
MA 23/1 (correspondence concerning Hirini Taiwhanga and petitions to England).
MA 23/13A–B (papers relative to the Native Committees Act 1883).
MA–MLA 5/1 (correspondence concerning the Native Land Administration Act 1886).

### II. Published Primary Sources

**(a.) Official Publications**
*Appendices to the Journals of the House of Representatives (AJHR)*
*Appendices to the Journals of the Legislative Council*
*Bills Rejected*
*Journals of the House of Representatives*
*New Zealand Gazette*
*New Zealand Parliamentary Debates (NZPD)*
*New Zealand Statutes*

**(b.) Newspapers**
*Bay of Plenty Times*
*New Zealand Herald*
*Te Waka Maori o Niu Tirani*
*Te Wananga*

**(c.) Books and Pamphlets**
Fenton, F.D., *Important Judgements Delivered in the Compensation Court and Native Land Court 1866–1879*, Auckland: Native Land Court, 1879.
Rees, W.L., *To the Honourable the Premier*, 1893 (published pamphlet; copy held at Alexander Turnbull Library).

## B. Secondary Sources

### I. Research Reports
Armstrong, D.A., 'Ngati Makino and the Crown: 1880–1960', 1995.
Ballara, A., and G. Scott, 'Crown Purchases of Maori Land in Early Provincial Hawke's Bay', 1994.
Boast, R., 'The Hot Lakes: Maori Use and Management of Geothermal Areas from the Evidence of European Visitors', 1993.
Cross, S., and B. Bargh, 'The Whanganui District' (Rangahaua Whanui Working Paper: First Release), Waitangi Tribunal, 1996.
Daly, S., 'The Background to the Urewera District Native Reserve Act 1896', (draft Rangahaua Whanui chapter), Waitangi Tribunal [1995].
Gilling, B.D., 'The Nineteenth Century Native Land Court Judges: An Introductory Report' (Report Commissioned by the Waitangi Tribunal), 1994.
Goldsmith, P., 'Wairarapa' (Rangahaua Whanui Working Paper: First Release), Waitangi Tribunal, 1996.
Moore, D. and S. Quinn, 'Alienation of Rotomahana Parekarangi Lands Within the Whakarewarewa State Forest', 1993.
O'Malley, V., 'The Crown and Ngati Ruapani: Confiscation and Land Purchase in the Wairoa–Waikaremoana Area, 1865–1875'

*Select Bibliography*

(A Report for the Patunamu State Forest [Wai–144] claim), 1994.
O'Malley, V., 'The Crown and Te Arawa, c.1840–1910: An Overview Report Commissioned by the Whakarewarewa Forest Trust', 1995.
O'Malley, V., 'The Crown's Acquisition of the Waikaremoana Block, 1921–25' (A Report for the Panekiri Tribal Trust Board), 1996.
Ward. A., 'Whanganui Ki Maniapoto' (Preliminary Historical Report Wai–48 and Related Claims), 1992.
Ward, A., *et al.*, 'Historical Report on the Ngati Kahungunu Rohe', Crown–Congress Joint Working Party, 1993.
Webster, S., 'Urewera Lands 1895–1926: A Tentative Historical Survey of Tuhoe and Government Relations as Reflected in Official Records', University of Auckland, 1985.

## II. Unpublished Theses

Andrews, C.L., 'Aspects of Development: The Maori Situation, 1870–1890', MA Anthropology thesis, University of Auckland, 1968.
Cole, S.M., 'The Repudiation Movement: A Study of the Maori Land Protest Movement in Hawke's Bay in the 1870s', MA History thesis, Massey University, 1977.
Gilmore, B.R., 'Maori Land Policy and Administration During the Liberal Period, 1900–1912', MA History thesis, University of Auckland, 1969.
McRae, J., 'Participation: Native Committees (1883) and Papatupu Block Committees (1900) in Tai Tokerau', MA Maori Studies thesis, University of Auckland, 1981.
Martin, R.J., 'Aspects of Maori Affairs in the Liberal Period', MA History thesis, Victoria University College, 1956.
Sorrenson, M.P.K., 'The Purchase of Maori Lands, 1865–1892', MA History thesis, Auckland University College, 1955.
Ward, A.D., 'The East Coast Maori Trust', MA History thesis, Victoria University College, 1958.

## III. Books and Articles

Bagnall, A.G., *Wairarapa: An Historical Excursion*, Masterton: Hedley's Bookshop for the Masterton Trust Lands Trust, 1976.

Binney, J., *Redemption Songs: A Life of Te Kooti Arikirangi Te Turuki*, Auckland: Auckland University Press/Bridget Williams Books, 1995.

Brooking, T., '"Busting Up" the Greatest Estate of All: Liberal Maori Land Policy, 1891–1911', *New Zealand Journal of History*, vol 26, no 1, 1992.

Butterworth, G.V., 'Maori Land Legislation: The Work of Carroll and Ngata', *New Zealand Law Journal*, August 1985, pp.242–249.

Cowan, J., *The New Zealand Wars: A History of the Maori Campaigns of the Pioneering Period*, vol 2, Wellington: Government Printer, 1922 [1983 reprint].

Cox, L., *Kotahitanga: The Search for Maori Political Unity*, Auckland: Oxford University Press, 1993.

Dalton, B.J., *War and Politics in New Zealand 1855–1870*, Sydney: Sydney University Press, 1967.

*The Dictionary of New Zealand Biography, Volume One, 1769–1869*, Wellington: Allen & Unwin/Department of Internal Affairs, 1990.

*The Dictionary of New Zealand Biography, Volume Two, 1870–1900*, Wellington: Bridget Williams Books/Department of Internal Affairs, 1993.

Gilling, B.D., 'By Whose Custom? The Operation of the Native Land Court in the Chatham Islands', *Victoria University of Wellington Law Review*, vol 23, no 3, 1993.

Gilling, B.D., 'Engine of Destruction? An Introduction to the History of the Maori Land Court', *Victoria University of Wellington Law Review*, vol 24, no 2, 1994.

Hill, R.S., *Policing the Colonial Frontier: The Theory and Practice of Coercive Social and Racial Control in New Zealand, 1767–1867*, Wellington: Government Printer, 1986.

Oliver, W.H. and J.M. Thomson, *Challenge and Response: A Study of the Development of the Gisborne East Coast Region*, Gisborne: East Coast Development Research Association, 1971.

Orange, C., 'The Covenant of Kohimarama: A Ratification of the Treaty of Waitangi', *New Zealand Journal of History*, vol 14, no 1, 1980.

Orange, C., *The Treaty of Waitangi*, Wellington: Allen & Unwin/Port Nicholson Press, 1987.

Pool, I., *Te Iwi Maori: A New Zealand Population Past, Present and Projected*, Auckland: Auckland University Press, 1991.

Sinclair, K., *Kinds of Peace: Maori People After the Wars 1870–1885*, Auckland: Auckland University Press, 1991.

Sorrenson, M.P.K., 'Land Purchase Methods and their Effect on Maori Population, 1865–1901', *Journal of the Polynesian Society*, vol 65, no 3, 1956.

Sorrenson, M.P.K., 'The Politics of Land' in J.G.A. Pocock (ed.), *The Maori and New Zealand Politics*, Auckland: Blackwood & Janet Paul, 1965.

Stafford, D.M., *The Founding Years in Rotorua: A History of Events to 1900*, Rotorua: Ray Richards Publisher/Rotorua District Council, 1986.

Stokes, E., et al., *Te Urewera: Nga Iwi Te Whenua Te Ngahere/ People, Land and Forests of Te Urewera*, Hamilton: University of Waikato, 1986.

Waitangi Tribunal, *The Pouakani Report 1993*, Wellington: Brooker & Friend, 1993.

Waitangi Tribunal, *Report of the Waitangi Tribunal on the Orakei Claim (Wai–9)*, Wellington: Waitangi Tribunal, 1987.

Waitangi Tribunal, *The Taranaki Report: Kaupapa Tuatahi*, Wellington: GP Publications, 1996.

Waitangi Tribunal, *The Te Roroa Report 1992*, Wellington: Brooker & Friend, 1992.

Ward, A., 'Law and Law-enforcement on the New Zealand Frontier, 1840–1893', *New Zealand Journal of History*, vol 5, no 2, October 1971.

Ward, A., *A Show of Justice: Racial 'Amalgamation' in Nineteenth Century New Zealand*, Auckland: Auckland University Press/Oxford University Press, 1973.

Williams, J.A., *Politics of the New Zealand Maori: Protest and Cooperation, 1891–1909*, Auckland: Oxford University Press, 1969.

# Index

Aborigines Protection Society 145-7
advance payments 89, 93, 127
alienation of land 241: Crown pre-emption 243; papakainga lands 244; Te Arawa 125; Te Urewera 238
Aotea Maori Council *161*
Aporo 92
Arney, Chief Justice 21, 28-9
assessors (Native Land Court) 29-30

Ballance, John: empowering of committees 177-8; Native Committees Act 171-3; Native Land Court 171-2; tour of North Island 174-9; *see also* Native Lands Alienation Restriction Act 1884
Bay of Islands Native Committee 167, 181-6
Bell, Francis Dillon 25, 26
Booth, James 75, 76
Brabant, Herbert 51; and the Komiti Nui 110-11
Bryce, John 68; and Native Committees Bill 150, 151-2; and Native Committees Empowerment Bill 137-43, 148; and Parihaka 143-4; and petition to Aborigines Protection Society 146-7; replacement of 171
Buchanan, John 141-2
Buckley, P.A. 196
Buller, James 76

Cadman, Alfred 223
Carroll, James 164, 206, 214, 215; and Native Committee Amendment Bill 210; Ruatahuna meeting with Tuhoe 226-7; Ruatoki meeting with Tuhoe 224-5; and Te Urewera survey 228; and Urewera District Native Reserve Bill 232-3
chiefs' delegation to Parliament 1891 209-10
Clarke, Henry Tacy 50-1; and Davis and Mitchell 96-7, 100-1; Te Arawa 96-7
committees: fight for legal status *see* legal status; powers under Native Committees Act 1883 150-1; *see also* Native Committees, runanga *and* unofficial committees
Cooper, G.S. 16-17
Council of 70 *see* Te Whitu Tekau
Council of Twelve 93-5, 99-100
Crown Grants 35
Crown purchasing in Te Urewera 238
customary land tenure v. individual title 32-4, 38

Dalton, J.E. 111
Dargaville, Joseph 108-9
Davis, C.O. 106; *see also* Davis and Mitchell
Davis and Mitchell: advance payments 88, 93, 127 appointment 83; Te Arawa negotiations 87-93, 97-9
De Lautour, Cecil 142
District Officers 49

East Coast runanga movement 17

Fenton, F.D. 28, 29; on collective title 33, 34; and Federated Maori Assembly Empowering Bill 212-4; and Hawke's Bay grievances 40; and

301

legal status issue 138; and Rotorua township proposal 119-20
Fox, William; and Native Lands Bill 1862 25-6; and native land title 23, 24

Gore Browne, Governor 21, 22: and Native Council proposal 19, 20; and Native Territorial Rights Bill 1858 19
Graham, Robert 107, 108, 109: prosecution of 113-4, 115
Great Committee of Rotorua *see* Komiti Nui
Grey, Sir George 20: Komiti Nui deputation to 114-15; and Native Lands Alienation Restriction Act 1884 195; and runanga proposal 22-3, 24

Hakuene, Ihaka 196
Hall, John 125
Hamlin, F.E. 51, 94
Harris, Major 141
Haultain, T.M. 41
Haupapa, Rotohiko 120
Hauraki committee 166
Hawke's Bay 39: impact of Native Lands Act 40; impact of Native Land Court 69; Native Committee elections 189-90; unofficial committees 69-74
Hawke's Bay Native Lands Alienation Commission 1873 48
Heke, Hone *253*: Native Rights Bill 214-5; Urewera District Native Reserve Bill 234-5
hereditary title 37-8
Hikairo, Wiremu 45-6
Himiona 93

individual v. collective title 32-4, 38

juries and Native Land Court 30, 43-4, 46

Kaihau, Henare 242-3
Kaikohe title disputes 182-3, 185-6
Kaipara: Maori Parliament 133; title determinations 27-8
Kaiwhaiki hui 77
Kaiwhaka Komiti 47
Kapa, Eparaima 210
Katene, Wiremu 54
Kawepo, Renata 73, 76
Kawhia Native Committee election boycott 187
Kelly, George 135
Kelly, William 54
Kemp, Major *see* Te Rangihiwinui, Te Keepa
Kereru, Numia 224, 225, 250
Kihikihi meeting of Te Wahanui with Ballance 175-6
King Committees 187-8
King Country 39: settlement negotiations 187-9; *see also* Te Urewera
King movement 17; and Kotahitanga 202
Kohimarama Conference 1860 19-20
Komiti Nui 107-27: attitude to settlement 115-16; composition 110; deputation to Sir George Grey 114-15; jurisdiction 110; and Native Land Court 110-11; official attitude to 111-12; petition for Henry Mitchell's removal 114-15; restructuring 122-3; and Robert Graham 107, 108, 109; Rotorua settlement negotiations 119-23; sittings 117
Kotahitanga 71, 135, 202: 1898 meeting 242-3; and Apirana Ngata 243-4; petition to Queen 241; Waitangi agreement 212
Kotua, Te Whare 226
Kurimate, Paora 174

legal status of committees, 129-30, 138: draft bill 137-8; petitions 129-30; and *Te Wananga* 130-1, 132; of Tuhoe elected committee 221-2
Liberal Government Maori land policy 206
Locke, Samuel 51, 222-3

## Index

Mackay, Thomas 206-7
Mair, Gilbert 102-3, 104
Maketu: Native Land Court conflict 106-7; Pukaingateru Block 46-7
mana and land claims 91
Mana Maori movement 135
Maori Council Constitution Bill 242-3
Maori Council proposal 200-1
Maori Councils Act 1900 244-7
Maori land: customary tenure v. individual title 32-4, 381; leasing to settlers 23
Maori Land Boards 246
Maori Land Councils 244, 245
Maori Lands Administration Act 1900 244-7
Maori Parliament: proposal 16-17; Orakei 133-4; petition to Queen 144; Waipatu 212;
Maori parliamentary seats 73
Maori Settlement Act 1905 246
Martin, Sir William 47-8
Matua, Henare 74; at Kaiwhaiki hui 77; and Hawke's Bay Native Committee 190; and repudiation movement 69-70
Maunsell, E.S. 66-7
McLean, Donald, 26: Native Councils Bill 54; and Te Arawa dispute 49-50; Maketu meeting with Te Arawa 97; Native Lands Frauds Prevention Act 1870 40
Mitchell, Henry: dismissal 117-18; payment to Komiti members 115, 116; Te Arawa petition for removal of 114-15; see also Davis and Mitchell
Morton, Henry 125-6
Moss, Frederick 140-1
Mueller, Gerhard 227
Murimotu boundaries 76
Muriwhenua and Mana Maori movement 135

Native Affairs Committee 52; and petitions for recognition of committees 129-30; Rohe Potae petition to 150; Te Arawa delegation to 86-8
Native Circuit Courts Act 1858 19
Native Committees: districts 166, 167; impact of Native Lands Administration Act on 202, 203; limitations on 73-4; members with interests in cases 179-80; revenue 175, 176; and summonses 173 174;
Native Committees Act 1883: appointments under 166; committee powers under 150-1; effects and failure of 163-5; Maori translation of 167; Rees-Carroll commission 164; tribal districts 166, 167
Native Committees Bill 150-5: Legislative Council debate 152-4
Native Committees Empowering Bill 137-43; parliamentary debate 140-3
Native Councils 53
Native Councils Bill 1872 54-7
Native Districts Regulation Act 1858 19
Native Land Act 1873 34-6, 48-9
Native Land Act 1838 204-6
Native Land Boards proposal 242
Native Land Court 1900 legislation 244; and Maori health 36; assessors 29-30; boycotts 211; Chief Judge Fenton see Fenton; costs to land owners 36; exclusion from Te Urewera 229; false evidence 31-2; juries 30, 43-4, 46; Maketu sittings 106; negative impacts 35-8; petition for abolition of 52; Rohe Potae hearings 189; Rees-Carroll on effects 207; Rohe Potae petition 149-50; rules of evidence 43; Te Arawa 124-5; Rotorua settlement negotiations 119-23
Native Land Purchase Board 210
Native Land Purchase Ordinance 1846 23
Native Lands Act 1862 25-8
Native Lands Act 1865 28-32 44; and hereditary title 37-8
Native Lands Act 1867: amendment 40; suspension over Te Arawa lands 91-2; and speculation 26;
Native Lands Act 1873 207
Native Lands Administration Act 1886 202-4, 207-8
Native Lands Alienation Restriction Act 1884 194-6
Native Lands Frauds Prevention Act 1870 40
Native Rights Bill 214-5

303

# Index

Native Territorial Rights Bill 1858 19
New Zealand Constitution Act 1852 15-16
New Zealand Native Land Settlement Company 193
Ngahuruhuru, Pererika 110
Ngai Tahu: Committee of all the Runangas of Ngaitahu 71; and repudiation movement 71-2; *see also* Hori Tairoa
Ngai Te Rangi 166
Ngapuhi: Bay of Islands Native Committee 168; Hone Mohi Tawhai *see* Tawhai; Rees-Carroll commission evidence 209; Wiremu Pomare *see* Pomare
Ngata, Apirana; and draft legislation 243-4
Ngata, Paratene 237
Ngatata, Wi Tako 196
Ngati Awa's request for own Native Committee 190-1
Ngati Kahungunu: Committee of Kahungunu 72-3; Henare Tomoana *see* Tomoana; Rees-Carroll Commission evidence 209; Renata Kawepo 76
Ngati Manawa 225-6
Ngati Maniapoto: dispute with King party 197; and Native Committees Act 1883 169; opposition to King movement 189; Rohe Potae petition 148-50; Te Wahanui 153-4, 171
Ngati Porou 167
Ngati Ranginui 166
Ngati Rangiteorere 180
Ngati Rangiwewehi: Wiremu Hikairo 45-6; Wiremu Maihi Te Rangikaheke, 86-7; and the Komiti Nui 108
Ngati Raukawa and the Rohe Potae petition 148-50
Ngati Tuwharetoa: Iwakau Te Heuheu, 16; Rees-Carroll commission evidence 209; response to Native Committees Act 165; Rohe Potae petition 148-50
Ngati Whakaue 55-6: committee 103-6; meeting with Ballance 178; and Robert Graham, 107, 108, 109; Rotorua settlement negotiations 119-23; opposition to Crown negotiations 88-92
Ngati Whare 225-6
Ngati Whatua Paora Tuhaere *see* Tuhaere
Ngati Hako 188
Niho-o-te-Kiore 105

Ohinemuri King committee 188
Ohinemutu: Ngati Whakaue committee 104; Tamatekapua meeting house opening 50-1
Opotiki Native Committee election 169
Orakei Maori Parliament, 133-4
Ormsby, John 175, 187-9

Paerau 226; and Te Whitu Tekau 218-21
Paeroa hui 99-100
Paeroa-Te Aroha rail line 188
Pakowhai hui 72-3
papakainga lands 244
Papatupu Block Committees 244, 247
Papawai land dispute 65
Parikino meeting 75
Parata, Wi 54
Parekarangi hui 105
Parihaka 143-4
Parikino hui 211
Patene, Wiremu 45
Pauru 92-3
Pere, Wi 252: Native Lands Administration Bill 216; Native Lands Alienation Restriction Act amendments 195-6; Waipatu meeting 203; Native Lands Act Amendment Bill 193
petition to Queen 1882 144-5
Pink and White Terraces 179
Pollen, Daniel 153-4, 196
Pomare, Wiremu 43-4, 209
Poutu meeting of King supporters 200-1
Poverty Bay Commission 70-1
Preece, George 190
Pukaingateru Block 46-7
Pukututu, Renata 209
Putaiki 93-5; Paeroa hui 99-100
Putiki hui 76, 205

304

*Index*

Ranana 174; Huriwhenua *159*
rangatiratanga Native Land Act 1873 35
Rawiri, Taekata 96
Rees, W.L. 164, 193-4, 206
Rees-Carroll Commission 48-9, 164, 206-10
Rehua, Rakuraku 191
repudiation movement 64, 69-70, 74: and *Te Wananga* 65
Resident Magistrates 19; and Native Councils 53-4
Richmond, C.W. 48
Richmond, J.C. 196
Rogan, John 27-8
Rohe Potae Native Land Court hearings 189; petition 148-50
Rongowhakaata 167
Rotomahana title dispute 93-4
Rotomahana-Parekarangi Block 178-9
Rotorua settlement negotiations 119-23
Rotorua Native Committee 168-9, 178-9
Ruatahuna: Council of 70 meeting 218; Tuhoe meeting with Seddon, 226-7
Ruatoki 224-5
runanga: control of land sales 23, 24; and Domett administration 25; Grey's proposal 22-3, 24; justice 17-18; and land sales 18; rights under Native Lands Act 26; state sponsorship 18-19; support for proposal 50-2; Te Wheoro's proposal 42; use against King movement 25; Whanganui 78-80
Russell, Captain 234
Russell, Henry Robert 70
Russell, Thomas 26

Seddon, Richard: Ruatahuna meeting with Tuhoe 226-7; Ruatoki meeting with Tuhoe 224-5; and Tuhoe delegation 229-30
Sheehan, John 70
Shortland, Edward 47-8
speculation and Native Lands Act 1862 26
Stout, Robert: Native Lands Alienation Restriction Act 1884 195; and Tawhiao's petition to Queen 198-9

Stout-Ngata Commission 241, 245, 246
summonses 173, 174
Supreme Court on native land title 21-2
surveys: Paeroa-Te Aroha rail line 188; Te Arawa opposition to 102-6; Te Urewera 223, 227-8; Tuhoe veto 218
Swanson, William 141

Tai Tokerau Land Boards 246
Taiaroa, Hori 199: and Native Councils Bill 54; Native Committees Empowering Bill 142; Aborigines Protection Society 145-6
Taiawhio, Hori 92, 179
Taipua, Hoani 210-11
Tairawhiti Land Boards 246
Taiwhanga, Hirini 144-5, 206, *254*
Takamoana, Karaitiana 44-5, *59*
Tamamatu, Hohepa 93
Tamatekapua meeting house *158*; opening 50-1
Tapapa committee 166
Taranui, Te Pokiha 69
Tarapipipi, Wiremu Tamihana 17
Tauaki, Hira 219-20
Taupopoki, Mita *61*
Tautari, Hemi 43
Tawhai, Hone Mohi 43, 96, *249*: and Bay of Islands Native Committee 167-8, 181-6; and Native Committees Empowerment draft bill 137-8, 141; petition to Aborigines Protection Society 145-6
Tawhiao, King *see* Te Wherowhero, Tawhiao
Te Aitanga-a-Mahaki 167
Te Amohau, Paora 107-8
Te Ao, Te Puke 195-6
Te Arawa: committees 85-127; delegation to Parliament 85-8; factional land dispute 49-50; and H.T. Clarke 96-7; land alienation 125; and Native Land Court 124-5; negotiations with Davis and Mitchell 87-93, 97-9; opposition to surveys 102-6; Petera Te Pukuatua 49; petition for Mitchell's removal 114-15;

305

petition to Queen 211; Putaiki 93-5, 99-100; response to Native Committees Act 165-66; Rotorua settlement negotiations 119-23; support for Native Councils Bill 55-6; and suspension of Native Lands Act 91-2; Te Pokiha Taranui 49; Wiremu Hikairo 45-6
Te Aroha Block hearing 46
Te Awekotuku, Ratema 180
Te Heuheu, Iwikau 16
Te Komiti Nui o Rotorua *see* Komiti Nui
Te Kooti 223
Te Ore Ore committee meeting 65
Te Paku-o-te-Rangi hui 81-2
Te Puke Block 99
Te Pukeiotu 226
Te Pukenui, Kereru 224
Te Pukuatua, Petera 49, *60*
Te Rangihiwinui, Te Keepa (Major Kemp) 76, 211; "Kemp's Trust" 82-3
Te Rangikaheke, Wiremu Maihi 86-7, 108
Te Rangipuawhe, Te Keepa 88-9: Maketu conflict 107
Te Rarawa 168
Te Uremutu, Eruera 114, 115
Te Urewera: Commission 231; committees 217-39; Council of 70 *see* Te Whitu Tekau; elected committees 229-30; Local and General Committees 231-2; subdivision of 236; *see also* Tuhoe
Te Wahanui 153-4, 171, 175-6, *251*: Native Lands Alienation Restriction Act 1884 196
Te Waiohiki hui 69, 73
*Te Wananga* 65, 74: influence on committee movement 133; John White 130-1, 132-3; Putaiki 94-5
Te Wharehuia, Makarini 218-19
Te Whatahoro 67-8
Te Whenuanui and Te Whitu Tekau 218
Te Wheoro, Wiremu 29-30, 41-2: and Native Committees Empowerment draft bill 137-8; petition to Aboriginal Protection Society 145-6; runanga title adjudication proposal 42

Te Wherowhero, Potatau 17
Te Wherowhero, Tawhiao *248*; and Maori Council bill 200-1; meeting with Ballance 176-7; petition to Queen 197-8, 199-201
Te Whiti 144
Te Whitu Tekau 52, 191, 218-21
Te Whiwhi, Matene 17
ten-owner system 33-4
Thames Native Committee 173-4, 177-8
title investigations: Bay of Islands Native Committee 181-4; Kaikohe 182-3
Tomoana, Henare 44, 74: Native Committees Empowerment Bill 137-40, 143; petition to Aboriginal Protection Society 145-6
Treaty of Waitangi Committee 181, 186
Trimble, Colonel 143
Tuhaere, Paora 20, 41-2, *58*: address to Legislative Council 205-6; at Maori Parliament, Orakei 133-4
Tuhoe: Commissioners 231; delegation to Wellington 1895 228-30; gathering 1894 224; meetings with Seddon 224-5; opposition to surveys 190-2, 218 ; request for own Native Committee 190-2; support for runanga proposal 52; Te Whitu Tekau 52; veto over Native Land Court 218-20; *see also* Te Urewera
Tuhourangi: capture of survey party 105-6; complaints about Davis and Mitchell 92-3; meeting with Ballance 178-9; meeting with McLean 92-4; Pink and White Terraces 179; Putaiki *see* Putaiki; Te Keepa Te Rangipuawhe 88-9
Turnbull, Richard 140

Uenukukopako 96
unofficial committees: emergence of 63-4; jurisdiction over land tenure 66-8; magistrates 65-6; veto over Native Land Court applications 66-7; Wairarapa 64-9
Urewera Commission 236-7; *see also* Te Urewera

*Index*

Urewera District Native Reserve Bill 230-6; *see also* Te Urewera

Validation Court 210

Wahanui *see* Te Wahanui
Waikato Native Committee: election boycott 187; and Native Committees Act 169-70
Waipatu: Maori Parliament 212; meeting with Ballance 203-4
Wairarapa 67-9: Native Committee 180-1; unofficial committees 64-9
Wairoa 190
Waitangi hui 1892 212; *see also* Treaty of Waitangi Committee
Waterhouse, George 52-3, 196
Whanganui: internal conflict 74; meeting with Ballance 1885 74-5; Native Committee boundaries 174-5; Native Committee election 169; and Native Lands Act 27; Parliament 81-2; repudiation movement 74-5 76-7; Rohe Potae petition 148-50; Te Paku-o-te-Rangi 81-2; tribal boundary disputes 75-6; unofficial committees 74-83; *see also* Te Rangiwhinui, Te Keepa (Major Kemp)
Whatiwhatihoe: Tawhiao's meeting with Ballance 176-7; King Committee 187-8
Whitaker, Frederick 26, 145
White, John 27, 130-1, 132-3
Whiteley, John 18
Whitmore, Sir George 152-3
Wilkinson, G.T. King Country settlement negotiations 187-9
Williamson, John 54
Woon, Richard 75-6, 78-82

Young Maori Party 243, 244